Consumer Credit Insurance

CONSUMER CREDIT INSURANCE

by

DANIEL P. KEDZIE, Ph.D.

Assistant Professor of Insurance and Finance
Marquette University
and
Former Insurance Examiner
Wisconsin State Insurance Department

1957

Published for

THE
CONSUMER CREDIT
INSURANCE ASSOCIATION

by

RICHARD D. IRWIN, INC.
Homewood, Illinois

First Printing, August, 1957

Library of Congress Catalogue Card No. 57–12639

PRINTED IN THE UNITED STATES OF AMERICA

FOREWORD

The Consumer Credit Insurance Association was organized in April, 1951 by a group of insurance companies specializing in the writing of credit life and credit disability insurance.

The purposes for which the Association was organized, set forth in the Articles of Incorporation, are:

1. To act as a trade association of insurance companies engaged in the business of underwriting creditors' life insurance and allied lines of insurance;
2. To promote high ethical standards for the consumer credit insurance business and related lines of insurance;
3. To disseminate information and provide for the exchange of ideas among and between its members.

The Association seeks to accomplish these objectives by compiling statistics concerning the industry; publishing booklets explaining various aspects of consumer credit insurance; conducting opinion surveys; and co-operating with state officials in developing effective laws and regulations.

In June, 1956, the Association appointed a Research and Education Committee whose principal functions are to assist scholars everywhere in the study of all aspects of this relatively new type of insurance; to stimulate original or more thorough research particularly in the misunderstood areas of the industry; to assist in the dissemination, through publication or co-operation with publishers, of such research findings and essays as the Association deems worthy and in the public interest; and generally to co-operate with eleemosynary institutions, associations, and conferences in better educating the American public, which has come to use the many and varied forms of consumer credit insurance so widely.

Pursuant to its responsibilities, the Association sponsors a pamphlet series, comprised of brief essays, or reports, and a monograph series, comprised of scholarly dissertations or theses.

The Association is pleased to sponsor Dr. Kedzie's work, the first book dealing solely with the subject of consumer credit insurance, and to have it published under the imprint of Richard D. Irwin, Inc.

By virtue of its sponsorship, the Association does not intend to signify its support of or sympathy with the author's interpretations. The decision to sponsor publications is based upon their academic merits and general contribution to the understanding of the subject.

It is our earnest hope that the willingness of the Association to publish these series will in itself provide impetus to scholarly study and writings. The Committee will be pleased to receive any works submitted for consideration at the Association headquarters.

Research and Education Committee
RICHARD B. DOSS, *Chairman*
ALLEN C. EASTLACK
ALLEN J. LEFFERDINK
JAMES S. RICE

MEMBERSHIP ROSTER
CONSUMER CREDIT INSURANCE ASSOCIATION

AMERICAN BANKERS LIFE ASSURANCE COMPANY
Miami, Florida

AMERICAN LIFE INSURANCE COMPANY
Birmingham, Alabama

BANKERS NATIONAL LIFE INSURANCE COMPANY
Montclair, New Jersey

BANKERS SECURITY LIFE INSURANCE SOCIETY
New York, New York

CENTRAL NATIONAL LIFE INSURANCE COMPANY
Omaha, Nebraska

CENTRAL STATES HEALTH AND LIFE COMPANY
Omaha, Nebraska

COLORADO CREDIT LIFE, INC.
Boulder, Colorado

CORNBELT LIFE COMPANY
Freeport, Illinois

CREDIT LIFE INSURANCE COMPANY
Springfield, Ohio

FEDERAL LIFE AND CASUALTY COMPANY
Battle Creek, Michigan

GREAT AMERICAN RESERVE INSURANCE COMPANY
Dallas, Texas

LIFE ASSURANCE COMPANY OF AMERICA
Thorp, Wisconsin

NATIONAL FIDELITY LIFE INSURANCE COMPANY
Kansas City, Missouri

NORTH AMERICAN LIFE & CASUALTY COMPANY
Minneapolis, Minnesota

NORTH CENTRAL LIFE INSURANCE COMPANY
Saint Paul, Minnesota

OLD REPUBLIC LIFE INSURANCE COMPANY
Chicago, Illinois

PLYMOUTH LIFE INSURANCE COMPANY
Austin, Texas

SOUTHERN LIFE INSURANCE COMPANY OF GEORGIA
Atlanta, Georgia

STUYVESANT LIFE INSURANCE COMPANY
Allentown, Pennsylvania

THE VOLUNTEER STATE LIFE INSURANCE COMPANY
Chattanooga, Tennessee

WESTERN NATIONAL LIFE INSURANCE COMPANY
Amarillo, Texas

WORLD INSURANCE COMPANY
Omaha, Nebraska

PREFACE

This text is the first known attempt at describing and discussing one of the fastest growing, controversial, and interesting forms of insurance. Consumer credit life, and accident and health insurance are considered. Both group and ordinary or individual policy systems of marketing are examined. Because the literature to date contains no comprehensive explanation of the operational aspects of the subject, it was necessary that the author confer extensively with officials of the industry. Without their co-operation this work would not have been possible. My sincere thanks are therefore extended to all who contributed to the completion of this text.

For their outstanding assistance rendered, special recognition is extended to Mr. John Colby, Director of Field Operations, and Mr. Theodore Wysocki, Actuary, of the CUNA Mutual Insurance Society; Dr. Richard B. Doss, Research Director of the Old Republic Life Insurance Company; Mr. John Kittredge, Actuarial Director of the Midwest Home Office of the Prudential Insurance Company of America; Mr. Howard Thoenig, District Manager of the Accident and Health Division of the Continental Casualty Company; Mr. W. Lee Shield, Associate General Counsel, the American Life Convention; Mr. William J. Walsh, General Counsel, The Consumer Credit Insurance Association; Messrs. Barrett, Dauer, and Dunning of the Household Finance Corporation; Mr. Edward A. Dunbar, Associate Counsel, Beneficial Management Corporation; the Honorable William Langer, United States Senate; the Institute of Life Insurance; the Life Insurance Agency Management Association; and the Wisconsin State Insurance Department.

To Dr. Charles C. Center, Professor of Commerce, University of Wisconsin goes an especial acknowledgement for his persistent and invaluable assistance evidencing to a singular degree his insight as an academician and practical businessman.

To Miss Ena Moll who typed the original manuscript goes my appreciation for her pains-taking care and excellent work.

To my wife Patricia goes my gratitude for her patience, encouragement, and prayers.

This work is dedicated to my children, Daniel and Kathleen, who are too young to understand why, but old enough to be aware of, their father's excessive absences from home.

DANIEL P. KEDZIE

MILWAUKEE, WISCONSIN
June, 1957

TABLE OF CONTENTS

LIST OF TABLES AND DIAGRAMS

Tables

xv

Diagrams

Chapter I

INTRODUCTION

THE SENATE JUDICIARY REPORT

Following a public hearing at Topeka, Kansas, on January 20, 1954, the Subcommittee on Antitrust and Monopoly Legislation of the Senate Judiciary Committee studying the tie-in sale of credit insurance in connection with small loans submitted its report containing this observation:

> Those who are associated with the credit insurance industry have the choice between the high calling of a great public service and yielding to a single temptation—greed. It is most regrettable that some few have brought disrepute to an industry so great as the insurance industry.[1]

As a final admonition to those who "abhor the thought of Federal interference" with the insurance industry and who desire "the continued regulation of the insurance industry by several States," the Committee report closes saying:

> The patience of the Federal Government with those who would abuse the good name of insurance some day may come to an end.
> > William Langer, Chairman
> > Everett McKinley Dirksen
> > Harley M. Kilgore
> > Estes Kefauver[2]

Thus, while this Senate investigatory body recognized that credit insurance (called consumer credit insurance here) "per-

---

[1] "The Tie-In Sale of Credit Insurance in Connection With Small Loans and Other Transactions," a report of the Subcommittee on Antitrust and Monopoly Legislation of the Committee on the Judiciary, United States Senate (83rd Cong., 2nd sess.) (Washington, D.C.: U.S. Government Printing Office, 1955), p. 14.

[2] *Ibid.*

1

forms a most admirable function," serious abuses have prompted several legislative investigations on the state and national level and cries for the repeal of Public Law 15.[3] Concern over the trends in consumer credit insurance is steadily increasing and should be, since the methods and practices of this small but rapidly expanding segment of the business may well effect the regulation of the majority. What was the nature of the abuses which warranted so firm and solemn a warning from such an august body?

Discovered Abuses

Among the abuses that this Committee found were instances where coercion and intimidation were used to force consumer credit insurance upon an unwilling borrower. In its investigation of unscrupulous practices, the Committee noted these additional devices employed in the sale of consumer credit insurance:

a) Sales of credit insurance far in excess of money loaned;

b) Failure to deliver the policy to the borrower, thus keeping the borrower in ignorance as to his coverage or other rights in the policy;

c) Payment of excessive commissions, in which instances little was left for the payment of claims;

d) Pyramiding of policies effected by requiring the borrower to purchase a second policy upon refinancing his loan without cancellation of the first policy purchased when the money was originally borrowed; failure to make a refund of unearned premium when insurance is canceled on payment of the loan, and other pernicious practices.[4]

Ethical vs. Unethical Lenders

To gain and maintain a proper perspective of the problem of these abuses, however, further reference to the Committee report is necessary. Fully aware that two distinct classifications of lenders existed, the Committee attributed the afore-

---

[3] Public Law 15, c. 20 (79th Cong., 1st sess.).

[4] "The Tie-In Sale of Credit Insurance in Connection With Small Loans and Other Transactions," *op. cit.*

mentioned abuses solely to the unethical lender who "employs subterfuge to circumvent the law." With the recent popularity of consumer credit insurance, the Judiciary Committee felt that these modern-day Shylocks are given an additional method of obtaining a pound of flesh.

The ethical lender, on the other hand, is one who "strictly complies with State laws and regulations." It was emphasized that "under no circumstance should those individuals and institutions who sell such insurance, without engaging in coercion, intimidation, or other unscrupulous activities, be condemned because other lenders sell credit insurance unethically."[5]

Incidence of Abuses

The investigation in Kansas, considered an unregulated state in the field of small loans, also alluded to the ineffective regulation of consumer credit insurance in the state at the time the report was made. Despite this absence of stringent regulation, the Committee reported that "an impressive number of borrowers testified before the subcommittee at Topeka that credit insurance paid their debt when they were beset by illness, accident, or by death of the head of their household."[6] The majority of the officials interviewed and many authors of current periodical articles accept the thesis that the magnitude of abuses is usually inversely related to the caliber of regulation within a given state. While regulation of consumer credit insurance per se is still in an embryonic state, considerable progress has been made in the regulation of small-loans operations.

At least thirty-six states, comprising about 79 per cent of the United States population, have effective to partially effective regulation.[7] Since 1954 when these estimates were compiled,

---

[5] *Ibid.*, p. 5.

[6] *Ibid.*, p. 14.

[7] F. B. Hubachek, "Progress and Problems in Regulation of Consumer Credit," *Law and Contemporary Problems,* School of Law, Duke University, Vol. 19, No. 1 (Winter, 1954), p. 8.

considerable progress has been noted in several states toward drafting new small-loan laws and the improvement of the old. Thus it would seem that the percentage of the populace currently subjected to consumer credit insurance abuses is small. Moreover, when it is remembered that abuses cited are attendant particularly to the small-loan field in which regulation has progressed and to a relatively smaller degree among other lenders, the problem assumes an even more realistic dimension.

Historical Analogy

It is interesting to note further that the consumer credit insurance segment appears to be following the pattern established by its predecessors in the industry. The life insurance segment, for example, was a juvenile delinquent of the pre-1900's, got spanked by the Armstrong Committee, and grew into a leading citizen of the business community. We might attribute to coincidence the fact that consumer credit life insurance purchases during the previously mentioned Langer investigation were reasonably close in amount to life insurance purchases at the time of the Armstrong investigations. This pattern was again repeated in 1910 when the Merritt Committee probed the abuses in the casualty insurance field.

All these investigations had a common element: the vast majority of abuses could be attributed to a small minority of offenders. Faced with a similar situation today, it is believed that in the near future the entire consumer credit insurance segment will begin to operate as a more respectable member of the insurance fraternity.

ABUSES AND THEIR REPERCUSSIONS

If the abusive practices of some few unscrupulous lenders and companies have accomplished any good, they have certainly made many people, both within and without the industry, cognizant of the existence of this type of insurance. From these highly questionable practices just noted, many and varied forms of action have resulted, among which the following might be mentioned:

  a) Agitation for and passage of new state statutes.
  b) New or revised insurance department rulings.
  c) A variety of opinions of attorneys general.
  d) Investigation by federal and state governmental bodies.
  e) Demands for rate regulation of consumer credit insurance in particular and life insurance in general.
  f) A deluge of articles, some of them biased, in trade journals, lay periodicals, and newspapers.
  g) An extremely bitter dispute between one of the largest writers of consumer credit insurance and one of the giants of the consumer finance industry.
  h) Heated testimony before, and factions within, the National Association of Insurance Commissioners.
  i) University-sponsored seminars.
  j) Detailed studies and publicized statements by insurance trade organizations.
  k) Promulgation and adoption of a new statistical exhibit to be submitted by companies writing consumer credit insurance to state insurance departments.
  l) A phenomenal growth of the consumer credit insurance business.

THE IMPORTANT ISSUES

It is probably true that a study comparable in size to this one could be made to encompass no more than the results of an investigation of abuses in this field and a description of recommended and resulting corrections. Allusion to these topics, although necessary to a complete exposition of this subject, will be treated as incidental to the main thesis of this text, since it is the author's belief that the magnitude of abuses connected with the sale of consumer credit insurance and the resulting remedial action taken and yet to come is of lesser importance in the long run than an explanation of the growth, operation, uses, benefits, and future developments of this coverage. This does not mean to suggest a discounting of the importance of the remedial action brought about by the crusading efforts of those bringing abuses to light. It means simply that this study will principally consider the current operation, status, and future possibilities of consumer credit insurance in its important role within the insurance industry.

With the subject in its proper perspective, a definition is now in order.

Chapter II

NATURE AND SCOPE

"ASSET" VS. "LIABILITY" INSURANCE

The term "credit insurance" contemplates two diverse forms of insurance coverage. They are probably best explained by adapting Dr. Shenkman's[1] terminology of "assets insurance" and "liabilities insurance." The former explains the effort of a creditor to insure his working capital in his accounts receivable against the loss resulting from the impossibility of collecting a debt, thus insuring his assets; the latter explains the effort of the debtor to insure the payment of his loan against the contingencies of death and disability, thus insuring his liabilities. They are similar in that both make the creditor the beneficiary; both are able to lubricate the credit system.

Credit insurance of the first type—assets insurance—written since 1891, is further described as "a guarantee to the policyholder that his working capital invested in accounts receivable will not be materially depleted through the inability of the policyholder's debtors to pay their obligations. The guarantee is issued to manufacturers, wholesalers, and advertising agencies. It is never provided to retailers or to any line of business where the customer is the ultimate consumer unless that customer be in some established business."[2]

Since this form of credit insurance preceded the "liability" type by twenty-six years, the term "credit insurance" is reserved for it out of respect for its seniority. Addition of the adjective

---

[1] Elia M. Shenkman, "Insurance Against Credit Risks in International Trade" (London: P. S. King and Son, Ltd., 1935), p. 83.

[2] J. L. McCauley, "Don't Be Confused About Credit Insurance," *The American Agency Bulletin*, April, 1955, p. 25.

"consumer" to this term should then serve to identify that form of coverage usually provided to those cash borrowers contemplating consumer purchases, or time purchasers at the retail level, which promises repayment of the outstanding balance of consumer loans or accounts in the event of the borrower's death. In the case of accident or sickness, the coverage pays installments due on behalf of the debtor during his disability.

A few examples of consumers who might utilize consumer credit insurance protection are a purchaser of a new automobile who finances a major portion of it by use of a conditional sales contract, a credit union member who borrows to pay his income tax, or a bank or finance company borrower who wants cash to purchase a major appliance. That such instances are not isolated is evidenced by the fact that 32 million policies and certificates were reported in force at the end of 1956.[3]

DEFINITION AND GENERAL NATURE

As of May 1, 1956, all insurers writing consumer credit insurance of the "liability" type were required to file with the state insurance departments a "Credit Life and Accident and Health Exhibit" if they had written such coverage in 1955. This new form, in addition to setting forth the manner of reporting the business, also defines consumer credit insurance as follows:

a) Credit life insurance is defined as that form of insurance under which the life of the borrower of money or purchaser of goods is insured in connection with a specific loan or credit transaction.
b) Credit accident and health insurance is that form of insurance under which a borrower of money or purchaser of goods is indemnified in connection with a specific loan or credit transaction against loss of time resulting from accident and sickness.
c) This definition shall not include life insurance or accident and health insurance sold on an individual contract basis in connection with real estate loans of more than 36 months duration.[4]

---

[3] Preliminary estimate of the Institute of Life Insurance, New York.

[4] "Credit Life and Accident and Health Exhibit," a supplement to the Annual Statement to be filed beginning May 1, 1955, with state insurance departments.

This definition confines the required information to policies issued on relatively short-term loans to the exclusion of those
covering longer terms, such as mortgage protection plans. Since
later statistical data will be based upon this definition, it shall
be used for the remainder of the book. Appendix A contains the
results of an earlier attempt at a comprehensive definition of
group consumer credit insurance by the National Association of
Insurance Commissioners, incorporated by many states into their
existing definitions of group life insurance.

Methods of Marketing

Two basic methods of writing consumer credit insurance
currently exist: group and ordinary. The latter is sometimes
called individual. Group consumer credit insurance is that form
of life and/or disability insurance which, in the event of the
insured borrower's death or disability, pays the remaining balance of the indebtedness or prorata payments to the creditor
as the beneficiary and master policyholder. As is true in other
group insurance contracts, the insureds under group consumer
credit insurance, in this case the borrowers, receive certificates
that give a summary of insurance benefits. It should be added
that, although consumer credit accident and health insurance
is included in the group definition, only a relatively small
amount is known to be written on this basis nation-wide, principally because of existing statutes which either expressly prohibit its being written or fail to include debtors as those eligible for such coverage. Some states have amended or are in
the process of amending existing laws to provide for the writing
of this coverage on a "blanket" basis, thus foreshadowing
a possible relative decrease in accident and health insurance
on an individual basis.

To be discussed later in more detail, these observations
seem pertinent at this point. Group credit insurance contracts
usually require 75 to 100 per cent participation and a minimum group of 100 new debtors per year. As are all group
rates, those for consumer credit insurance are lower than ordinary policies, usually $0.75 per $1,000 per month on the out-

standing balance. Premiums are paid by the creditor, although generally passed on to the borrower.

The ordinary, or individual, policies have no participation or minimum requirements, being sold on an optional basis to the borrower. Rates on the most popular form of this policy, the decreasing term, are generally $1.00 per year per $100 on the initial amount of indebtedness. The premiums are paid by the borrower in addition to finance charges. In most states, an employee of the lending agency is also licensed as an agent to write this business and receive a commission. Individual accident and health contracts are sold at varying rates, the majority of the business written by carriers operating on the ordinary basis for consumer credit life insurance.

Importance of Group and Ordinary

Table I shows the relative importance of group and ordinary consumer credit life insurance since 1940. It will be observed

TABLE I

CONSUMER CREDIT LIFE INSURANCE PURCHASES, 1940–54
(000 Omitted)

	Ordinary			Group	
Year	Number	Amount	Master Policies	Certificates	Amount
1940	421	$ 73,000	1	204	$ 32,000
1941	479	84,000	1	304	56,000
1942	428	69,000	1	136	17,000
1943	394	66,000	1	80	12,000
1944	424	76,000	1	75	17,000
1945	614	118,000	1	112	30,000
1946	1,092	208,000	1	481	171,000
1947	1,399	330,000	1	563	166,000
1948	1,778	443,000	1	605	220,000
1949	2,044	519,000	2	987	449,000
1950	2,718	730,000	2	1,746	839,000
1951	3,445	1,071,000	3	1,600	521,000
1952	4,254	1,470,000	3	1,487	915,000
1953	4,871	1,818,000	5	2,511	1,432,000
1954	4,786	2,143,000	5	2,386	955,000
1955		(Compilation discontinued)			

Source: Institute of Life Insurance.

Figures for group credit purchases exclude increases and replacements except for increases occurring in the first one or two years of the group contract.

that ordinary consumer credit life insurance purchases are currently more than twice that of group purchases in both insurance amount and number of insureds. When the "in force" figures are compared, as in Table II, group consumer credit life maintains an appreciable edge over ordinary.

TABLE II

CONSUMER CREDIT LIFE INSURANCE IN FORCE, 1940–56

(000 Omitted)

	Ordinary		Group		
Year	Number	Amount	Master Policies	Certificates	Amount
1940	392	$ 62,000	5	2,171	$ 318,000
1941	445	74,000	6	2,574	395,000
1942	417	66,000	6	2,047	289,000
1943	382	57,000	6	1,474	218,000
1944	335	66,000	5	1,417	224,000
1945	561	101,000	6	1,549	264,000
1946	1,024	180,000	6	2,366	549,000
1947	1,355	291,000	7	3,490	919,000
1948	1,475	372,000	8	4,666	1,357,000
1949	1,781	482,000	9	6,170	2,049,000
1950	2,225	720,000	10	8,609	3,169,000
1951	3,033	1,110,000	12	9,355	3,708,000
1952	3,596	1,464,000	14	10,851	4,971,000
1953	4,311	1,851,000	19	13,550	6,855,000
1954	4,760	2,324,000	23	16,238	7,917,000
1955	5,001	2,379,000	27	22,965	12,371,000
1956 (EST.)	—	—	—	—	17,000,000

Source: Institute of Life Insurance.

Based on the data for purchases alone, it appears that, although both group and ordinary are increasing, the latter has increased at a faster rate. This may partially be explained by giving consideration to the nature of each policy.

The group policy, being a master contract, tends to remain in force for many years, while the number of insureds increases from year to year as the creditors to which these contracts are issued increase their business.

The ordinary policy, on the other hand, usually is in force for slightly over one year on the average. Because this policy expires within a relatively short period of time, it is necessary to obtain a much greater number of new policies each year to show a substantial increase in the number and amount of ordinary business in force. Thus, not only must a great bulk of expiring policies be replaced, but many new ones must be purchased to produce increases in business in force.

Kinds of Ordinary Life

Two types of consumer credit life insurance policies sold by ordinary insurers to individuals are level-term life and decreasing-term life. The former, illustrated in Diagram 1, is merely a term life policy for the period of the loan, the face of which is constantly equal to the initial amount of the loan. The cost per $100 of insurance is usually $2.00 per year, paid at the inception of the loan.

DIAGRAM 1

LEVEL-TERM LIFE INSURANCE

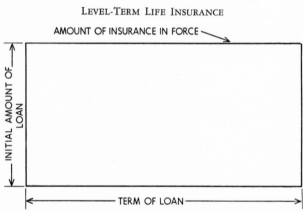

Level term is usually sold in conjunction with loans of the noninstallment variety. One example of this use is the so-called "balloon" loan in which very small periodic payments might be made during the loan period, being insufficient to amortize the loan, or no repayments at all, resulting in a "balloon" or large payment at the end of the loan period.

Under the level-term plan the full amount of insurance remains in force for the entire period of the loan. If death occurs any time within the insured period, the loan balance due is paid the creditor, any excess being returned to a second beneficiary, usually the insured's relative. If the loan has been repaid and the policy is still in force, the entire face amount is paid to the second beneficiary.

Of much more relative importance currently is the decreasing-term policy. Under this plan the amount of insurance declines as the balance of the installment loan decreases by periodic payments, thus making the insurance equal to the anticipated unpaid loan balance. Death of the insured results in full payment of the loan to the lender as beneficiary. Since the coverage is automatically decreasing, a policy of a given duration costs less than level term by about 50 per cent, or $1.00 per year per $100 of initial loan.[5] Diagram 2 pictorially

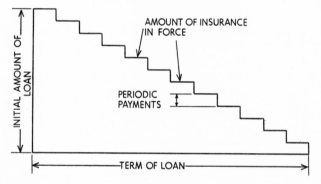

DIAGRAM 2
DECREASING-TERM LIFE INSURANCE

illustrates its use. Since more than three fourths of the current consumer indebtedness is of the installment variety,[6] the decreasing-term plan is more widely sold than the level-term plan.

Kinds of Ordinary Accident and Health

As mentioned, consumer credit disability insurance is sold principally by companies specializing in the sale of ordinary

---

[5] It is customary and proper in a comparison of this kind to consider age in those lines of life insurance where the rate varies with the age of the insured. In ordinary consumer credit life insurance, however, a single rate applies generally to all borrowers 18 to 65.

[6] See "Consumer Credit Statistics," *Federal Reserve Bulletin,* February, 1957, p. 190.

consumer credit life insurance.[7] It covers the hazard of disability resulting from accident or sickness. Prorata payments are made to the creditor during the period of disability.

In an attempt to provide lower rates, use is made of the "deductible principle" by incorporating waiting periods into consumer credit accident and health policies. The Elimination Plan, for example, provides that no payment shall be made on the debtor's behalf until he has been disabled for a period of time, fourteen days being a popular waiting period, after which prorata payments are paid by the company until either the disability ends or the loan runs out. Policies with from three to thirty days' eliminations are available. The purpose here is to bring down the cost of insurance by eliminating payment for the first few days of disability as well as disability resulting from common, short-term illness and accident.

The Retroactive Plan provides for a waiting period which, if exceeded during disability, makes payment on behalf of the debtor for the entire period of disability retroactively. Here again a fourteen day waiting period is typical, with a range of three to fourteen days available. Diagram 3 illustrates the differences between the two plans in a typical situation.

Total and Permanent Disability Plans

Certain lenders and companies do not wish to offer an insurance plan that pays benefits equal to the monthly installment of the borrower for a period of either temporary or permanent total disability until such disability ends or the term of the loan expires. These lenders and companies would rather offer a borrower protection against very long-term disability, defined as "permanent and total," and usually further described as a condition that precludes the debtor's performance of each and every duty associated with his occupation.

Such long-term disability plans are written in conjunction with a few group consumer credit life insurance contracts and require that, when such disability is incurred during the period

---

[7] One large writer currently offers a package of group consumer credit life insurance and an individual accident and health insurance policy to its clients.

of insurance, the claim is treated, in effect, as a death claim in that the entire loan balance on that date is paid to the lender with no further payments on the loan or insurance being required of the borrower. Under one plan,[8] it is required that the outstanding balance of the loan be paid upon the receipt by the home office of satisfactory proof of permanent and total

DIAGRAM 3

DISABILITY PAYMENTS MADE UNDER THE FOURTEEN-DAY ELIMINA-
TION PLAN AS CONTRASTED TO THE FOURTEEN-DAY RETROACTIVE

ELIMINATION PLAN

RETROACTIVE PLAN

disability. A similar plan[9] pays the outstanding balance of the loan on behalf of any borrower who remains totally disabled for at least ninety days. Any disability in excess of such period is considered to be permanent and total disability per se and is paid even though the insured borrower were to return to work on the ninety-first day after commencement of disability. Here again, no further payments on the loan or insurance are necessary, the debt and insurance being fully canceled.

---

[8] Written by a mutual company specializing in group consumer credit life insurance to credit unions.

[9] Written by a stock life insurance company writing multiple lines.

SPECIAL PLANS AVAILABLE

It must be remembered that these plans are the fundamental types upon which tailor-made plans are constructed. Because of the varying needs and philosophies of the many different lenders making consumer credit insurance available to their customers, many variations of this basic plan are requested and made available. Indeed it seems that flexibility of this kind is necessary to remain competitive.

With the subject thus defined, its development and growth may now be traced.

Chapter III

DEVELOPMENT AND GROWTH

THE DAWN OF INSTALLMENT SALES

The history and development of consumer credit, especially of the installment variety, and that of consumer credit insurance closely parallel each other. A trickle of installment purchases was noted as early as 1800 in New York City.[1] By 1900 this method of selling was used in connection with such items as furniture, sewing machines, and books. Up to this time the volume of consumer credit was insignificant, the majority of lenders requiring airtight negotiable instruments and easily accessible assets as requisites to a loan.

The Morris Plan Bank

The year 1910 marked the advent of the Morris Plan Bank which was to offer installment credit facilities to borrowers who had "nothing more" than character and potential ability to repay, truly revolutionary requisites for loans made to finance personal and family needs. Purchases of consumer goods now came within the financial reach of many who previously did not qualify for consumer loans. The phenomenal results and repercussions of this bold undertaking are known to all students of finance. Of lesser note but of equal importance were the results of Mr. Morris's conviction that a currently missing but valuable adjunct to his loan operations should be had. The idea stemmed from the recognition that death might take the debtor before his loan could be paid. If the borrower did die, the cosigner, who was many times a relative or close friend,

---

[1] Reavis Cox, *The Economics of Installment Buying* (New York: The Ronald Press Co., 1948), p. 62.

would be called upon to pay the remaining balance. Cosigners, as a result, became reluctant to bind themselves to such an uncertain burden.

The obvious answer, to Mr. Morris at least, was life insurance on the debtor. He conceived of a plan whereby the outstanding balance of the loan as of the date of the borrower's death would be paid by the insurance company to the lender. Upon presentation of his idea to various insurance companies in an attempt to secure such insurance for his borrowers, Mr. Morris met with indifference and discouragement. This being an area in which statistical information was unavailable, with mortality for such classes of insureds unknown and a potentially high initial expense on a relatively short-term contract evident, the insurance companies declined to underwrite this bold, new venture.

Morris Plan Insurance Society

On September 18, 1917, again evidencing a pioneer spirit, Mr. Morris incorporated the Morris Plan Insurance Society as a stock company under the laws of New York. Rates were based upon individual ages. In the first year of its operation 1,432 borrowers took advantage of the plan for $170,950 in coverage.[2] Today the Society has $305,463,408 in force.[3] With the slogan, "No man's debts should live after him," the Society has flourished to become one of the industry's mainstays.

OLD REPUBLIC LIFE INSURANCE COMPANY

Another pioneering company, originally organized in 1923 as the Garfield Casualty Company, of Washington, Illinois, finally evolved after a series of mergers with several other

---

[2] Frank J. Scott, "Memorandum on the Origins of Credit Life Insurance," discussion of the Morris Plan Banks and the development of the Morris Plan Insurance Society. The Society has changed its name recently to Banker's Security Life Insurance Society and now extends its services to other financial institutions in addition to offering accident and health coverage to debtors.

[3] Convention Statement, Banker's Security Life Insurance Society, December 31, 1956.

insurance companies into the Old Republic Credit Life Insurance Company (changed to Old Republic Life Insurance Company effective January 1, 1956). In 1933, it abandoned its writing of regular life insurance lines for the purpose of writing consumer credit insurance exclusively. As a specialty company originally writing the bulk of its business on the individual contract basis, it experienced an amazing growth emerging today as the giant in its field. Appendix B contains pertinent financial data reflecting its rapid rise.

DEVELOPMENT OF THE GROUP CONTRACT

James B. Jacobson attributes the inception of consumer credit life insurance on a group basis to the efforts of three men:

In 1927, Reynolds Pomeroy, a prominent New York insurance broker and close friend of Robert Steffan, an officer of the National City Bank of New York, conceived the idea of covering all of the Bank's personal loan borrowers under a blanket group policy. Steffan, being a progressive officer of a progressive bank, was readily receptive to the idea. Pomeroy, like Morris, presented his idea to various New York life insurance companies, all to no avail. None of the companies he contacted were willing to extend their group operations into the credit field by formulating a new coverage. Their reasons were much the same as those given to Morris some ten years earlier. In due time, Pomeroy met James Little, Vice-President and Actuary of The Prudential Insurance Company of America. Little, a creative thinker of extraordinary ability, accepted the problem as a challenge to formulate a group coverage for a new field.

As a result of the combined interest of these three men, the first credit life insurance policy on a group basis, Group Creditors Insurance, was introduced in 1928. The policy, issued by the Prudential to the National City Bank of New York, covered the Bank's unsecured personal loans. During the period 1928–1952, 15,400 individual debtors of the Bank died before completing their loan repayments, leaving outstanding balances at death, all insured, totalling $3,300,000.[4]

---

[4] James B. Jacobson, *An Analysis of Group Creditor's Insurance,* a thesis presented to the faculty of the Department of Finance, University of Southern California, and published by The Prudential Insurance Company of America, 1955, p. 15.

At the end of 1954, the company insured some seven million people for $3.5 billions under group consumer credit life insurance.[5]

By 1930, although only three companies wrote consumer credit life insurance, business in force totaled $73 million.[6] This rapid rise can be attributed to the increased use of installment credit, especially automobile purchases, which became very prominent after World War I.

CUNA MUTUAL INSURANCE SOCIETY

Of great importance in the development of consumer credit insurance was the emphasis given it by the credit union movement. By 1934, the movement hit a new peak of popularity resulting in the organization of the Credit Union National Association. The demand for the Association to write its own insurance was heard at the very first board meeting. Because of the peculiarities of the credit union mechanism, the members felt their own insurance company "could do a better job than was being done."[7] Consequently, the CUNA Mutual Insurance Society began operations on August 16, 1935, under Wisconsin statutes, devoting itself exclusively to the insuring of credit union members. Its success was characterized by Mr. Thomas Doig, managing director, who stated:

Our rate of growth has been remarkable. One insurance journal recently pointed out that it took CUNA Mutual 6 years to grow from nothing to $100,000,000 coverage, 7 years more to reach $200,000,000, another 2 years to hit $500,000,000, and only 2 years more to arrive at $1,000,000,000. There seems to be no tapering off in prospect.[8]

At the end of 1956, CUNA Mutual Insurance Society had

---

[5] E. B. Whittaker, vice-president of The Prudential Insurance Company of America, a statement made on February 15, 1955, before the Senate Judiciary Committee of the State of Kansas.

[6] *Fact Sheet on Consumer Credit Insurance* (Chicago: Consumer Credit Insurance Association, July, 1953), p. 1.

[7] Roy F. Bergengren, *Crusade* (New York: Exposition Press, 1952), p. 258.

[8] Thomas W. Doig, in the CUNA Mutual Insurance Society's Annual Report, 1954, p. 4.

$1,599,203,314[9] of consumer credit life and disability insurance in force, testifying to its important contribution to the consumer credit insurance industry. Appendix C attests to the company's remarkable growth in recent years in the field of consumer credit life and disability coverages available to credit union members by CUNA Mutual Insurance Society.

THE PRUDENTIAL–GMAC CONTRACT

Another extremely significant development in the group form of consumer credit life insurance took place just prior to World War II. In one of the most notable success stories in insurance history, two leaders of different industries were cast in the leading roles. About 1940, G. ArDee Ames, vice-president of the General Motors Acceptance Corporation (GMAC), considered the possibility of insuring the lives of General Motors' customers whose time purchases were financed through GMAC.[10] Several insurance companies were asked by GMAC to provide an insurance plan whereby consumer credit life insurance could be issued at low cost to the public, at the same time being optional to the dealer and its customers. The Prudential Insurance Company of America underwrote GMAC beginning September 27, 1941. Its growth was slow in the early years due to its being promoted slowly on a state by state rather than a national basis. Credit restrictions of the federal government during the war were also greatly responsible for its meager beginnings.

Despite a slow start, the contract now covers "more people than are insured under any other life insurance policy in the world."[11] Over 2,100,000 persons were insured for more than

---

[9] This figure was taken from a statistical compilation made up at the author's request by the CUNA Mutual Insurance Society's accounting department and does not include Canadian business.

[10] *In the Best American Tradition*, a brochure prepared by the Group Department of The Prudential Insurance Company of America, October 1952, p. 2.

[11] Edmund B. Whittaker, "Group Creditors Life Insurance," *The Journal of the American Society of Chartered Life Underwriters*, Vol. VII, No. 3, June, 1953, p. 223.

$1.3 billion as of 1952. Since its inception, over $7 million in claims have been paid to people in every state of the United States and parts of Canada. Presently, the contract insures 3,286,578 customers of GMAC for an outstanding indebtedness of $2.9 billion.[12]

HISTORICAL TREND OF CONSUMER CREDIT LIFE INSURANCE

Table III and Diagram 4 show the growth of all consumer credit life insurance from its inception. As can be seen, the Great Depression brought a significant halt and subsequent downturn to purchases of this coverage.

From 1934 to 1941, consumer credit life insurance experienced a fairly steady growth. However, on August 12, 1941 President Roosevelt issued Executive Order 8843 directing the Federal Reserve Board to curtail consumer buying power. "Regulation W" followed on August 21, 1941 and required larger down payments and general contractions of credit. Production of consumer goods came to a virtual standstill. Both consumer credit outstanding and credit life insurance in force dropped drastically as it had during the Great Depression, but this time under completely different circumstances. A further credit restriction on May 6, 1942 resulted from the President's Special Message to Congress. Table IV demonstrates this marked decrease of both consumer credit life insurance in force and consumer credit insurance outstanding during the early years of World War II as well as the tremendous upsurge in the premium volume subsequent to 1945.

About 1946 credit restrictions began to ease. As consumer credit began to increase rapidly, it presented a potentially lucrative field for consumer credit insurance cultivation. Both mushroomed, the latter at a faster rate.

---

[12] This data was obtained through correspondence with the General Motors Acceptance Corporation.

TABLE III

CONSUMER CREDIT LIFE INSURANCE PURCHASES IN THE UNITED STATES, 1917–54
(000 Omitted)

| | Ordinary | | | Group | | Total | |
Year	No. of Policies	Amount	Master Policies	No. of Certificates	Amount	Number*	Amount
1917	1	$ †	—	—	$ —	1	$
1918	20	3,000	—	—	—	20	3,000
1919	25	4,000	—	—	—	25	4,000
1920	25	5,000	—	—	—	25	5,000
1921	32	7,000	—	—	—	32	7,000
1922	35	8,000	—	—	—	35	8,000
1923	35	8,000	—	—	—	35	8,000
1924	49	11,000	—	—	—	49	11,000
1925	80	17,000	—	—	—	80	17,000
1926	113	23,000	‡	8	1,000	121	24,000
1927	138	28,000	‡	7	1,000	145	29,000
1928	148	34,000	‡	33	8,000	181	42,000
1929	176	39,000	‡	70	8,000	246	47,000
1930	193	44,000	‡	65	9,000	258	53,000
1931	160	32,000	‡	85	18,000	245	50,000
1932	128	23,000	‡	30	6,000	158	29,000
1933	116	20,000	‡	31	7,000	147	27,000
1934	136	23,000	‡	40	9,000	176	32,000
1935	178	29,000	‡	73	15,000	251	44,000
1936	202	33,000	1	164	22,000	366	55,000
1937	241	44,000	1	262	46,000	503	90,000
1938	315	53,000	1	242	32,000	557	85,000
1939	360	62,000	1	275	37,000	635	99,000
1940	421	73,000	1	204	32,000	625	105,000
1941	479	84,000	1	304	56,000	783	140,000
1942	428	69,000	1	136	17,000	564	86,000
1943	394	66,000	1	80	12,000	474	78,000
1944	424	76,000	1	75	17,000	499	93,000
1945	614	118,000	1	112	30,000	726	148,000
1946	1,092	208,000	1	481	171,000	1,573	379,000
1947	1,399	330,000	1	563	166,000	1,962	496,000
1948	1,778	443,000	1	605	220,000	2,383	663,000
1949	2,044	519,000	2	987	449,000	3,031	968,000
1950	2,718	730,000	2	1,746	839,000	4,464	1,569,000
1951	3,445	1,071,000	3	1,600	521,000	5,045	1,592,000
1952	4,254	1,470,000	3	1,487	915,000	5,741	2,385,000
1953	4,871	1,818,000	5	2,511	1,432,000	7,382	3,250,000
1954	4,786	2,143,000	5	2,386	955,000	7,172	3,098,000

* Includes group certificates.
† Less than 500 master policies.
‡ Less than $500,000.
Source: Institute of Life Insurance.

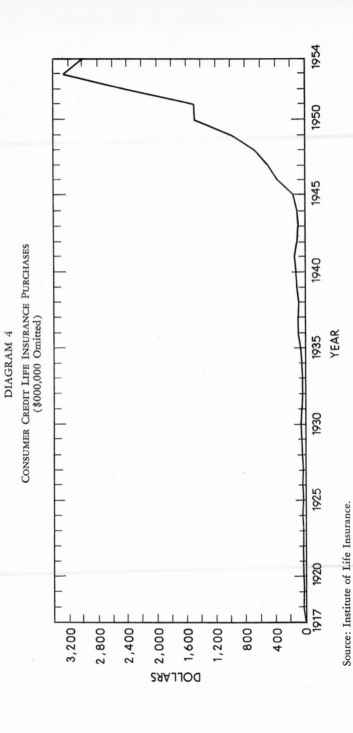

DIAGRAM 4

CONSUMER CREDIT LIFE INSURANCE PURCHASES
($000,000 Omitted)

DOLLARS

YEAR

Source: Institute of Life Insurance.

TABLE IV

CONSUMER CREDIT OUTSTANDING AND
CONSUMER CREDIT LIFE INSURANCE IN FORCE
1929–56
(In Millions of Dollars)

Year	Total Consumer Credit Outstanding*	Consumer Credit Life Insurance in Force†
1929	$ 6,444	$ 57
1930	5,767	73
1931	4,760	85
1932	3,567	69
1933	3,482	63
1934	3,904	75
1935	4,911	101
1936	6,135	138
1937	6,689	216
1938	6,338	256
1939	7,222	307
1940	8,338	380
1941	9,172	469
1942	5,983	355
1943	4,901	275
1944	5,111	290
1945	5,665	365
1946	8,383	729
1947	11,570	1,210
1948	14,398	1,729
1949	17,305	2,531
1950	21,395	3,889
1951	22,617	4,818
1952	27,401	6,435
1953	31,243	8,706
1954	32,292	10,241
1955	38,648	14,750
1956	41,863	17,000‡

* Federal Reserve Bulletin, August, 1956, p. 878; February, 1957, p. 190.

† *Credit Life in the United States* (New York: Institute of Life Insurance).

‡ Estimated.

REASONS FOR GROWTH

Diagram 5 illustrates the marked advance made by consumer credit insurance as a per cent of consumer credit in force. It will be noted that, from a low point during the war and postwar years when 6 per cent of the outstanding consumer credit was insured, the tremendous rate of increase outstripped that of consumer credit, resulting in 41 per cent insurance to consumer credit at the end of 1956.[13] From 1945 to 1955 consumer credit life insurance increased over 4,000 per cent while regular group life insurance experienced a 500 per cent increase for a comparable period. This tremendous

DIAGRAM 5

CONSUMER CREDIT LIFE INSURANCE IN FORCE AS A PERCENTAGE OF CONSUMER CREDIT OUTSTANDING, 1929–55

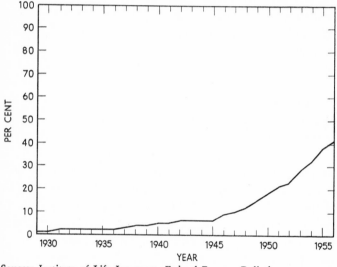

Source: Institute of Life Insurance, Federal Reserve Bulletins.

increase in consumer credit insurance purchases can be attributed to several underlying causes.

Composition of Consumer Credit

First to be noted is the quality of consumer credit outstanding. Because consumer credit of the installment variety most readily lends itself to the mechanism of consumer credit

---

[13] A more impressive but less accurate picture can be had by comparing total installment credit outstanding to consumer credit insurance in force. To the extent that the latter is sold to cover debts of the noninstallment variety, such an exposition is distorted.

life insurance on the decreasing-term basis, any growth of such form of buying would tend to result in a higher potential market for such insurance protection. As of December 31, 1956, consumer credit outstanding reached $41.8 billion.[14] Of this total, installment credit represented about three-fourths, while noninstallment debt, principally single payment loans and charge accounts, constituted the remaining quarter of the total.

Emphasizing the tremendous importance of automobile sales in the total installment buying picture, the Department of Commerce recently stated: "By far the largest single factor in the expansion of installment credit has been the booming sales of automobiles."[15] During 1955, the increase in automobile paper outstanding accounted for more than 60 per cent of the consumer debt total. In recent years, three-fifths of total new car purchases have utilized the installment plan. The year 1955 proved to be one of the best for automobile sales, and although repayments of consumer debt exceeded extentions in 1956, it is generally agreed that such a decline is not indicative of a trend.

As previously mentioned, although relatively more noninstallment debt is being insured, the bulk of the insured debt is of the installment variety. To a large extent the continued success of consumer credit insurance is dependent upon the continuing high rate of installment automobile sales.

Lending further insight into the quality of consumer credit debt, the Federal Reserve Board's Survey of Consumer Finances for 1955 revealed that 65 per cent of installment debt was to be paid off in one year or less, with less than 10 per cent exceeding two years or more. Because of the essentially short-term composition of current installment debt, giving it the characteristic of rapid turnover, it is easier to understand the very great increase in consumer credit life insurance as related to total consumer credit.

The extent of the dependence of the high standard of living

---

[14] Federal Reserve Bulletin, February, 1957, p. 190.

[15] U.S. Department of Commerce, "Recent Trends in Consumer Credit," *Survey of Current Business*, Vol. 35, August, 1955, p. 7.

enjoyed in America upon the availability and use of consumer credit is evident when it is noted that approximately three out of five spending units have installment debts of some kind.[16] Without discussing the ability of the present economy to support a short-term debt of this magnitude, it must be remembered that consumer credit, particularly installment buying, has been responsible to a very great extent for the sustenance of much of the consumer goods industry, if not the entire economy. Furthermore, it is generally conceded that installment buying will persist as part of the American way of life, and that consumer credit insurance will co-exist with it.

Variety of Publicity

A second reason for the rise in consumer credit life and accident and health insurance is the publicity given it in various forms. Although impossible to measure, favorable word-of-mouth advertising has been claimed by most officials connected with the business. They cite with pride many examples of borrowers who take the initiative in requesting the coverage without being asked. They point to the many borrowers who tell of being advised by a friend or relative of the many advantages of this coverage. Several have related their experience of their lender-clients who have gained a distinct competitive advantage in their operations because of their making this coverage available.

These cases, although scattered and statistically unreliable for purposes of generalization, are important nevertheless. Many good advertising men realize that favorable word-of-mouth advertising of a few faithful and satisfied customers is at least equal in desirability to any other advertising medium.[17]

---

[16] R. D. Shepard, "Thirty-six Year Story: Insuring Credit," *The Spectator,* Vol. 161, p. 18.

[17] Evidencing an even stronger conviction regarding the effectiveness of word-of-mouth advertising, Harry P. Bridge, in his book *Practical Advertising* (New York: Rinehart and Co., 1949), states on page 32: "You cannot for instance, expect to advertise once or twice and sell a Ford automobile to a man who has just bought a Chevrolet. But keep pounding away and you may succeed a year or two hence when he's again in the market for a car. Moreover, once your advertising has sold him on buying a Ford, the quality and performance of the product may then lead him to become so enthusiastic that he will

In 1951, several consumer credit insurers banded together to form the Consumer Credit Insurance Association (CCIA). Besides acting as a trade organization in the dissemination of consumer credit insurance advertising for companies specializing in writing this coverage, it also attempts to promote higher standards of the business. Another purpose is "to disseminate information and provide for the exchange of ideas among and between its members."[18] In addition to providing consumer credit insurance information to the public and exchanging ideas among its members, the organization has been an effective spokesman before legislative and investigatory bodies and has generally rallied to the defense of the ordinary method of doing business, although recently many of its members have acquired substantial amounts of group coverage. CCIA members are listed in the front part of the book.

Of no small consequence in publicizing the existence of this form of coverage is the publication by newspapers, periodicals, and trade journals of the abuses connected with the sale of this insurance by a few "sharp" leaders, overambitious agents, and volume-hungry companies. Abusive practices such as those previously cited are considered "news"; ethical business undertakings rarely, if ever, receive such notoriety. In most cases, it subsequently comes to light that such practices are in the minority, the majority of the companies retaining their reputations for integrity. The end result, besides frequently suggesting needed and desirable remedial action to legislative and administrative officials, is that the consumer credit insurance industry acquires "free" advertising of an institutional nature.

Increase in the Number of Insurers

A third reason for the growth of this coverage is the increasingly large number of companies entering the field in

---

make a point of recommending this car to all of his friends. *This word-of-mouth advertising is the most valuable, most convincing kind of advertising in the world."* (Italics added.)

[18] Articles of Incorporation of the Consumer Credit Insurance Association, Chicago.

recent years adding additional facilities to what, in the postwar period at least, appeared to be an excessive demand for an inadequate supply. Despite the remarkable increases in consumer credit purchases during this period, the demand for the coverage increased as the demand for consumer credit grew.

As mentioned, by 1930 only three companies competed for business. By 1946 approximately 51 companies wrote some form of consumer credit life insurance in the United States.[19] At the end of 1955, no less than 237 companies were writing the coverage on the group and ordinary basis.[20] Appendix E contains the names of those companies currently writing the coverage and their method of selling it.

Because of the relatively few companies offering this insurance just after the war, and due to the spectacular upsurge of consumer credit already noted, it became a fairly simple task to market and sell such coverage. As one interviewed industry spokesman put it: "The sky's the limit and it keeps getting higher," which was his way of saying that, although sales of consumer credit insurance were very great in absolute terms, the industry had a difficult time in keeping a given percentage of consumer credit insurance over a period of time. As more companies entered the field this goal was more easily attainable.

A fair number of those companies entering the field as specialty insurers, that is, companies writing consumer credit insurance exclusively, branched out into regular forms of life and accident and health insurance as well. Indeed it has been said by many company officials that one of the quickest and simplest ways of entering the regular life and allied insurance lines is through the doorway of consumer credit insurance.

Security-Minded Populace

The recent awareness and demand for security by the public accounts for a fourth reason for the demand for consumer

---

[19] Correspondence with the Institute of Life Insurance.
[20] *Ibid.*

credit insurance. Mr. Edmund B. Whittaker, whose company pioneered group consumer credit life insurance, stated recently: "The amazing growth of group life and accident and health insurance in this country can be traced to the increasing awareness of the importance of security in our political and economic thinking."[21] To this can be added the spectacular gains made in individual life and accident and health policies and individual and group annuities. Since consumer credit insurance does seem to afford security to the borrower, particularly in the form of peace of mind regarding the contingencies of premature death or prolonged disability, its appeal to a security-minded populace is extremely great.

Reversal of Cause and Effect

Finally, it seems that the phenomenal growth of this coverage may be partially attributed to its ability to make people eligible for credit, who but for the availability of consumer credit insurance could not qualify or avail themselves of the facilities of consumer credit. Indeed it would seem that a significant reversal has taken place in recent years in the cause and effect relationship between consumer credit and the coverage which insures it.

From 1917 until the early 1940's, the volume of consumer credit insurance closely followed the growth of consumer credit. In recent years, however, lenders have come to appreciate the value of being made a beneficiary to a life and/or accident and health policy thereby eliminating the possibility of nonpayment of a loan by reason of premature death or sudden accident or sickness. Thus more people have become eligible for credit *because* of the availability of consumer credit insurance, thus contributing to the potential purchasing power of the populace. Mr. E. J. Faulkner, distinguished accident and health underwriter, maintains that "to the extent that (con-

---

[21] Edmund B. Whittaker, "Group Creditors Life Insurance," *The Journal of the American Society of Chartered Life Underwriters,* Vol. VII, No. 3, June, 1953, p. 220.

sumer) credit insurance has underwritten consumer credit it has contributed to our expanding economy."[22]

Bruce E. Shepherd, manager of the Life Insurance Association of America, recently stated: "The remarkable development of [consumer] credit insurance from virtually insignificant proportions within the decade can be read as both a reflection and as a facilitating factor in the expanding utilization of credit."[23]

We might well add to the previous definitions of this insurance by stating that it is a form of coverage which in some cases insures the receipt of credit by making one an eligible recipient. Although measurement of the frequency of this result would be difficult, the results are clear. The availability of consumer credit insurance is now a causal contributing "ingredient" to the volatile consumer credit "brew."

Such is the history, development, and importance of the mechanism to be explained in operational detail.

---

[22] E. J. Faulkner, "An Underwriter Looks at Insurance in Connection with Lending," *Quarterly Report,* Winter 1951, p. 13.

[23] "Credit Life Has 40-Fold Gain in Ten-Year Period," *The American Banker,* December 22, 1955.

Chapter IV

SALES AND ADMINSTRATION

INTRODUCTION

Simplicity of operation has been the marketing hallmark of insurers offering consumer credit insurance. In an attempt at securing a mass market for the coverage at a relatively low rate, bold operating concepts have been adopted. Liberalization of underwriting has resulted in the waiving of physical examinations by the companies and, with the usual exception of insureds under 18 and over 65, a single rate for all ages. Policies containing a minimum of exclusions and a constant endeavor to streamline management and sales operations characterize this trend. Because of the many variables in operations encountered among banks (both commercial and industrial), consumer and sales finance companies, credit unions, department stores, and other retail outlets, most companies provide custom-tailored plans to fit a particular lender's needs. It would be nearly impossible to describe the details of each plan. With but few exceptions, the discussion in the following chapters will apply generally to all types of lenders.[1]

TYPES OF COMPANIES WRITING CONSUMER CREDIT INSURANCE

It is particularly in the area of sales and administration that the greatest differences in operating procedures and philosophies exist between the group and ordinary, or individual,

---

[1] One such notable exception is the insurance of consumer debt held by the credit unions, which, in the main, is underwritten by the CUNA Mutual Insurance Society. However, because this text is devoted primarily to an explanation of proprietary lenders, rather than those operating on a co-operative basis, discussion of this type of lending institution has been necessarily minimized.

method of insuring. In general, the bulk of the consumer credit life insurance of the group variety is marketed by several large, old-line mutual life insurance companies whose consumer credit life insurance sales, although substantial in dollar amount, are a relatively small part of their total life and accident and health insurance premium income.[2] Most of the ordinary insurance business is sold by the smaller stock life and accident and health insurers among which are many whose sole or main coverage is consumer credit life and accident and health written on the ordinary insurance basis. It should be noted that, although the large mutual life insurance companies mentioned do not write consumer credit life insurance on the ordinary basis, several of the stock life and accident and health companies writing ordinary insurance business do have a relatively large and growing volume of group consumer credit life insurance in force. Thus it appears that, although all companies engaged in the sale of this insurance recognize and agree upon the feasibility of administering such coverage on the group basis, the large, old-line, predominantly mutual companies do not uphold the ordinary insurance method and philosophy of doing business. The latter group's principal objection stems from the amount and method of compensating lenders, to be discussed presently.

Consumer credit accident and health insurance paying monthly installments to the creditor on behalf of the insured while disabled is written generally, though not exclusively, on the ordinary insurance basis.[3] In any event, although more companies offer ordinary consumer credit accident and health insurance than do not, the large old-line life and accident and health insurers do not generally make such coverage available. Reasons for this will become apparent as the operation of, and differences within, the consumer credit insurance mechanism

---

[2] Although several very large stock life insurance companies are writing this coverage, their volume is relatively small, entry into the consumer credit insurance field being quite recent.

[3] Group consumer credit accident and health insurance is relatively new and not generally permitted by most states at this time. However, a trend toward legalizing the sale of such coverage appears to be developing.

on the group and ordinary insurance basis of administration are discussed.

In conducting insurance operations on the group basis, the lending institution becomes a master policyholder under a one-year renewable term policy. Insured borrowers are issued certificates of insurance as they become debtors of the lender. If premiums are paid entirely by the lender under a noncontributory plan, current debtors may be insured.[4]

Unlike the group method, individual policies are sold to each borrower under the ordinary insurance method. The insurer enters into an agency agreement with the lender who becomes an agent of the company rather than a master policyholder. As agent, the lender is thus in a position to receive commissions. It is in this area that one of the great differences in operation and philosophy arises. Who receives the commissions and the size of such commissions are considerations of vital importance to group and ordinary insurers and the public as well.

MARKETING ON THE GROUP BASIS

Agency System

The vendors of consumer credit life insurance written on the group basis have generally utilized the existing agency channels. A similarity in marketing does exist between regular group life and group consumer credit life insurance, which is usually considered a subdivision of regular group life insurance. Agents and brokers working on a commission basis are commonly assisted by a salaried home office representative variously titled "group representative," "home office representative," or "fieldman." Use is made of the local agent's contacts and it is not uncommon for such a local agent to find prospects among

---

[4] Issuance of coverage to existing debtors where the premium is paid by the borrower is rather impractical in that it involves contacting each borrower individually. This is necessary because the effective date of the master policy may fall somewhere in between installment due dates. Also, many debtors use the mails rather than go to the lender's office personally to make payment. The opportune time to effect coverage would thus seem to be the date of issuance or renewal of the loan.

those of his clients to whom he has sold insurance for personal and/or other business needs. Most times, however, mere personal contact with such clients is not enough to result in a sale because of the specialized nature of consumer credit insurance and its varying applicability to a given lender's needs. The fieldman who is a specialist in consumer credit insurance and allied plans is called in to render technical assistance to the local agent. Except for large metropolitan brokerage firms, very few local agents would have sufficient need to acquaint themselves with the details of this coverage and its applications. The fieldman, as a home office specialist, is constantly dealing with this insurance coverage and the problems of the lenders and is thus thoroughly familiar with them.

Compensation of Agents

Compensation to the fieldman takes the form of a salary. In a few cases a year-end bonus is paid also. Commissions paid to the local agents and brokers as producers are based upon the graded commission scale commonly used to compensate agents selling regular group life insurance. This scale has been so constructed as to adequately compensate the agent while still holding acquisition costs at a reasonable level.[5] Table V relates typical commissions paid to such producers.

Companies operating under this plan are quick to emphasize that no other commissions are paid (besides those in Table V) to their regular producing agents and brokers, and under no circumstances are they paid to the lender. One of the largest writers in the field maintains that commissions would not be paid to any official of a lending institution even if he were legally entitled to receive them.[6] It appears that the companies

---

[5] L. W. Ilse, *Group Insurance and Employee Retirement Plans* (New York: Prentice-Hall, Inc., 1953), p. 129.

[6] See, for example, the statement given by E. B. Whittaker, vice-president of The Prudential Insurance Company of America, before the Senate Judiciary Committee of the State of Kansas, February 15, 1955.

If the commissions, as such, *were* paid to a lender in the case of group consumer credit life insurance, serious consideration would have to be given the legal right of such lender as a holder and beneficiary under a master policy, to also collect commissions in the capacity of an agent.

writing consumer credit insurance solely on the group basis are making a sincere effort to pay commissions only to those persons directly responsible for the acquisition of consumer credit

TABLE V

AGENTS AND BROKERS COMMISSION SCHEDULE FOR
GROUP CONSUMER CREDIT LIFE INSURANCE

Annual Premium	First Year Commission, %	Renewal Commission for Nine Years, %
First $1,000	20	5
From $1,000 to $5,000	20	3
From $5,000 to $10,000	15	1.5
From $10,000 to $20,000	12.5	1.5
From $20,000 to $30,000	10	1.5
From $30,000 to $50,000	5	1.5
From $50,000 to $100,000	2.5	1
From $100,000 to $200,000	1	0.5
Over $200,000	0.5	0.1

insurance accounts. Such a system is in support of the American agency system.

MARKETING ON THE ORDINARY BASIS

Agency System

The foregoing may be contrasted with the practices of the group of companies exclusively devoted to, or heavily emphasizing, the sale of ordinary consumer credit insurance. Their employment of salaried representatives is generally, though not exclusively, utilized to secure the agency agreement, or account, between the lender and insurer. One of the largest specialty companies in this group retains salaried representatives schooled primarily in the operation of consumer credit insurance, only occasionally accepting business from a few selected general agencies. It is the belief of this company and others like it that the American agency system is not generally capable of procuring such business because of the intricacies of the coverage and its variability among differing lending operations resulting in the need for a specialist. An official of this company expressed the belief that his company's method of acquisition was more efficient since it embodied the functions of acquisition and technical knowledge into one individual.

Although the utilization of the American agency system by the old-line, predominantly mutual life insurance companies and employment of salaried representatives by the newer stock specialty writers are the prevalent methods, at least one large stock life and accident and health insurer departs from this pattern. In its offering of a "package policy" of group consumer credit life insurance and ordinary consumer credit accident and health insurance, this company offers a 20 per cent commission of which 15 per cent is retained by the lender and 5 per cent is paid the company agent who acquires the account. This method would seem to support the thesis that both the agent who acquires the account and the lender who makes the coverage available have a role significant enough in the marketing of the insurance to merit compensation.

It should again be emphasized that the legal relationship between the lender and insurance company is different as between the group and ordinary insurance methods of operation. In the former, the lender is a policyholder; in the latter, he is an agent. In the majority of states, statutes permit the lender to act as an agent and receive commissions. In those states that specifically prohibit the lender from receiving compensation, various means are employed to nullify the effect of such laws.

A lender may, for example, establish an insurance agency as a separate wholly-owned business entity. Since the lender will have an interest in both the lending operations and the agency operations, any profits which accrue to either will also eventually accrue to the lender. Another subterfuge is to use an employee who works "free," his income actually consisting of commissions paid on the sale of insurance. Another may receive a relatively small salary in addition to payment of commissions. A few instances have been discovered where the lender creates or buys control of a credit insurance company so that profits on both lending and insuring operations are received.[7] The most devious method of securing commissions is through a reinsurance subsidiary. Professor Wallace P. Mors described the operation as follows:

> Here the X creditor turns over collected premiums to the Y insurance company. The X creditor then organizes Z insurance subsidiary which reinsures a specified amount of the insurance written by the Y insurance company and gets a substantial tax advantage by organizing its own insurance or reinsurance subsidiary. This tax advantage results from the fact that the underwriting income of insurance companies is not taxable under the federal income tax law.[8]

Compensation Rates

Rates of compensation to lender-agents of consumer credit life and accident and health insurance written under the ordinary method of insuring are substantial, ranging from a minimum of 40 to 55 per cent of each premium dollar. Besides these known and established rates, a few instances were brought to light of payments of 60 and 65 per cent, and at least one of 85 per cent.[9] Commissions of such great magnitude are difficult to justify by all parties concerned. The problem of high commissions is recognized by many people associated with consumer credit insurance administration, but it appears that the companies are fearful of diminishing commissions at the expense of losing a competitive tool and business as well. Since maximum rates and commissions are not generally controlled by legislation, it appears that there is nothing to prevent an insurance company from securing the business of commission-hungry lenders by tendering successively higher commissions than those of its competitors. Obviously, if such were the tendency, it would not work to the benefit of the insured

---

[7] See, for example, "The Tie-In Sale of Credit Insurance in Connection With Small Loans and Other Transactions," a report of the Subcommittee on Antitrust and Monopoly Legislation of the Committee of the Judiciary, United States Senate (83rd Cong., 2nd Sess.) (Washington, D.C.: U.S. Government Printing Office, 1955), pp. 7–8.

[8] Wallace P. Mors, "Consumer Installment Credit Insurance," *The Insurance Law Journal,* No. 400, May 1956, p. 300.

[9] United States Senate Judiciary Report, *op. cit.,* p. 4.

since the impact of such increases will almost certainly be borne by him, resulting in higher premiums for the same insurance coverage. Such practices have given rise to the terms "reverse competition" and "captive markets."

"Reverse Competition"

The term "reverse competition" refers to the tendency of the cost to the borrower of ordinary consumer credit insurance to increase or remain high because of the practice of the insurance company's bidding for the lender's business through tendering the lender successively higher commissions. As a result of rising compensation, rates tend to increase or remain at an excessive level. Competition for business, then, instead of being on the basis of low rates to the insured borrower, is on the basis of commissions paid to the lender. That this practice has occurred is known and admitted by most lenders and insurers. Because insurance is a highly competitive business, however, the frequency of occurrence of such bidding and the exact range of commissions tendered is unknown, since these are among the insurer's closely guarded business secrets.

"Captive Markets"

The term "captive market" attempts to express the unique position of the lender who, because of the borrower's generally embarrassed financial and inferior bargaining position, is able to foist this insurance upon the debtor. Unlike other lines of insurance where the insured generally has a choice of coverages, companies, agents, and rates, an individual who secures a loan from a lender offering consumer credit insurance and elects, or is required, to carry such coverage has automatically, by the selection of his creditor, chosen his coverage, company, agent, and rate.[10] Because either the group or ordinary form

---

[10] The ordinary method of insuring does offer the borrower a choice of level- or decreasing-term life, the retroactive or elimination plan of accident and health insurance, and varying lengths of waiting periods. The group method usually offers only decreasing-term life insurance, although one company surveyed and previously mentioned offered a group life and ordinary accident and health insurance "package." There are a few cases where group level-term life insurance is being written, but the volume appears insignificant.

of consumer credit insurance offers incentive to the creditor to make an effort to sell such protection to as many borrowers as possible, the term "captive market" might be used to describe a lender's superior position whether utilizing the group or ordinary insurance method of operations, so long as the cost of such coverage is paid by the borrower.

Already mentioned as one incentive to the creditor operating on the ordinary insurance basis was the minimum 40 to 55 per cent commission retained. The group method returns the "retrospective credit," "premium refund," or "dividend" to the lender, the amount of which is dependent, among other things, upon the amount of premiums and losses attributed to the individual lender. This latter system admittedly provides a lesser over-all incentive to the lender to promote this coverage, since the return is usually less direct, being paid contingently at the end of a policy year. Furthermore, the return to the lender as a percentage of premium dollar is generally smaller than commissions under the ordinary insurance plan.[11] In either case, however, once the creditor has agreed to furnish insurance to his customers, the mechanism is such that active promotion of the coverage results in pecuniary return of some kind to the lender.

Depending on the quality of the "captive market" and the return realized by the lender over and above his actual cost of providing the insurance, the system offers a potential for abusive practices. One of the most serious is that of coercion of the borrower. A lifting of the eyebrow, a certain inflection of the voice, and a "suggestion" that the borrower ought to have insurance might result in a degree of coercion, their very description attesting to the difficulty of measuring the frequency of

---

[11] See Chapter VI for a further explanation of the "retrospective rate." As will be noted later, a system of "retrospective rating" was also used by some ordinary insurers. This device led to flagrant abuses because it permitted direct and almost independent control of the insurance monies by the lender-agent, including both collection from, and payments to, policyholders and claimants. There was thus established a pecuniary incentive to avoid the payment of legitimate claims since any claims payments would directly effect the lender's retention. Today this abuse appears as the exception rather than as the rule, since most jurisdictions disallow such practices.

occurrence. Several factors might be mentioned as influencing both the frequency and severity of coercive practices by the lender. Included would be the extent of competition among and within the various classes of lenders in the vicinity, the statutes regulating the lender's operation and their degree of enforcement, the urgency of the borrower's financial position, and finally the ethics of the lender. This latter factor is important not only in determining the extent to which lenders may take advantage of their "captive markets," but also influences the extent of the operation of "reverse competition." If one accepts the view that lenders are ruthless, unethical, and commission-hungry, the problem of coercion appears to be acute and one must completely disregard the fact that the lender must meet ethical standards prescribed by law before being permitted to operate. On the other hand, the attitude that the lender "can do no wrong" creates too idealistic an approach and the tendency to discount or overlook any existing abuses. If the situation is viewed with any amount of objectivity, one sees that advantage has been taken of the debtor in several instances.[12] The abuses have generally occurred among a minority of small-loan operators in states having no small-loan legislation, inadequate legislation, or poor enforcement. It would appear, however, that most lenders taking the long-run view have the best interests of their customers in mind because most businessmen recognize that customer satisfaction is their guarantee of long-run success.

OPPOSITION TO LENDER COMPENSATION

As might be expected, associations of insurance agents have voiced strong protests against the system of licensing lenders and paying them commissions. Their objections are several. Since the lender-made-agent is primarily engaged in the business of lending money, and only incidentally in the sales and administration of consumer credit insurance, the agents' groups

---

[12] For example see "The Tie-In Sale of Credit Insurance in Connection With Small Loans and Other Transactions," *op. cit.*, p. 8.

contend that the assureds suffer from lack of agent's services and experience. It must be remembered in considering the argument, however, that for consumer credit life insurance, the amount of servicing is limited since a claim is paid but once, if at all, for an individual insured debtor. Also, the type of insurance protection received from such coverage is temporary in nature and contributes little, if anything, to a person's permanent insurance program. The criticism is more justifiable for accident and health insurance, where the contract is more elaborate and subject to experienced interpretation. Furthermore, the amount of servicing necessary is considerably greater than with life insurance since, when claims are presented, they may continue for a lengthy period of time.

Some agents believe that the sale of consumer credit insurance infringes upon their regular life and accident and health business and thus object to the lender's becoming a vendor. For consumer credit life insurance, it can be argued that this protection lessens the need for a clean-up fund, at least to the extent that consumer loans are insured.[13] However, because the average balance due on consumer installment debt is small[14] in comparison to the size of the clean-up fund,[15] it is doubtful that such coverage is a real threat to the sale of regular and permanent forms of life insurance.[16] To the extent that consumer credit accident and health insurance lessens a debtor's installment payments during periods of disability, the sale of such coverage encroaches upon the regular sales of accident and health insurance. Here the financial impact of

---

[13] This fund ordinarily includes funeral and burial costs, provision for medical expenses, accrued taxes and other expenses, and balances due on consumer goods.

[14] A prospectus issued by the Household Finance Corporation, January 14, 1957, indicated the company's average size loan to be $365 for 1955. The "Life Insurance Fact Book" for 1955 reports that the average insured consumer credit loan was $490.

[15] See Robert Mehr and Emmerson Cammack, "Principles of Insurance" (Homewood, Ill.: Richard D. Irwin, Inc., 1953), p. 491. "Typically, from $2,000 to $3,000 is considered a minimum cleanup fund."

[16] Neither ordinary nor group consumer credit insurance has any conversion privileges.

monthly installment debts due is relatively small during disability, medical bills and living expenses many times constituting a greater potential loss.

Naturally any invasion of the agent's right to sell insurance and earn compensation for his sales can be expected to meet with opposition. Owen D. Pritchard,[17] representing the National Association of Life Underwriters, recently summarized the agents' opposition to the system by stating:

> The position of the National Association of Life Underwriters has not changed from that previously expressed that no commissions, fees, or emoluments whatever should be paid to the lending institutions or to any employee or executive thereof in connection with the negotiation of a small loan.

So strong is the agents' feeling on payment of commissions to any lender that one officer of a state association, in speaking for his members and the National Association of Life Underwriters to a state investigatory body, went on record "in favor of legislation which would prohibit the payment, directly or indirectly, of any commissions, fees, or other compensation to the lending institutions or their representatives in connection with the sale of credit life insurance."[18] It is apparent that the associations recognize that compensation may take a form other than commissions and thus favor legislation to bar any return to the lender, whatever its form. This presumably would include any form of "retrospective rates" which is a form of pecuniary return to the lender and which is offered by those companies that support the American agency system.

Opposition to any form of compensation being paid the lender has also arisen from one of the giants in the consumer finance field. The position of this company stems basically from an interpretation of the Model Small Loan legislation sponsored by the Russel Sage Foundation. The position, briefly

---

[17] Owen D. Pritchard, in a statement to the Subcommittee of the Life Insurance Committee of the National Association of Insurance Commissioners, November 28, 1955, New York.

[18] Cecil N. Peterson, vice-president of the Kansas State Association of Life Underwriters, in a statement before the Senate Judiciary Committee of the State of Kansas, Topeka, Kansas, February 16, 1955.

summarized, is that *based upon their interpretation,* the Model Small Loan Law contemplates but one all-inclusive charge being made by the lender to the borrower. According to this view-point, the charge is usually stated as a per cent and represents the maximum charge permissible for *all* costs connected with the lending operations regardless of their nature. It follows from this reasoning then that an insurance premium paid by the borrower is in violation of the all-inclusive charge which is set by the legislatures at a level so as to include *all* risks to which the lender is subject, *including* death and disability of his debtors. It is significant to note that, despite the violent opposition to the current method of paying commissions evidenced by these groups, neither has condemned consumer credit life insurance in principle.[19]

AN INDUSTRY PROPOSAL

A noteworthy development connected with the problem of high commissions recently took place when the American Life Convention and the Life Insurance Association of America, after a joint study, issued a proposal to the National Association of Insurance Commissioners which they believed would "go to the root of many if not most of the remaining problems" connected with the sale of this coverage. Recognizing the effectiveness of existing model laws, while at the same time believing that "they do not necessarily protect the borrower from excessive charges resulting from excessive compensation paid the lender for his services in furnishing insurance," the following proposal was submitted to the National Association of Insurance Commissioners:

---

[19] The National Association of Life Underwriters is apparently in favor of both consumer credit life and accident and health insurance. Household Finance Corporation issues consumer credit life insurance to its customers, on a group basis only, at no extra charge in several states. Company officials have described consumer credit accident and health as "impractical" in public statements and interviews with the author. Household issues no consumer credit accident and health in any form, nor does it seem that the company is likely to do so in the future.

We propose to your subcommittee for incorporation in model legislation the establishment of a fixed limit, expressed in dollars and cents per $100 of initial indebtedness, on the compensation a lender may receive for his services in marketing credit life and credit accident and health insurance. To preclude the possibility that compensation may be paid by means other than commissions, we would propose that this limit apply also to dividends, premium adjustments, policy writing fees, underwriting gains, etc. Specifically, we propose that the NAIC rules be reduced to model legislation which, with respect to credit life and credit accident and health insurance written by or through a creditor, its affiliate, associate, or subsidiary, or a director, officer or employee of any of them, in connection with an indebtedness of $500 or less, will limit the compensation for writing such insurance to such creditor, affiliate, associate, subsidiary, director, officer or employee, in whatever form, including commission, dividends, premium adjustment, policy writing fee, or underwriting gain, to 40¢ per annum per $100 of initial indebtedness in the case of credit life insurance, to 60¢ per $100 of initial indebtedness in the case of credit accident and health insurance with a 14 day non-retroactive elimination period on an indebtedness of one year's duration, and to consistent amounts in the case of other credit accident and health insurance.

It will be observed that the proposal suggested above is limited in this application to loans of $500 or less. This restriction is suggested for two reasons. First, the credit insurance abuses which have been so publicized in this field have, by and large, been confined to small loans. Second, we believe that limitations with respect to loans of $500 or less will have a pace-setting effect on the maximum compensation paid for larger loans, without standardizing the compensation rate to the lender at a floor higher than the lender may require or the forces of competition may produce on these larger loans where the borrower can be more selective in his choice of lender.[20]

As time did not allow the subcommittee to hold an executive session following the foregoing statements and those of other interested parties, no questions were resolved at this meeting, they being deferred to subsequent sessions.

The joint American Life Convention–Life Insurance Association of America proposal brought mixed reactions from interested groups. Mr. Pritchard, of the National Association

---

[20] Joint statement of the American Life Convention and the Life Insurance Association of America to the Subcommittee on Credit Life and Accident and Health Insurance of the Life Committee of the National Association of Insurance Commissioners, November 28, 1955, New York.

of Life Underwriters, expressed his belief that it was not possible to control "the evils of Credit Life Insurance or Health and Accident by merely limiting the amount of profit which they [the lenders] may obtain."[21] A representative of Household Finance Company sharply criticized the industry proposal by saying:

> As treatment for this problem they have prescribed an aspirin tablet whereas what the patient really needs is a handful of sulfa pills and a hundred thousand units of penicillin.[22]

The Consumer Credit Insurance Association, representing twenty-three companies engaged mainly in the sale of ordinary consumer credit insurance, seemed to concur with the American Life Convention–Life Insurance Association of America proposal.

It must be remembered that, because their very survival depends upon the legislation enacted by the various jurisdictions, lenders have resorted to extensive lobbying. Because proposals to limit lender compensation have been made, adoption by the National Association of Insurance Commissioners would immeasurably increase its chances of becoming law. Undoubtedly the organizations that proposed this limitation on commissions did so fully cognizant of the lender's ability to exert considerable legislative pressures. Proposal of commissions lower than those suggested would probably have little chance of becoming law. As a "practical"[23] solution then, the joint proposal to limit commissions to lenders in the manner cited was submitted. Once the momentous step of placing commissions under the scrutiny of the several states is taken, it should then become a simpler chore to effect reasonable compensation scales.

---

[21] Owen D. Pritchard, in a statement to the Subcommittee of the Life Insurance Committee of the National Association of Insurance Commissioners, November 28, 1955, New York.

[22] Paul F. Boyer, representing the Household Finance Corporation in a statement before the Credit Life Insurance Subcommittee of the Life Insurance Committee of the National Association of Insurance Commissioners, November 28, 1955, New York.

[23] So termed by several interested parties interviewed.

INSURANCE COMPANY ADMINISTRATION

Once the lender has been contacted and has accepted a program of consumer credit insurance, the insurer will usually require that certain preliminary information be submitted to the insurer's home office for underwriting purposes. In addition to being a formal application for coverage, the form used may also inquire as to the nature of the lender's business, the rate of interest charged debtors, the kinds of indebtedness to be insured, the current volume of such loans as well as anticipated growth, a statement as to who will bear the cost of the insurance and in what proportion and, if necessary, a statement of the financial affairs of the lender. This information is of value in underwriting and classification of a risk for rating purposes.[24]

If the lender is acceptable to the underwriters, a company representative delivers the necessary materials to execute the insurance program. The essential kinds of materials needed for the group and ordinary programs are set forth in tabular form in Table VI. Not all these types are issued by all lenders; neither does the list exhaust the kinds in use by the various companies. For example, a lender who made no additional charge for the insurance would not have need of the monthly installment payment tables containing insurance charges for varying sizes of loans. One would also find a variation in computing premiums between the group and ordinary insurance method. The group monthly premium statement contains return premiums, renewals, additions, and so forth in a single figure representing the outstanding balances of a given class of loans. Most group writers accept the balance outstanding on a given day of the month, usually the last, as the amount used to calculate a premium, as few companies use the average of the opening and closing balance for the month.

The ordinary method, which requires a record of such information as each individual's cancellations, return premiums,

---

[24] As will be seen in the following chapters, the rate may vary by the type of lender and premium volume.

TABLE VI

Usual and Necessary Material for Executing a Consumer Credit
Insurance Program by a Lending Institution under the Group and
Ordinary Insurance Methods

Group	Ordinary
Master Policy—Sets forth the insuring agreements between the insurer and lender.	*Agency Agreement*—Sets forth the agency contract between insurer and lender.
Monthly Premium Statement—Gives current month's outstanding loan balances to which group rate is applied to get premium due company.	*Periodic Premium Statement*—Lists insured debtors and amounts and duration of the loan to which ordinary rate is applied to get premium due company.
Certificate of Insurance—Issued to debtors as evidence of existing insurance.	*Policies of Insurance*—Issued to debtors as evidence of existing insurance.
Claim Forms—Give identifying information regarding the debtor and his indebtedness.	*Claim Forms*—Give identifying information regarding the debtor and his indebtedness plus medical information on accident and health claims.
Monthly Installment Payment Tables—Show finance charges at various rates of interest and premiums on life insurance to cover the amount financed.	*Monthly Installment Payment Tables*—Show finance charges at various rates of interest and effect of advance premiums to cover amounts financed by life and accident and health insurance.

renewals, purchases, and additions, would require a separate listing not necessary under the aggregative method of group coverage where these items are incorporated into a single figure. The name and address, age, loan number and date, amount and duration of the loan, and the plan of insurance (decreasing term or level term, the retroactive or elimination plan in accident and health, and the number of days in the waiting period) would be used to calculate the premium for one individual. Once the gross premium for all insureds is ascertained for the current month, refunds must be deducted or applied for to give an adjusted gross figure. If commissions to the lender are deducted from this figure, as is quite common under the ordinary plan, the remittance forwarded the company is an amount net of commissions representing a minimum 40 to 55 per cent retention by the lender.

After the plan has been in operation for some time, or upon request, the company representative will return to the lender's place of business to answer any questions that may have arisen regarding such matters as administrative procedure, policy interpretation, and methods of reporting. In addition to assisting the lender in this manner, it is not unusual for the insurer's representative to make an informal examination of the lender's operations as it applies to the administration of the insurance program. Most policies specifically make it the contractual right of the insurer to audit such financial data as are pertinent to the insurance program. Among the checks made by the company are those to see that only eligible classes of debtors are being insured, to see that insured loans are segregated from noninsured loans, and, for group coverage, to make certain the proper kinds and numbers of debtors are being covered.

Most companies require proof of death or disability to be sent to the home office for final disposition of the claim,[25] although it is known that in some instances a lender may have had complete discretion in the matter of payment of claims. The latter seems to be rapidly becoming an obsolete and illegal method of administration of claims. When claims are handled by the home office, a check is issued, or for larger accounts, the drafts executed by the lender and made payable to himself are approved for payment by the insurance company.

Accounting for premiums is a relatively simple operation in group coverage. A mere multiplication of the outstanding loan balance times the rate applicable to the particular lender is required. As previously mentioned, the ordinary method necessitates the auditing of considerably more figures.

A discussion of retrospective rating in more detail will be found in a later chapter. However, calculation of such returns

---

[25] The recent trend by large life insurance companies toward decentralization is resulting in claims being processed through the main office in a given geographical area.

to the lender should be mentioned as constituting the remaining function of the insurer. Here a mathematical formula is applied to a lender's experience to determine the premium credit returned to him, if any. At this time, postselection underwriting is conducted and consideration is given to the renewal of the legal insurance relationship.

LENDER ADMINISTRATION

Completion of the insurance certificate under the group method or the individual policy under the ordinary method of insuring is a fairly simple operation, with the latter method requiring more information. Although certificates are not required by law in most states, many of the insurers require their issuance to the insured debtors. For ordinary insurance, the original policy is issued to the debtor, a copy of the policy is retained by the lender, and one is sent to the insurance company. Model legislation proposed by the National Association of Insurance Commissioners requires that evidence of insurance be given each borrower at the time the loan is consummated or as soon thereafter as is practicable. It is generally agreed that such legislation is sound.

Considerable speculation has arisen over the question of what would happen to the frequency of claims when a group of insured borrowers is suddenly given evidence of insurance which they previously did not have. It has been suggested that claims would generally tend to rise appreciably, and such has proven to be true in at least one instance.[26] This occurs because, without evidence of insurance, the estate or survivor may not be aware of the coverage or be reluctant to press such a claim without possession of evidence. Also it is found that the estate or the survivor pays the loan balance off without

---

[26] See, for example, the *National Underwriter,* December 11, 1952, p. 19, which quotes Commissioner Cheek of North Carolina as stating: "the accident and health loss ratio was very low until the department required companies to mail policies to the borrower. Then the ratio jumped about 500 per cent."

notifying the lender of the death of the debtor because of ignorance of the borrower's protection being in force.[27]

The claims procedure itself is relatively simple, the lender's principle function being to transmit proof of death and information regarding the loan to the home office. The procedure is slightly more involved in accident and health claims where the lender must secure completed forms from the attending physician of the insured borrower attesting to the condition of disability of the insured. This, together with information regarding the loan, is forwarded to the company, which reviews the claim. If the claim is questionable, the lender may be asked to assist in getting additional information. When a claim is paid, the draft is usually drawn in favor of the lender who in turn credits the insured account and notifies the survivors, under a death claim, or insured, under accident and health insurance.

The ease with which the lender is able to complete the monthly premium report will depend upon the adequacy and method of accounting for his business. As suggested previously, group consumer credit life insurance requires a simple statement of the outstanding balance of a given class of loans on a given date. Application of the proper rate gives the premium due the company. Under the ordinary insurance method, somewhat more involved computations are required since more information is needed by the company because of the availability of the various types of coverages.

One of the most important functions that the lender performs on behalf of the consumer credit insurer is the introduction of this coverage to his customers. When the insurance is issued to the borrower at no additional cost, an explanation of

---

[27] Where evidence of insurance is not given the assured, the survivor of the estate is in a position comparable to one in which the debtor had no insurance at all since it cannot be expected that the lender knows when a borrower dies unless so notified. Edward A. Dunbar, in a paper presented to the American Finance Association on December 30, 1955, in speaking on consumer installment credit insurance stated: "When there is no insurance there is no reason for the survivor to bring the death to the attention of the lender, and, if payments (on the loan) are made regularly, there is no occasion for the lender to inquire."

the coverage in a general way should suffice.[28] When the premium is paid entirely by the borrower, considerably more resistance is encountered. To alleviate the task of selling, assistance may be obtained from various sources. The recommendation of a friend or relative and the use of attractive brochures and posters have acted to ease a buyer's reluctance. In the majority of cases it seems quite clear that an explanation of the coverage and its advantages are sufficient to elicit a premium from the borrower; however, the amount of effort needed to sell this coverage will vary considerably among individuals. In any event, a sales presentation usually becomes necessary to secure a premium from a borrower just as it is necessary in other forms of life and accident and health insurance.[29] Such presentations involve a varying amount of the lender's time.[30] To varying degrees within the business world it is generally conceded that time costs money. Time spent in selling results in expense to the lender insofar as the lender is prevented from performing other useful tasks or to the extent that additional

---

[28] Exceptions have been reported where an employee under a noncontributory group insurance plan has refused to accept "free" insurance because of some religious or economic belief. No cases of this sort pertaining to consumer credit insurance were found.

[29] On the necessity of having to sell life insurance, see, for example, Charles C. Center, "An Experiment in State Insurance—The Wisconsin State Life Fund," *Journal of the American Society of Chartered Life Underwriters,* Vol. V, No. 3, June, 1951, p. 232. In describing the failure of the Life Fund to grow, Dr. Center says: "Such a slow growth is believed to be primarily the result of (1) lack of knowledge by citizens of the State generally that such a Fund exists, and (2) the acknowledged fact that people do not "buy" life insurance of their own accord but must be solicited by agents."

Although a few accident and health insurance companies operate successfully on a nonagency basis, utilizing media such as the mails, radio or television advertising, and tie-ins with newspaper subscription promotions, the bulk of the business is written through agency companies.

[30] A representative of a large consumer finance company, when asked about his company's administration of ordinary consumer credit life insurance, expressed his surprise at the results of a time-study survey conducted within his company to determine the cost of administering its insurance program. Considerably higher expense than expected resulted from the designation of the loan office manager as agent. This caused him to spend considerable time in sales presentation to the borrowers. Since his salary was the highest in the office, the expenses charged against his time were much higher than would have been realized had a clerk, for example, handled the transaction.

help is required because of the lender's providing the insurance program to his customers.[31] Incentive to sell insurance coverages, other than consumer credit, stems from the system of compensation, generally of the commission variety. In consumer credit insurance the major methods of compensation and incentive to the lender already noted were commissions and retrospective rates. These represent tangible returns to the lender for handling the details of administration cited previously. There also exist intangible returns that accrue to the lender who offers such coverage to his debtors. Included among them are the competitive advantage the lender enjoys over those of his competitors who do not make such coverage available, possible goodwill gained as a result of not having to collect outstanding balances of deceased or disabled debtors, ability to make loans to persons who, except for the availability of consumer credit insurance, would not qualify for consumer loans, and so on.

Since the return to the lender is of both a tangible and intangible nature, it might be argued by some opponents of compensation to lenders, as well as critics of the level of compensation, that the intangible advantages cited, as well as others not mentioned, would result in sufficient pecuniary return to the lender for the expense of handling the insurance. This argument does have some validity. For example, to the extent that availability of such coverage by a lender results in an increased volume of loans, an additional return does accrue to the lender. Similarly, to the extent that insurance on the debtor's life lessens the cost of collecting outstanding balances from a survivor or a disabled debtor, a return is realized in the form of possible decreased costs of operation.[32] To the

---

[31] It seems surprising that one specializing in the study of the subject of the cost of such credit could state that the selling function results in no expense to the lenders. See "Consumer Instalment Credit Insurance," a paper presented to the American Finance Association by Wallace P. Mors, December 31, 1955.

[32] The amount of savings here would depend upon the lender's collection policy of whether or not, and to what extent, accounts of deceased borrowers are written off. Available information indicates that very few lenders do write

extent that more borrowers may qualify for loans when consumer credit insurance is available as additional security, the lender may benefit from increased loan volume. It is readily apparent that measurement of the amount of such return realized is of great difficulty, as is the measurement of the effects of any single factor in an economic, dynamic whole. Because of the questionability of any results secured through measurement and their application to a given situation in time, there necessarily can be no easy method of calculating a single dollar and cents amount that could be cited as a return to be realized by a lender brought about solely by making consumer credit available to its customers which would be universally applicable to all lenders.

Among the many advantages cited as enjoyed by the insured borrower, the following list cannot be considered exhaustive:

1. Replacement of uncertainty with certainty that insured debts will not have to be paid by a cosigner or survivor in the event of the debtor's death, or by the insured if disabled.
2. An opportunity to purchase life and accident and health insurance without being required to take a physical examination usually up to age 65, sometimes beyond.
3. Increased security to the lender resulting in a possible willingness to loan additional funds to the debtor when needed.
4. A special custom-designed coverage used exclusively by financial institutions keyed precisely to the borrower's needs.
5. Provision of security and peace of mind.

Because the lender assists in the administration of consumer credit insurance to the extent just described, and since the advantages to the borrower appear to be at least equal to those enjoyed by the lender, it does not seem unconscionable to compensate a lender reasonably.

---

off the accounts of deceased debtors without an attempt at collecting from the cosigners, endorsers, or estate.

See, for example, "Statement on Credit Insurance," submitted to the Subcommittee of the Indiana Legislative Advisory Commission, March 15, 1956, by the Indiana Consumer Finance Association, Inc., at Indianapolis.

THE LENDER'S IMPORTANCE

From the description of the lender's functions in the program just described, it is significant that the insurance company has no direct contact with its insured borrowers. It is true that under the ordinary insurance plan the lender becomes the insurance company's agent. However, this relationship cannot be construed as comparable to the usual insurance company agent since the lender-made-agent acts in such capacity only for the purpose of effecting the ordinary method of insuring debtors and still is primarily a lender and but incidentally an insurance agent. From most outward appearances, however, because the borrower deals exclusively with the lender, either under the ordinary or group method of insuring, he is easily led to believe that the lender is the insurance company's legal representative. Because an unethical lender might thus possibly be able to damage an insurance company's good name, it behooves each insurer to view a lender with an eye to its reputation for integrity and fair dealing. The next chapter attempts to demonstate the methods of doing this and obtaining for insurance companies a safe and profitable distribution of insureds.

It is clear then that the lender plays a role of pivotal importance in the success or failure of consumer credit insurance and the insurance companies which make it available. It is hoped that the craving for volume evidenced by a few companies will not result in poor selections of lenders and subsequent disrepute to the industry.

Chapter V

UNDERWRITING

INTRODUCTION

The process of underwriting has been defined as the "selection of risks for the insurer and the determination in what amounts and on what terms acceptable risks will be insured."[1] Consumer credit insurance is generally available from most lenders and many retail outlets without a physical examination of the borrower. There is no difference in rate or protection between the sexes or among hazardous and nonhazardous occupations. An eligible borrower of any race, color, or creed, usually between the ages of 18 and 65, may secure such coverage containing a minimum of exclusions. It might appear that such liberality affords little, if any, underwriting to the insurers. In the insurance business it is axiomatic that unless the insurer selects his risks it will be selected against. This means that the less desirable individuals from an underwriting standpoint will tend to secure coverage resulting in adverse selection to the insurer. Regarding consumer credit insurance specifically, this adverse condition would assume two basic forms. First, the less physically fit persons would consent more readily to become insured once the availability of the coverage was made known by the lender. Second, and more important, an individual might actively seek out a lender for the primary purpose of obtaining insurance and only incidentally for the purpose of obtaining a loan. Thus it becomes incumbent upon

[1] Albert H. Mowbray and Ralph H. Blanchard, *Insurance: Its Theory and Practice in the United States* (New York: McGraw-Hill Book Co., Inc., 1955), p. 388.

the insurer to minimize the effects of adverse selection without imposing an undue administrative burden upon the lender, while at the same time keeping losses within bounds so as to result in an attractive premium to the borrowers. A description of how this task is attempted is the purpose of this chapter.

LEVELS OF UNDERWRITING

The process of underwriting or of selection in the consumer credit insurance field is performed at three different levels. The first and immediate level of selection is performed by the agents or insurance company representatives making this coverage available to their clients. This function may be likened to the role of the agent in regular types of life and accident and health insurance where personal contact allows him to make a preliminary and ofttimes superficial appraisal of the prospective insured. In regular forms of this coverage, this stems from the obvious difficulty of being unable to appraise with any degree of accuracy an individual's physical condition and moral character solely through a personal interview.

The second level of underwriting is noted when the home or branch office underwriters of the insurance company review the experience of insureds at various intervals. Under either the group or ordinary method of insuring, the underwriters are primarily concerned with the aggregate experience of this line of coverage so that the insurer may know whether or not consumer credit insurance is contributing to the company's growth.

Next in importance is the consideration of the experience of individual debtors of a given lender, or the parts which make up the whole. This third level of underwriting is performed by the lender when acceptance or rejection of an applicant for a loan is made. The major factors considered by these various "underwriters"[2] in their quest for a safe and profitable distribution of insureds is the next issue considered.

---

[2] Underwriter is used here in the functional sense only.

CLASSES OF ELIGIBLE LENDERS

Ethical Lenders

All insurers have definite underwriting rules regarding the types of lenders eligible to act as vendors for their consumer credit insurance. The majority of companies, for example, do not wish to insure any lender who was known to be or strongly suspected of being unethical. Lenders who charge more than the statutory rate of interest or who coerce the borrowers into paying for unwanted "security" could be so described. Insuring such lenders might well result in adverse effects, either directly through the contingency of poor underwriting experience for the group due to poor and arbitrary standards of debtor eligibility, "ghost accounts," fake claims, and the like, or indirectly through the damage caused to an insurance company's good name when such abusive practices become publicly associated with a particular insurer. As one company official put it: "An insurance company has to be very careful not to risk its good name by getting tied up with concerns of doubtful reputation."[3]

It is not too difficult for the insurance company representative to ascertain the integrity of the lenders with whom he is not well acquainted. Former customers, supervisory officials, Better Business Bureaus, and even competitors may be relied upon in varying degrees to divulge information of this sort. An additional safeguard arises from the practice of most insurers of requiring submission of a rather detailed account of the lender's operations before any insurance is effected.

One student of group consumer credit insurance sent questionnaires to nine of the major insurance companies in the field to discover the types of lenders which these companies considered eligible for group consumer credit life insurance. Table VII shows his compilation of those creditors who qualified for the coverage among these nine large insurers.

---

[3] E. B. Whittaker, "Creditor's Insurance Under Group and Allied Plans," *The Record,* American Institute of Actuaries, Vol. XXVI, Nos. 53 and 54, 1937, p. 199.

TABLE VII

CLASSES OF LENDERS CONSIDERED ELIGIBLE FOR GROUP CONSUMER
CREDIT LIFE INSURANCE BY NINE MAJOR WRITING INSURERS

Type of Creditor	*Number of Major Writing Companies Which Consider Such Type Eligible*
Credit union	9
Bank	8
Finance company (other than small-loan company)	8
Furniture and appliance dealer	6
Department store	6
Motor vehicle dealer	5
Small-loan company	4
Other vendors	3
Investment trust	2
Cemetery or funeral director	0

Source: James B. Jacobson, *An Analysis of Group Creditors Insurance* (M.B.A. thesis, University of Southern California, 1955), published by The Prudential Insurance Company of America, p. 21.

Because one of the insurers surveyed wrote credit unions exclusively, the first three creditors listed (credit unions, banks, and finance companies other than small-loan companies) were considered acceptable classes of lenders by all companies. The basis of their qualification was:

These institutions generally are better organized and equipped to administer a loan program than the remaining types of creditors. Furthermore, their loan and credit departments are generally operated on a more formal basis. Because of this, the insurance companies feel that a better community of interest with respect to the debtors insured exists with these types of creditors.[4]

Credit Unions

Although all companies surveyed, and many of those not included, consider the credit union an acceptable debtor for consumer credit insurance, the bulk of the insurance sold to this type of lender is written by the CUNA Mutual Insurance Society, an insurance company established by the Credit Union

[4] James B. Jacobson, *An Analysis of Group Creditors Insurance* (M.B.A. thesis, University of Southern California, 1955), published by The Prudential Insurance Company of America, p. 21.

National Association, the parent organization of approximately 88 per cent of United States credit unions. The close business, social, and sometimes religious ties between the credit union and its members is largely responsible for the former's wide acceptibility for consumer credit insurance purposes.

Commercial Banks

Prior to and during World War II, banks traditionally were the purchasers of the commercial paper of finance companies and retailers. The postwar years witnessed a tremendous upsurge of consumer credit and with it an awareness by the banks that direct consumer credit loans were not only lucrative but relatively safe as well. Thus the installment loan departments of banks began to function as competitors and finally as the leaders in the consumer credit lending field. Table VIII

TABLE VIII

CONSUMER CREDIT BY TYPE OF HOLDER
(Financial Institutions)
(In Millions)

Year	Total	Commercial Banks	Sales Finance Companies	Credit Unions	Consumer Finance Companies*	Other*
1939	$ 3,065	$ 1,079	$1,197	$ 132	$ ...	$ 657
1940	3,918	1,452	1,575	171	...	720
1941	4,480	1,726	1,797	198	...	759
1942	2,176	862	588	128	...	598
1943	1,413	532	252	103	...	526
1944	1,486	574	262	99	...	551
1945	1,776	745	300	102	...	629
1946	3,235	1,567	677	151	...	840
1947	5,255	2,625	1,355	235	...	1,040
1948	7,120	3,529	2,011	334	...	1,246
1949	9,257	4,439	2,944	438	...	1,436
1950	11,805	5,798	3,711	590	1,286	420
1951	12,124	5,771	3,654	635	1,555	509
1952	15,581	7,524	4,711	837	1,866	643
1953	18,963	8,998	5,927	1,124	2,137	777
1954	19,450	8,796	6,144	1,342	2,257	911
1955	24,441	10,601	8,443	1,680	2,656	1,061
1956	27,038	11,682	9,100	2,048	3,049	1,159

Source: "Consumer Credit," *Business Statistics*, July, 1955, and *Survey of Current Business*, June, 1956, Federal Reserve Bulletin, February, 1957, p. 190.
* Consumer finance companies included with "other" financial institutions until September, 1950.

testifies to the rapid growth and continuing leadership of the banks as holders of consumer credit obligations. Adding further emphasis to their prominence in this area, it was observed in a recent banking publication that:

> Commercial banks are the most important source of instalment credit. They provide funds not only through direct loans to consumers and through purchases of instalment paper but also through loans to financial institutions and retailers to finance their holdings of instalment credit receivables.
>
> In July 1954, banks held 39% of all instalment credit outstanding. About one-half was in the form of direct loans and one-half in purchased paper.[5]

Because of the standards established by the commercial banks, the caliber of an individual who qualifies for a bank loan is usually expected to be good for insurance purposes.[6] This is one of the important reasons why insurers consider banks eligible for coverage and accounts for the large number of banks presently insured.[7]

Sales Finance Companies

In recent years the sales finance companies have grown to take their place among the leading financial institutions. The three leading sales finance companies accounted for approximately $6 billion of consumer credit outstanding as of the end of 1955.[8] The largest of the three, General Motors Acceptance Corporation, has already been discussed as the holder of

---

[5] "Consumer Instalment Credit," *Federal Reserve Bulletin*, Vol. 40, No. 9, September, 1954, p. 934.

[6] See Chapter VI for the mortality experience of a major small-loan company which indicated a considerably higher mortality than that recorded by insurers primarily insuring bank debtors.

[7] In recent years the leading metropolitan banking houses of the nation as well as the small rural banks have recognized the benefits of consumer credit insurance. Included among such insured institutions are: The First National City Bank, New York; The Citizens and Southern National Bank, Atlanta; Manufacturers Trust Co., Baltimore; The Chase National Bank, New York; Bank of America, Los Angeles; The Second National Bank, Houston; The First Wisconsin National Bank, Milwaukee; Bank of Lebanon, Lebanon, Oregon; Citizens State Bank, New England, North Dakota; and Palatka Atlantic National Bank, Palatka, Florida.

[8] "In a Boom Built on Credit," *Business Week*, March 10, 1956, p. 59.

the largest insurance policy in the world. The other companies, the Commercial Investment Trust Financial Corporation and the Commercial Credit Corporation, have group contracts in force on the lives of their debtors also.[9] Reference to Table VIII will indicate their position as a close second to the consumer credit volume of commercial banks. These companies, as their names imply, finance the sale of various products, generally through the media of various forms of negotiable instruments. Their major operations at the retail level have been and still are in the field of automobile financing. Through the use of a chattel mortgage, conditional sales contract, and the like, credit is extended to both the purchaser of the product and the dealer who is unable to handle his own financing. The consumer credit insurance is written on a group basis in the name of the sales finance company and all purchasers of automobiles or other goods financed through the policyholder's corporation are eligible for coverage.

Small-Loan Companies

These finance companies are not to be confused with the small-loan lenders who make cash loans to borrowers for various reasons. Traditionally, the majority of abuses, both in lending practices and sales of consumer credit insurance, have been associated with this group. Because of this, group insurers willing to accept small-loan companies as policyholders have exercised more stringent underwriting rules than for other classes of lenders. These rules or standards reflect degrees of stringency ranging from blanket nonacceptance of such risks to acceptance on an equal basis with other lenders, with many shades in between.

It will be noted from Table VII that five of the nine insurers surveyed would not accept the small-loan lender for

---

[9] It should be noted that these corporations have substantial business dealings with customers other than at the retail level. For example, a sales finance company may also lend money to retailers to buy stocks from factories and also may buy accounts receivable for collection, a process known as factoring, especially in the textile trade. The insurance, however, usually covers only those borrowers at the retail level.

group coverage under any conditions. This aversion apparently stems from the reluctance of these insurers to subject their good reputations to possible defamation.

Other group insurers will accept small-loan lenders only if the volume of loans is relatively large;[10] some will insure this group only at higher rates than other insurers or apply a rate scale that provides for an increased premium for a decreasing amount of outstanding loans, lending recognition to the fact that, as the size of the group decreases, the relative expense and risk of insuring generally tends to increase. An additional requirement that some insurers may exercise is to have the creditor pay the entire cost of the premiums. This requirement is used by some companies in the hope that it will prevent any abuses arising out of possible unauthorized rate differentials between the charge made to the insured debtor under a contributory group plan and the amount paid by the policyholder to the insurer. Because the distinct possibility exists that the amount charged to the contributing debtor may be in excess of the premium paid to the company, some insurers require the entire payment to be made by the lender without contribution from the debtor before a policy may be issued.

Insurers operating under the ordinary plan for consumer credit insurance have fewer underwriting restrictions than group insurers for all classes of lenders, small-loan licensees included. Most ordinary insurers, in accepting a small-loan lender, require that it be an ethical organization and seek assurance that the company's established underwriting rules will be followed. Because the policy is written on an individual basis, no minimum balance is necessary to qualify or continue coverage with the company. The rate of $1.00 per $100 on the initial amount of the loan generally prevails for all classes of lenders.

Retail Outlets

Of great future importance to all insurers of consumer credit is the cultivation of the accounts of department stores, mail-

---

[10] One insurer requires $500,000 of outstanding loans for eligibility in the hope that such volume is indicative of a sound and reputable company.

order houses, and furniture, appliance, and automobile dealers. Several large Eastern department stores have recently placed into effect programs of consumer credit insurance.[11] Among the many plans available, two general types exist. The first plan insures installment accounts only and is limited to major appliances or so-called "big ticket" items. The plan is available on both the optional and automatic basis, the latter applying to all purchases in specifically named departments. The second plan applies to all installment purchases of both "big ticket" items and soft goods (nondurables) as well. This is a recognition of the recent attempts by department stores to encourage customers to use their credit to purchase all types of goods, not merely the traditionally high-priced, easily repossessed, and salable items. This plan would be particularly applicable to the recently popularized "revolving credit account" which is designed to increase and simplify installment purchasing.

Under the "revolving credit account" plan, once the customer's credit rating has been established he is granted a credit limit which he may utilize in whole or in part. If he elects to use it all, required monthly payments will again allow him to purchase up to the maximum limit. If he elects to use but part, he may still buy on credit the difference between his current time purchases and the maximum allowed. Attesting to the growing importance of this type of consumer credit sales, a recent issue of the Chicago Federal Reserve Bank's monthly publication stated:

Revolving credit plans have grown rapidly in the last five years, especially in large department stores. The National Retail Dry Goods Association reports that 42% of stores with annual credit sales over 20 million dollars offered a revolving credit plan in 1950; at the beginning of 1955, 65% did so. On the other hand, it has only been since 1952 that stores with smaller credit volumes have become greatly interested in the plan. Between that year and 1954 the proportion of department stores offering revolving credit plans rose from 24 to 44%.[12]

---

[11] Among the larger department stores and mail-order houses now utilizing some form of consumer credit insurance are Hess Brothers, of Allentown, Pennsylvania, and Spiegel, Inc., of Chicago.

[12] "Changing Fashions in Department Store Credit," *Business Conditions,* a review of the Federal Reserve Bank of Chicago, December, 1955, p. 11.

It is expected that the increasing use of such credit accounts will further increase the volume of consumer credit insurance.

Until recently, most insurers would not consider department stores as eligible because of the potential of adverse selection against the insurer. One anticipated abuse by the customer was the placing of the credit account in the name of the member of the family in poorest health. This problem has been met satisfactorily by naming the principal wage earner as the insured. It appears that the initial fears of insuring such accounts have not materialized as predicted.

Establishing accounts used to purchase soft goods such as clothing, for example, has been criticized by some as unsound because such items are not easily resold, thus making such

TABLE IX

CONSUMER CREDIT BY TYPE OF HOLDER
(Retail Outlets)
(In Millions)

Year	Total	Department Stores*	Furniture Stores	Household Appliance Stores	Auto Dealers†	Other
1939	$1,438	$ 354	$ 439	$...	$123	$ 522
1940	1,596	394	474	...	167	565
1941	1,605	320	496	...	188	601
1942	990	181	331	...	53	425
1943	723	127	235	...	31	330
1944	690	127	230	...	33	300
1945	686	131	240	...	28	287
1946	937	209	319	...	47	362
1947	1,440	379	474	...	101	486
1948	1,876	470	604	127	159	516
1949	2,333	596	740	178	236	583
1950	2,898	743	827	267	287	771
1951	3,170	924	810	243	290	903
1952	3,822	1,107	943	301	389	1,082
1953	4,042	1,064	1,004	377	527	1,070
1954	4,118	1,242	984	377	463	1,052
1955	4,579	1,511	1,052	381	535	1,100
1956	4,514	1,407	1,020	378	572	1,137

Source: "Consumer Credit," *Business Statistics*, July, 1955, and *Survey of Current Business*, June, 1956, Federal Reserve Bulletin, February, 1957, p. 190.

* Includes mail-order houses.

† Represents automobile paper only; other installment credit held by automobile dealers is included with "other" retail outlets.

credit sales potentially less secure. However, it is submitted that if such accounts are predicated upon satisfactory credit investigations, they should be no less desirable to consumer credit insurers than accounts extended for "big ticket" items which are more readily resalable. As a result, an increasing number of insurers can be expected to enter and vie for this business.[13] Table IX shows the volume of consumer credit by the various types of retail outlets and indicates to some degree their potential for consumer credit insurance coverage.

Of extreme importance to the successful operation of the consumer credit insurance mechanism is the selection of the proper kind of loan for insurance purposes. Not all types of loans qualify, nor should be expected to qualify, for this coverage. According to the definition adopted by the National Association of Insurance Commissioners and used in this paper, a loan must be less than thirty-six months' duration. This eliminates mortgage redemption insurance which is generally written on the individual or ordinary basis by an insurance company agent. Although no exact maximum limit has been set, with the exception of automobile loans, which are generally higher, the typical insured loan is well under $1,000.

CLASSES OF ELIGIBLE LOANS

One convenient and effective method of segregating eligible from ineligible loans is to classify them as secured and unsecured. The latter are considered to be more desirable, and in many companies, the only type of loan that may be considered as insurable. The reason for this is clearer when the nature of an unsecured loan is examined.

Unsecured Loans

Under ordinary circumstances, a person may be considered eligible for an unsecured loan if he is employed. This has

[13] One large life insurance company which had previously engaged solely in regular lines of coverage recently decided to enter the consumer credit insurance field to write department stores exclusively, attesting to their belief of the great potential of this line.

been verified by David Durand in an extensive study of consumer installment financing. He stated:

> The result is almost always the same: the good loans contain a larger percentage of borrowers with long periods of employment than do the bad loans, and the average number of years of tenure of occupation among the good loans is longer than that among the bad. This fact implies that in the past there has been a causal relation between stability of employment and good loan experience, and that in the future applicants with stable employment records are more likely to turn out well than those with unstable records. Stability of occupation it will be remembered, is one of the factors considered extremely important by the lenders.[14]

If a person also meets with the other usual requirements, such as ability to repay and favorable credit history, he most likely will be granted a loan. What is of primary importance here is that, if these requirements for loans are faithfully enforced by the lender, the borrower, in meeting these requirements, at the same time meets with the major underwriting requirement of the consumer credit insurance companies.

One of the main reasons for the success of regular group life and disability insurance has been the requirement that the insured be actively engaged in work. An employed individual generally represents a good subject for insurance protection since "the fact that a person is able to drag himself down to the office often enough to retain his job indicates at least a certain minimum of stamina and health."[15] This applies with equal intensity to consumer credit insurance of the group or ordinary variety since either type of company must have certain standards by which it may judge a risk. Because this single standard of employment has been very effective in other lines of insurance, there is no reason to suspect that it will not continue to work well in consumer credit insurance. This principle then emerges: eligible consumer loans based upon sound lend-

---

[14] David Durand, *Risk Elements in Consumer Instalment Financing,* (technical edition), National Bureau of Economic Research, 1941, p. 3.

[15] Robert Mehr and Emmerson Cammack, *Principles of Insurance* (Homewood, Ill.: Richard D. Irwin, Inc., 1953), p. 470.

ing principles are also generally acceptable for consumer credit insurance.

Secured Loans

It might well be argued that a secured loan is a much safer investment in the eyes of a lender. The reason for this is again found in the nature of the loan. Because the major concern of the lender on the secured loan is the value of the collateral offered as security, the lender may well overlook or waive the requirement that the borrower be employed. Moreover, the health of the borrower may be given a superficial consideration if the caliber of the collateral is acceptable. Some underwriters of consumer credit insurance have thus envisaged the sale of this coverage to the infirm and dying collateral-posting borrower. As one industry spokesman said:

> Suppose a man about to undergo a serious operation walked into a bank with collateral they could hardly refuse to grant him a personal loan repayable in instalments, although they would probably refuse to grant an unsecured personal loan. While there would not be many cases such as this, there might be enough to make insurance of collateral loans an uncertain venture.[16]

Here again arises the fear that the individual will seek out the lender with the primary purpose of securing insurance. In addition to this higher potential mortality, it is also suggested that the over-all losses would tend to be greater since the size of collateral loans would tend to be larger than unsecured loans.

Conditional Sales Contracts

Because of the great amount of financing being done through the use of the conditional sales contract, some thought should be given to their nature. It might well be argued that durable consumer goods financing, such as for television sets, refrigerators, and freezers, is actually a form of a secured loan when sold under the conditional sales contract and thus subject to

---

[16] E. B. Whittaker, "Creditor's Insurance Under Group and Allied Plans," *The Record,* American Institute of Actuaries, Vol. XXVI, Nos. 53 and 54, 1937, p. 197.

the objections just mentioned. The sales made using the contract are in fact a form of secured loan in that the title of the goods generally remains in the seller's name until all installment payments are completed, the contract is as negotiable as other commercial paper, and in the event of default the seller may repossess the goods.

However, this popular form of financing varies from the usual secured loan in several instances. It has been found, for example, that the purchaser of such items generally has as his primary goal the possession of the goods, not the insurance protection. Since in many instances the conditional sales contract is used as a method of financing the purchases of recently married people, the age of such buyers has been found to be relatively young. Also the type of collateral offered, that is, the television set, refrigerator, or freezer, itself, is not as readily marketable as a bond, stock, or other easily converted assets. As a result, there is a tendency on the part of the lender to be reluctant in allowing a known poor credit risk to take possession of an item if he has reason to suspect that he will be forced to conduct a repossession action for these less marketable goods knowing the market for such goods to be very limited. Thus, although having many elements of a secured loan, the goods sold under the conditional sales contract are generally accepted types of indebtedness for consumer credit insurance purposes.

LEGAL UNDERWRITING REQUIREMENTS

Minimum Number of New Entrants

The legal requirements for the writing of group consumer credit life insurance generally provide that the lender insure at least 100 new borrowers a year.[17] Similar provisions are noted in the regular group life insurance statutes which also require a given minimum number of insureds before the issuance of a group contract. Most states today require a minimum of 50 participants to effect a regular group life policy. It should not

---

[17] See, for example, Wisconsin Statutes 206.60 (2) (c).

be concluded from this that the minimum of 100 new entrants as applicable to group consumer credit life insurance is necessarily more stringent a requirement. One hundred new borrowers annually is equivalent to less than one new borrower every three days. It is doubtful whether any lender could operate profitably and competitively with only this minimum.

Minimum Participation

State laws also generally require a minimum participation of eligible debtors to effect and continue a group policy of consumer credit insurance. The majority specify 75 per cent.[18] Lenders generally do not appear to have difficulty in securing the required percentage participation to qualify for group coverage. In fact, all of the lending institutions surveyed by the author had no difficulty in securing considerably more than this minimum.

Where contracts and companies require 100 per cent of eligible debtors to be insured, the risk of antiselection is minimized. A growing number of people, however, are concerned with the effects of the 100 per cent participation requirement by consumer credit insurers. It is feared that in the event the lender is unable to secure full participation, resort to "pressuring" the borrowers into purchasing the coverage may occur. Because ordinary insurers have no such minimums, they feel that the tendency of the lender-agents to coerce clients into purchasing consumer credit insurance is reduced.

Maximum Amounts of Coverage

The maximum amount of insurance permissible on the life of any one debtor under a group credit life insurance policy is also subject to statutory regulation. These maximums range from $5,000 to $10,000,[19] with two states, Kentucky and South Carolina, specifying no dollar amounts. Most group insurers set their own maximum coverage on individuals, fully recog-

---

[18] See, for example, Wisconsin Statutes 206.60 (2) (b).

[19] See, for example, "Wisconsin Statutes 206.60 (2) (d).

nizing the dangers to an insurer of having too much insurance in force on the life of any one individual in proportion to the total coverage for the group. Setting such maximums reduces the potential of antiselection since it limits each borrower within the group to a definite maximum amount of coverage and also limits a given group to a stated maximum loss. This tends to decrease the chance of wide fluctuations in the experience of the group, providing it with greater stability. Typical maximums on the life of any one debtor are given in Table X.

TABLE X

TYPICAL MAXIMUM AMOUNTS OF CONSUMER CREDIT LIFE INSURANCE FOR EACH INSURED DEBTOR UNDER A GROUP CONTRACT

Total Amount of Insurance in Force under the Group Policy	Maximum Amount of Insurance on the Life of any Debtor*
Less than $100,000	$1500
$100,000 or more but less than $250,000	2500
$250,000 or more but less than $400,000	3000
$400,000 or more but less than $550,000	3500
$550,000 or more but less than $700,000	4000
$700,000 or more but less than $850,000	4500
$850,000 or more	5000

* Or such lesser amount as may be required by the law of the state in which the policy is issued. If such lesser maximum amount is applicable, the policy will so indicate.

ADDITIONAL UNDERWRITING FUNCTIONS

Premium Billings and Refunds

An additional function ascribed to the underwriting segment of the industry is the handling of premium billings, refunds, and cancellations. The method and calculation of premiums under the group consumer credit insurance policy has been described previously in considerable detail. It was then noted that the outstanding balance method in general use by such insurers resulted in a simplified procedure for checking at the insurer's offices. In most cases all that is necessary is a simple multiplication check consisting of the outstanding balance times the rate for that particular group. Because cancellations and premium refunds are presumed to have been handled by the creditor, home office routine is minimized.

For ordinary consumer credit life and accident and health insurance, the procedure is more complicated because of the amount of information needed from the lender-agent. In addition to a complete record of individual insureds, the company will also want the details of new business written by the lender-agent as well as refunds of premiums to policyholders. Each of these figures in turn influence the amount of commissions to be paid the lender and must be considered in that light. Despite the use of a simplified form, the home office staff is faced with considerably more details for checking than under the group method of insuring.

In the chapter on policy provisions,[20] it will be seen that the insurance on the life of a debtor under the group plan usually ceases when the loan is repaid. With ordinary life and accident and health insurance, however, the insured generally has the option of continuing the coverage or applying for a refund in the event the loan is repaid or refinanced before the expiration of the original term. If the insured remains silent, the insurance is kept in force until such time as it would normally have expired. If he requests cancellation, he is then required to sign a statement requesting such cancellation. At the same time, receipt of the unearned premium refund is acknowledged.

Cancellations

Because the entire business of consumer credit insurance has traditionally received no more regulation than the life insurance industry in general, there remains today a considerable difference in the manner of handling cancellations and renewals among insurers and lenders. It appears, however, that despite these differences the "Rule of 78" is generally followed. This "rule," accepted by the American Bankers Association and many lending institutions, is used to determine minimum refunds for installment loan charges upon repayment. It is currently being used extensively by lenders as the basis for in-

---

[20] See Chapter VIII.

surance premium refunds in case of prepayment, refinancing, or renewal. Based on a $120 loan, Table XI indicates the operation of the "Rule of 78" in the computation of finance charge refunds.

TABLE XI

DERIVATION AND USE OF THE "RULE OF 78" BASED UPON A
$120 ANNUAL INSTALLMENT LOAN AT INTEREST OF 1 PER CENT PER
MONTH ON THE UNPAID BALANCE

End of Month	Principal Balance	Loan Charge	Proportion of Each Month's Loan Charge to Total Loan Charge	Proportion of Total Loan Charge Saved by Prepayment in Full at End of Month
1	$120	$1.20	12/78	66/78
2	110	1.10	11/78	55/78
3	100	1.00	10/78	45/78
4	90	0.90	9/78	36/78
5	80	0.80	8/78	28/78
6	70	0.70	7/78	21/78
7	60	0.60	6/78	15/78
8	50	0.50	5/78	10/78
9	40	0.40	4/78	6/78
10	30	0.30	3/78	3/78
11	20	0.20	2/78	1/78
12	10	0.10	1/78	0/78

Source: J. Reuben Darr, "Refund of Installment Loan Charges and Consumer Credit Insurance Premiums," the Bankers Security Life Insurance Society, New York.

It will be noted that, the first month, 12 installment units are outstanding; the second month, 11 units, and so on. The sum of these installment units totals 78. This method is sometimes termed the "sum of the digits method," but more commonly, the "Rule of 78."

For consumer credit decreasing-term insurance, the "Rule of 78" is applied, whereas under level-term insurance a "pro-rata" table is used. These tables may be found in Appendix F.

Although the "Rule of 78" and the "prorata" table appear to be used most frequently, most states do not prescribe a standard table. Therefore, it is confusing and sometimes irritating to the insured borrower who is never sure of the method or correctness of the calculation of his return premium. Uniformity in cancellation and refunding would eliminate a present source of ill will and misunderstanding.

A GUIDING PRINCIPLE

It was noted that the process of underwriting consumer credit insurance is performed to various degrees by three distinct groups. For group consumer credit insurance, the commissioned agent, home office underwriter, and lender-policy-holder play the leading roles. The ordinary insurers employ the services of a salaried representative, home office underwriter, and lender-agent to perform comparable functions.

Along with legal considerations, the two most important considerations noted regarding the eligibility of the borrower for consumer credit insurance were the type of lenders and the type of loans. Acceptability standards relating to the type of lenders varied considerably between group and ordinary insurers, the former being more selective. Also noted were the variations among companies within these two groups. It is generally conceded by both group and ordinary insurers that the unsecured loan is best suited for consumer credit insurance.

It is clearly evident that close adherence to these principles by insurers is necessary to the sound underwriting of this coverage. Once these standards have been met, the lender carries forward the process by maintenance of sound lending practices. As has been demonstrated, once the lender and the type of loan are accepted, an eligible borrower becomes an acceptable insured.

Chapter VI

THE RATE AND ITS COMPONENTS

Probably the most controversy to date regarding consumer credit insurance has arisen in connection with discussions of the rate and its constituent parts. Because the components of the rate entail considerations of losses, expenses, reserves, profits, and costs of acquisition, it is evident that attention must be given each of these topics in any comprehensive discussion of the consumer credit insurance rate. This chapter attempts to review these important aspects as well as the level of rates currently in use by most consumer credit insurers.[1]

RATE VS. PREMIUM

A rate may be defined as the cost per unit of insurance. The most common unit in consumer credit insurance is $100, although sometimes it may be expressed in terms of $1,000. A premium, on the other hand, is defined as the product of the rate times the number of units purchased. Thus a premium of $3.00 results from the purchase of an individual consumer credit life insurance policy at the rate of $1.00 per $100 on an initial loan balance of $300. This premium is paid by the

---

[1] No discussion of current rates for group or blanket consumer credit disability insurance will be found here because coverage under these forms is presently limited to a relatively few number of states. Several jurisdictions have recently amended their statutes to provide such coverage, but the companies are proceeding slowly in their expansion in these states. Valid generalizations could not presently be made concerning these coverages so as to lend any substantial contribution to this text.

borrower as an additional cost if the insurance is desired. With group consumer credit life insurance, the premium is paid by the policyholder according to the terms of the master policy. If the cost is not passed on to the borrower as an additional charge or in the form of increased interest or discount rates, the plan is termed noncontributory. Sometimes, however, the cost of the insurance may be shared in some predetermined proportion, thus being called a contributory plan. Insurers and lenders generally decide if the plan is to be contributory or not based upon the type of loan insured. As one industry spokesman stated:

> While there are exceptions, the greatest number of policies issued with a contribution from the borrower toward the cost of insurance are those which involve the extension of credit by means of a conditional sales contract or its substitute. Where a loan is based largely upon the character and earning power of the individual, the creditor frequently absorbs the cost of Group Creditor Life Insurance without any identifiable charge to the borrower.[2]

At the present time, although the exact apportionment of contributory and noncontributory plans among the various types of financial institutions is not known, it is doubtful that the greatest number of contributory policies still involve sales financing.

The most common method of passing the charge on under the group plan is through a separate additional charge or an increase in the interest or discount rate to the borrower.

Two ways of paying the premiums for this coverage are utilized. They might be paid in advance at the time the loan is made, a method used principally in the ordinary method of insuring. An alternative is a method in which the rate is applied to the outstanding balance of loans of the lender on a particular date, usually the first or last day of the month. The rate might also be applied to an "average" amount outstanding calculated by dividing the sum of the month's opening and closing balance by two.

---

[2] E. B. Whittaker, "Statement on Behalf of The Prudential Insurance Company of America on Proposed Colorado Small Loan Legislation," March 9, 1953.

THE RATE FOR ORDINARY CONSUMER CREDIT INSURANCE

Life

Under the advance payment premium plan used in ordinary consumer credit life insurance the rate is usually $1.00 per year per $100 of initial indebtedness payable in one sum at the time the loan is made. The $1.00 rate provides the borrower with decreasing-term life insurance in which the face amount decreases by such amounts as to be approximately equal at all times to the anticipated outstanding indebtedness. Table XII shows typical credit life insurance premiums at the $1.00 rate for loans of varying amounts and durations.

TABLE XII

DECREASING-TERM LIFE PREMIUMS ON INSURED LOANS OF VARYING AMOUNTS AND DURATIONS UNDER THE ORDINARY METHOD OF INSURING AT $1.00 PER YEAR PER $100 RATE

Initial Amount of Loan	Repayable in Equal Monthly Installments Over a Period of				
	6 Months	12 Months	18 Months	24 Months	36 Months
$ 100	$0.50	$ 1.00	$ 1.50	$ 2.00	$ 3.00
200	1.00	2.00	3.00	4.00	6.00
300	1.50	3.00	4.50	6.00	9.00
400	2.00	4.00	6.00	8.00	12.00
500	2.50	5.00	7.50	10.00	15.00
1000	5.00	10.00	15.00	20.00	30.00

Ordinary consumer credit life insurance on the level-term plan may be written to cover consumer loans which do not decline by periodic installments. Since the insurance protection is at all times equal to the initial amount of the loan and the average amount of insurance in force is about double that of decreasing-term, the rate is about double that of decreasing-term insurance. To approximate the premiums on insurance policies covering loans of various sizes and durations for level-term insurance merely double the amounts found in Table XII.

Accident and Health

Ordinary consumer credit accident and health insurance is that form of insurance which pays monthly payments equal to the installment repayments of a loan on behalf of the borrower while he is disabled due to accident or sickness. A waiting period is necessary under the two basic forms available before benefits can be received. Under the Retroactive Plan, payments are made for the entire period of disability once the waiting period is exceeded. The Elimination Plan provides benefits only for that disability occurring beyond the waiting period. Naturally the Retroactive form can be expected to be more costly since it pays first dollar benefits retroactively for the entire waiting period if the period of disability is exceeded.

As with ordinary credit life insurance, consumer credit accident and health insurance is paid in advance. The rate is frequently expressed in cents per $100 of original indebtedness

TABLE XIII

TYPICAL PLANS, WAITING PERIODS, AND RATES FOR ORDINARY
CONSUMER CREDIT ACCIDENT AND HEALTH INSURANCE

Waiting Period	Elimination Plan Rate per $100 of Loan	Term in Months	Retroactive Plan Rate per $100 of Loan
3 days	$3.50	up to 12	$6.00
7 days	2.50	up to 12	3.00
	3.00	13–18	4.00
	3.50	19–24	4.50
	4.00	25–36	5.00
14 days	1.50	up to 12	2.20
	2.00	13–24	3.00
	2.50	25–36	3.80
30 days	0.5125*	...	...

* The company writing this coverage offers it as part of a "package plan" including consumer credit life insurance. The rate is for 12 months or less.

or as a percentage of that amount. The rate is also dependent upon the length of the loan period since the longer the period, the higher the insurer's potential payment on behalf of a disabled policyholder. The term of the waiting period is also considered since, on the average, the longer the waiting period, the smaller the probability that the insured will be disabled for the entire period. Typical plans and rates are contained in Table XIII.

It will be noted that most accident and health rates are promulgated for periods of six or twelve months and not subdivided into months as are consumer credit life insurance rates. Consequently, under an accident and health policy the same rate for any plan would be charged for a $100 loan of three months as for one of six months in duration. Under the rates in effect on consumer credit life insurance on the ordinary basis, the rate on the former loan would be one half of the latter.

To derive a premium on a $300 eighteen-month loan under an ordinary decreasing-term consumer credit life and fourteen-day accident and health Elimination Plan, for example, the following computations would be made:

Rate for consumer credit life insurance: $1.00/yr./$100.
Amount of the loan: $300.
Term of the loan: 18 months.
Premium on consumer credit life insurance: $1.00 times 3 (units of $100) times 1½ (years) = $4.50.

Rate for 14-day elimination consumer credit accident and health insurance as per Table XIII: $2.00.
Amount of the loan: $300.
Term of the loan: (Already considered in the $2.00 rate).
Premium on consumer credit accident and health insurance: $2.00 times 3 (units of $100) = $6.00.

Total cost of ordinary credit life and disability insurance on a $300, 18 month loan: $4.50 + $6.00 = $10.50.

RATE FOR GROUP CONSUMER CREDIT LIFE INSURANCE

Minimum Rates

From the very beginnings of group consumer credit life insurance, the New York State Insurance Department expressed an interest in the subject of rates by the issuance of bulletins to insurance companies doing such business in that state. In 1929, New York State Insurance Superintendent Conway saw fit to promulgate a Tentative Initial Average Premium per Month per $100 for "borrowers from banks on unsecured paper, repayable in instalments."[3] Two other classes of borrowers mentioned in the letter were "employees purchasing stock from employer" and "purchasers of merchandise," the former reflecting the department's recognition of speculation in stocks during this era. Promulgation of such minimum rates was necessary,

---

[3] "Creditors and Debtors Group Life Insurance," State of New York Insurance Department, a bulletin dated September 20, 1929, p. 1.

in the Department's opinion, because of the peculiar operation of the group credit insurance mechanism. Unlike the usual group life contract, group consumer credit life insurance did not cover the current debtors of a creditor at the time the contract was consummated, but rather only those who became debtors after the effective date of the master contract between the creditor and the insurer. As a result, rates had to be based upon some minimum amount until a reasonable number of new debtors had become insured so that a rate based upon the actual age could be calculated. Table XIV shows a typical schedule used to calculate rates for debtors giving consideration to each debtor's individual age. "A common procedure was to use the tentative rate until 500 debtors had become insured under the policy. At that time, an actual rate was calculated, based upon the ages of the 500 insured debtors."[4]

It became evident that these minimum premiums were more than adequate, with the result that the formality of calculating a premium based upon the actual age of the group was waived by many companies, if not verbally, then by inaction in failing to require the calculation based on individual ages to be made. It is interesting to note that, although most companies still maintain a schedule or table of rates by individual ages in their policies to this date, they are used rarely, if ever.

On August 22, 1940, Superintendent Pink, recognizing the adequacy of the previous $1.00 group rate for consumer credit life insurance, circularized the companies advising them of a new tentative initial monthly rate of $0.75 per $1,000 for all classes of debtors.[5]

The latest revision of minimum rates came on April 29, 1955. At that time, because of the insistence of several of the large writers of this coverage, the New York Insurance Department approved a minimum rate of $0.60 to be used rather than the $0.75 rate in appropriate cases. "In order to recog-

---

[4] James B. Jacobson, *An Analysis of Group Creditor's Insurance*, a thesis submitted to the faculty of the Department of Finance, University of Southern California, and published by the Prudential Insurance Company of America, 1955, p. 23.

[5] "Creditors Group Life Policies," State of New York Insurance Department, a bulletin dated August 22, 1940, p. 1.

TABLE XIV

SCHEDULE OF MONTHLY PREMIUM RATES PER $1,000 OF INSURANCE
BASED ON POLICYHOLDER'S ATTAINED AGE

Attained Age Nearest Birthday	Premium	Attained Age Nearest Birthday	Premium
15	$.20	48	$ .98
16	.20	49	1.05
17	.21	50	1.13
18	.21	51	1.22
19	.22	52	1.31
20	.22	53	1.42
21	.23	54	1.53
22	.24	55	1.65
23	.25	56	1.78
24	.26	57	1.93
25	.27	58	2.08
26	.28	59	2.25
27	.29	60	2.44
28	.30	61	2.64
29	.31	62	2.86
30	.33	63	3.10
31	.34	64	3.36
32	.36	65	3.64
33	.38	66	3.94
34	.40	67	4.27
35	.42	68	4.63
36	.45	69	5.02
37	.47	70	5.44
38	.50	71	5.89
39	.54	72	6.39
40	.57	73	6.92
41	.61	74	7.50
42	.65	75	8.13
43	.69	76	8.80
44	.74	77	9.54
45	.79	78	10.32
46	.85	79	11.17
47	.91	80	12.09

nize the higher proportionate expense on small cases and to provide an appropriate graduation between the 75¢ and 60¢ rates," the Department promulgated the following rates:[6]

Average Amount of Insurance	Minimum Monthly Premium per $1000
Less than $250,000	$0.75
$250,000 but less than $500,000	Pro rata between $0.75 and $0.60
$500,000 or more	$0.60

[6] "Minimum Premiums for Group Creditors Insurance," State of New York Insurance Department, a bulletin dated April 29, 1955.

Although the $0.60 rate has been rather widely adopted, it would seem that most group contracts are still written at the $0.75 rate because of the many accounts averaging less than $250,000 of insured loans and partially because some companies are not licensed in the state of New York and therefore not subject to such minimum rates. For this reason most illustrations used here will be on the basis of the $0.75 rate.

The $0.75 Rate and Its Equivalent

The $0.75 per $1,000 rate is sometimes expressed as 7½ cents per $100 per month on the outstanding balance so as to

TABLE XV

CALCULATION OF THE TOTAL GROSS RATE PER $100 OF GROUP
CONSUMER CREDIT LIFE INSURANCE AT A RATE OF 75 CENTS PER $1,000
PER MONTH ON THE OUTSTANDING BALANCE
(Equal Monthly Repayments of $8.3333)

Month	Outstanding Loan Balance	Rate on Outstanding Balance
1	$100.0000	$0.0750
2	91.6667	0.0675
3	83.3334	0.0625
4	75.0001	0.0562
5	66.6668	0.0500
6	58.3335	0.0437
7	50.0002	0.0375
8	41.6669	0.0312
9	33.3336	0.0250
10	25.0003	0.0187
11	16.6670	0.0125
12	8.3337	0.0062
	APPROXIMATE Total Gross Premium	0.4875

make a comparison between group and ordinary consumer credit life insurance easier. When this rate is applied each month to an outstanding balance of an installment loan, the cost is not $0.90 per $100 (7½ cents times 12 months), but actually a lesser amount because the 7½ cent rate is being applied to a constantly decreasing balance. The actual result is a total cost of 48¾ cents per $100 of loan repayable in 12 equal monthly installments. The derivation of this amount is demonstrated in Table XV.[7]

[7] Under the so-called "flat payment" plan used by many loan companies, payments of both principal and interest are made over the life of the loan. This results in the initial payments being used primarily to pay off interest and only

Table XVI shows the typical gross credit life insurance premiums at the $0.75 per $1,000 rate for loans of varying amounts and durations.

On a comparable basis of total gross rates it will be seen that when the rates for group consumer credit life insurance are compared to those used in the ordinary method of insuring, the former are approximately one half of the latter or 48¾ cents as compared to $1.00 per $100 of coverage per year respectively.

TABLE XVI

GROSS PREMIUMS ON INSURED LOANS OF VARYING AMOUNTS AND DURATIONS UNDER THE GROUP METHOD OF INSURING AT A $0.75 PER $1,000 RATE

Initial Amount of Loan	Repayable in Equal Monthly Installments Over a Period of				
	6 months	12 months	18 months	24 months	36 months
$ 100	$0.27	$0.49	$0.72	$0.94	$ 1.39
200	0.53	0.98	1.43	1.88	2.78
300	0.79	1.48	2.14	2.82	4.17
400	1.05	1.95	2.85	3.75	5.55
500	1.32	2.44	3.57	4.69	6.94
1000	2.63	4.88	7.13	9.38	13.88

It must be remembered that the group rates just discussed, promulgated by the New York Insurance Department, are minimum rates only and apply only to initial premiums. On the policy anniversary date this rate may be reduced substantially by the process of retrospective rating. This procedure also allows a company to increase its rates if the experience so dictates; however, such increases are relatively few.

COMPARISON OF COSTS OF CONSUMER CREDIT LIFE INSURANCE WITH OTHER FORMS OF LIFE INSURANCE

Industrial Life Insurance

Comparisons between the current rates of consumer credit life insurance with other more common types of life insurance

secondarily applied to the principal. In the latter months of the loan, the reverse is true, that is, most of the monthly payment goes to pay off the principal and a relatively small amount is applied to the interest. As a result of the application of this system, the gross unpaid loan balance is in excess of the amount of the gross unpaid loan balance which would be outstanding if an equal payment of principal were applied monthly to a given loan. The average balance outstanding under the "flat payment" plan then, is somewhat in excess of 48¾ cents per $100 of initial loan as shown in Table XV.

have been made recently on several occasions. One such attempt resulted in a demonstration which attempted to show that the rate for consumer credit life insurance, written on the ordinary basis, was even more favorable than industrial life insurance, "the only type of life insurance available to individuals in amounts of less than $1,000."[8] The statement was made by a trade organization representing insurers who primarily emphasized individual consumer credit life and disability insurance. Using an industrial whole life policy which was paid up at age 75 and premiums payable weekly or monthly, annual costs per $100 of insurance at various ages were given based upon the rates charged by "one of America's largest life insurance companies."[9] Assuming the average age of consumer borrowers to be age 40,[10] it appears from this illustration that the annual cost per $100 of this type of coverage is $4.90. Since ordinary consumer credit life insurance is offered at $1.00 per $100 for all ages 18 to 65, it is suggested that "as temporary insurance protection, the figures are comparable to the much lower cost of credit life insurance." The brochure concedes that a difference does exist between the two policies in that industrial policies do have some cash value which consumer credit life insurance does not, but that is paid only after three years. No other distinction is made.

It should be pointed out, however, that most industrial policies issued today contain additional benefits besides the cash value just mentioned. For example, disability benefits are usually included in the policy which provide payment under certain conditions of an amount equal to the face of the policy at

---

[8] "How Consumer Credit Insurance Protects You and Your Family," a brochure published by the Consumer Credit Insurance Association, Chicago, Illinois, p. 7.

[9] *Ibid.*

[10] This age appears to be approximately correct as an average for most types of consumer credit borrowers. The Beneficial Management Corporation, one of the largest consumer finance companies in the United States, reports the average age of their borrowers to be about age 40. See "Consumer Instalment Credit Insurance," a paper by Edward A. Dunbar, presented to the American Finance Association, December 30, 1955, New York.

The CUNA Mutual Insurance Society, insurer of credit unions exclusively, has found the average age of their borrowers to be about age 40 also.

the time of the disability and continuance of the policy at the full face amount, payable at death or maturity. A further common benefit is the inclusion of an accidental death benefit similar to the so-called "double indemnity" provision. Then too, the policy is necessarily expensive because of the cost of handling the premiums, which are collected at frequent (weekly or monthly) intervals rather than at one time on an advance single premium basis as is common in ordinary consumer credit life insurance. To further invalidate the comparison, reference must be made to the "intermediate" policy, which is a form of life insurance available from most companies writing industrial life insurance. Such policies may be paid for on a monthly basis and bought in amounts of less than $1,000, a common minimum being $500, and afford savings in premium costs as compared with industrial policies. Finally, the comparison is inaccurate because the policies in question are dissimilar, one being a decreasing-term policy, the other a level, whole life coverage.

"Jumbo" Life Insurance

On the other hand, a comparison based on the similarity of rates has been made between ordinary consumer credit life insurance and a relatively new form of "jumbo" life insurance policy, so named because it is sold in minimum amounts of $10,000. In addition to its being sold in such large amounts, the rate per $1,000 is lower than for similar coverages purchased in lesser amounts. The lower rate is principally justified by a savings in commissions and general expenses.

A decreasing-term life policy of the "jumbo" type sold by a large mutual life insurance company and available from any of its agents, carries a premium of $89.90 per year before dividends for a $10,000 policy. This gross premium is equivalent to a rate of approximately $0.90 per $100; therefore, it is argued that the rate of $1.00 per $100 for ordinary consumer credit life insurance is thus proven to be reasonable.

If this comparison is not one of apples to oranges, it is certainly one of oranges to tangerines. To begin with, the "quantities" being compared ($10,000 to $25, $50, etc.) are greatly dissimilar. The "jumbo" policy generally involves expenses not common to ordinary consumer credit life insurance. For example, the former is paid for by annual, semiannual, or quarterly premiums, the latter by a single payment. Costs relating to the collection of premiums will undoubtedly be lower with a single payment. Also, since the term of coverage is ten years for the "jumbo" policy, and perhaps one and one-half years average and three years maximum for consumer credit life insurance, the cost of mortality is necessarily higher because the period of protection is some seven years longer. Then too, the "jumbo" policies require physical examinations and the assemblage of the usual underwriting information such as credit and medical reports, none of which is required under consumer credit life insurance. The application of dividends to the gross premium will make the rate per $1,000 less than $0.90, invalidating a comparison even further.

Although several other differences could be noted, this conclusion is apparent: Because of the unique nature of consumer credit insurance, comparisons of rates with other types of insurance results in conclusions of questionable validity.

The difficulty in comparing consumer credit insurance costs with other forms of insurance stems substantially from the following causes:

1. *Manner in Which It Is Sold.* Unlike most other insurance coverages, consumer credit insurance is available almost exclusively through lending institutions which, when sold under the ordinary system of marketing, are agents, and with group coverage, become policyholders.

2. *Persons Eligible to Purchase It.* It follows from this that only a debtor (more likely an installment debtor) will be eligible for the coverage. Since a common prerequisite to a loan is that an individual be working or expected to return to work, the eligibility requirements are different from companies marketing regular individual life and accident and health insurance policies in which employment of the insured is not usually required before insurance may be issued.

3. *Small Average Policies.*   Because the average consumer credit loan is approximately $365,[11] there is a tendency toward small average policies. For example, the Institute of Life Insurance reports the average consumer credit life insurance policy to be $530,[12] while the average size of policies for regular ordinary life insurance was $2,720.[13]

4. *Short Term of the Policy.*   Because the average consumer credit loan is of a relatively short duration, consumer credit insurers are faced with a relatively short time in which to amortize relatively high fixed expenses. Furthermore, even though the policies are considered noncancellable by the insurance company for the length of the loan period, the amount at risk (on installment loans at least) is decreasing constantly as the loan reaches maturity.

5. *Nature of Policy Coverage.*   As will be explained, consumer credit insurance policies have a minimum of exclusions so that, despite the trend in liberalization of underwriting in most other lines of insurance, from the standpoint of exclusions, consumer credit insurance is most liberal.

6. *Inadequacy of Reliable Statistical Information.*   At the present time, experience of the various companies writing this coverage appears to be a closely guarded secret except in a few isolated cases where statistical information was volunteered. It is hoped that the companies, either individually or in concert, will see fit to maintain and release adequate statistical information so that consumer credit insurance may stand on its own merits without questionable and sometimes invalid comparisons being made with other coverages.

Beginning May 1, 1956, an improvement in the quality of statistical information was forthcoming. At that time the new "Credit Life and Accident and Health Insurance Exhibit" was filed with State Insurance Departments. Until that time, all

---

[11] A prospectus issued by the Household Finance Corporation, January 14, 1957, indicated the companies' average size of loan to be $365.

[12] Based on Estimates and Prelimanary Data for 1956 Business, Institute of Life Insurance.

[13] Institute of Life Insurance, *Life Insurance Fact Book,* New York, 1956, p. 22.

company experience for consumer credit insurance was lumped together in the annual statement, and because many companies wrote several other types of coverages besides consumer credit insurance, it was impossible to get an accurate account of this coverage alone. Although a considerable improvement over the information formerly available, the Blank is subject to interpretation and judgment on the part of the companies filing it. In a few instances, the Blank left out important required data,[14] and in some instances requested irrelevant information.[15] Despite this, the National Association of Insurance Commissioners, particularly its Blanks Committee, should be commended for their efforts in adding to the inadequate supply of statistical information in this area.

There is a practical limitation to acquiring access to the aggregate experience of consumer credit insurers through use of this Blank, however. This difficulty arises because all companies are not licensed to do business in all states, Blanks and experience of a given company will be available only in the states in which it is licensed. To get a comprehensive view of all companies engaged in this line, it would be necessary to survey Blanks filed with most, if not all, insurance departments.

COMPONENTS OF THE RATE

Mortality

Because statistics on consumer credit insurance are limited in scope, where available, a discussion of experience of companies can be of a cursory nature. Considerable information on mortality under group consumer credit life insurance has become available from The Prudential Insurance Company of

---

[14] For example, return premiums on group consumer credit life insurance were not requested.

[15] For example, the Blank requests experience of consumer credit accident and health policies in which benefits are not limited to the loan period. In a study of 50 consumer credit insurers in Wisconsin, the author found no companies reporting business under this column. Because the National Association of Insurance Commissioners Model Code applying to this coverage requires the period of the loan and the insurance to be closely related, it is extremely doubtful that many insurers would issue such coverage at all.

America, which claims to be the largest writer of this insurance on the group basis. At the end of 1954 the company had 766 consumer credit life insurance contracts in force on the lives of 6,800,000 persons for $3,462,000; it was estimated in February of 1955 that this coverage then amounted to $3.5 billion under 800 policies insuring 7 million lives.[16] Most insureds included in these figures were bank borrowers, although debtors of finance companies, automobile dealers who finance their own paper, furniture and department stores, and vendors of cemetery lots on the installment plan were included. In reporting the company's experience, Mr. E. B. Whittaker, vice-president and actuary of the company, stated:

> In response to a letter from the Honorable Frank Sullivan, Commissioner of Insurance of the State of Kansas, I wrote on April 15, 1954, giving particulars as to our commission rates and mortality experience. I will quote just one paragraph of this letter: "The mortality rate under Group Creditors Life Insurance for the last five years has averaged 4.5 per 1000, or 50% of the scheduled premiums. On our smaller cases we have deemed it advisable to retain the 75¢ rate, but where there is a substantial volume, leading to a savings both in expenses and downscale commissions, it has been our practice to reduce the rate to the policyholder. This means that, if he makes any identifiable charge to the borrower, this charge will go down commensurate with the decrease on our premium rate."
>
> Translating a mortality of 4½ per thousand per annum into a pure claim cost per $100 of initial loan repayable in equal instalments over a year gives an arithmetical equivalent of 25¢, and we certainly feel that our rate of 49¢ is more than adequate except on smaller cases.[17]

The losses of this company, at least, seemed unaffected by the geographical location of its insureds as there was no appreciable variation among different sections of the country.

While these figures show the great volume of consumer credit insurance written by one insurer on the group basis, as well as its relatively low cost, it should be pointed out that it is extremely doubtful that *all* consumer credit life insurance

---

[16] A statement by E. B. Whittaker of The Prudential Insurance Company of America, before the Senate Judiciary Committee of the State of Kansas, February 15, 1955.

[17] *Ibid.*

could ever be written on this basis at the same rate. As was noted in the preceding chapter, one type of lending operation may be more or less desirable than another from the point of view of insurance company underwriting standards. Moreover, the size of a given lender's operations should, and does, influence his classification and rate. Finally, it was seen that legal requirements and regulations might preclude the sale of consumer credit life insurance on the group basis to debtors of certain types of creditors. To a great extent, it is for these reasons that the $1.00 per $100 ordinary rate has persisted as an effective competitor of the traditional 48¾ cents per $100 group rate.

The State Farm Life Insurance Company recently completed a five-year study of its experience with group consumer credit life insurance which substantially duplicated the experience of Prudential. Although the premium volume for a five-year period was relatively small ($344,824.50) and represented a select group of bank borrowers, the loss ratio proved to be 45.5 per cent of collected premiums.[18] In this case, however, the rate was $0.70 per $100 on the outstanding balance as compared to Prudential's $0.75 rate.[19] A further breakdown of results is contained in Appendix G.

M. R. Neifeld, vice-president of the Beneficial Management Company, recently completed a study of consumer credit life insurance experience for his company.[20] An initial survey taken in 1950 revealed a mortality of 37 per cent, or about 4 out of 1,000 outstanding Beneficial accounts. Since 1950 the corporation has experimented with several types of consumer credit insurance, the program now covering 169,016 accounts for $22,996,322 of insurance in force. Since the original survey,

---

[18] "Creditors Group Life Insurance," the results of a survey of consumer credit life insurance by the State Farm Life Insurance Company from 1950 to 1955.

[19] This company is not licensed in the state of New York and was therefore not required to use the 75 cent rate as prescribed by the New York Insurance Department.

[20] This study is referred to in "Consumer Instalment Credit Insurance," a statement by Edward A. Dunbar delivered before the American Finance Association, New York, December, 1955.

however, the figure has changed substantially. For example, in 1954 mortality was calculated at 6¾ per 1,000 outstanding accounts. In 1955 this figure was found to be 6½ per 1,000. Because the initial 1950 survey of mortality was made when there was no insurance in force on the lives of borrowers, it was the company's belief that mortality experience for that year was low because there was little reason for the survivors to report the debtor's death to the finance company and the debtor's family continued the payments on the loan. The increase in those years subsequent to 1950 might then be attributed to the issuance of consumer credit life insurance, which gave an incentive to survivors to notify the loan company of the borrower's death.

It is apparent that a considerable difference in mortality is found between Beneficial's study and those previously cited. It would be logical to assume that the difference between 4½ per 1,000 and 6¾ per 1,000 results primarily from the classes of borrowers insured. Because most of Prudential's and State Farm's insureds are bank borrowers, it is very likely that the higher qualifications for a bank loan as compared with the loan qualification of a small-loan company are responsible for the less favorable mortality recorded by the Beneficial Management Corporation which insures small-loan borrowers.

In an effort to supplement the currently inadequate compilation of experience in this field, an original study was completed. The details are given in Appendix F; the conclusions are used throughout this chapter. Based upon the experience of fifty consumer credit insurers who accounted for 58 per cent of total premiums for this line, a loss ratio for group consumer credit life insurance was calculated, to be 57.8 per cent during the calendar year of 1955 based on earned premiums and incurred losses. Ordinary consumer credit life insurance experience, representing 61 per cent of the business in force, registered an earned-incurred loss ratio of 22.6 per cent and 25.5 per cent for level-term and decreasing-term respectively.

To clearly understand the significance of these figures, one should be aware of the kind of premiums and losses used in deriving a given loss ratio. Premiums, for example, may be described as "written" or "earned." The former are those amounts which the insurer sells in a given fiscal period; the latter are those amounts which, only through the passage of time, the company is able to withdraw from its unearned premium reserve and classify as "earned." Because "earned" premiums tend to be the smaller of the two types in periods of increasing business, the choice of one type of premiums in preference to another for use in a loss ratio, may produce substantially different results.

Similarly, one should clearly understand and identify the kind of losses used in deriving a given loss ratio. Two of the more common types used are "paid" and "incurred." Paid losses are readily ascertained at year end by consulting an account showing the atcual disbursements made to claimants. Incurred losses, on the other hand, would include those reported to the company but not yet paid, plus those for which an insurer becomes liable in a given fiscal period but does not become aware of nor make payment until a subsequent fiscal period. Here again, the choice of one or the other kind of losses might result in different and possibly erroneous conclusions when used in a loss ratio.

As a result, if the loss ratio is to be used at all in a review of rates, it is essential that the components of this ratio relate the most accurate information. Authorities in this field are agreed that earned premiums and incurred losses are the most desirable and accurate constituents of this ratio.[21]

Morbidity

Even more limited than the experience of consumer credit life insurers is that of companies writing consumer credit accident and health insurance. To date, no individual company studies have been made available. The Consumer Credit Insurance Association has, on various occasions, claimed a minimum 40 per cent loss ratio for its member companies. This

---

[21] See, for example, G. F. Michelbacher, *Casualty Insurance Principles* (New York: McGraw-Hill Book Co., Inc., 1942), p. 317.

was echoed by a representative of a pioneer company in this field who maintained that the loss ratio (presumably on the earned-incurred basis), was "about 40."[22] My own study shows a 29.0 and 26.9 per cent loss ratio for group and ordinary consumer credit accident and health insurance respectively for companies doing business in Wisconsin and representing approximately 25 per cent of the total consumer credit accident and health business. It must be added that these figures for accident and health insurance are average loss ratios and that among surveyed companies the loss ratios of companies with over $50,000 in annual premiums for this coverage varied from 14.3 to 42.7 per cent.

Several reasons might be noted as accounting for this range of loss ratios. For example, the type of policy which a given company might issue could vary from a 3-day Retroactive to a 90-day Elimination plan. A substantial concentration of business by one company in the former policy and by another company in the latter might account for a difference in loss ratios each might experience. Also, even though the rates are somewhat standardized, there are many variations, which would again account for changes in the loss ratio among the various insurers. Finally, it is extremely questionable that the premium volume involved is sufficient to produce full statistical credibility. Where credibility is not complete, the element of chance may play an important role in determining the variation in loss ratios among insurers.

Reserves

As in most other lines of insurance, consideration of the reserve is important to a better understanding of the rate problem. In general, the system of reserves employed by consumer credit insurers is similar to that used in regular forms of life and accident and health insurance.

When consumer credit insurance is being paid on a monthly basis, the problem of reserve requirements is generally nil or

---

[22] "Credit Life, A. & H. Practices, Theories Sharply Challenged," *The National Underwriter,* December 11, 1952, p. 19.

not very great. It appears that a few writers effect all policies of the monthly premium variety on the first day of the month, the premium being due on the 10th or 15th of the following month. In this case there is no reserve problem since by the time the premium is actually received it has been fully earned and no reserve for an unearned premium is then required. The same would also be true where all policies are tabulated as of the end of the month and the premium is due sometime during the following month. In rare instances, the premium for group consumer credit life insurance is paid in advance by the lender, thus necessitating full pro-rata reserves.

There are cases in which the lender wishes to have immediate coverage. Thus many companies are requested and do inaugurate coverage at various times throughout the month other than the first or last day. In such a situation, insurers will set up an unearned premium reserve equal to one half of their gross premiums on the assumption that business is distributed evenly throughout the month. Essentially the same procedure is used for consumer credit accident and health insurance on the monthly premium basis.

Reserves for single-premium consumer credit life insurance are generally based upon the recommendations of the Credit Life and Credit Accident and Health Insurance Committee of the National Association of Insurance Commissioners.

Reserves should be held which are not less than the value, at the valuation date, of the risk for the unexpired portion of the period for which the premium has been paid, such value to be on a basis which in the aggregate is not less than that determined on the basis of mortality tables and interest rates as specified in the valuation laws of the individual states. For simplicity, since the insurer often does not have details as to ages, some reasonable assumption should be permitted as to the ages at which the net premiums should be determined. As an alternative, reserves based on unearned gross premiums may be used. However, it must be remembered that the amount of insurance often decreases each month and this may be taken into account rather than merely pro-rating the total premium for the period involved.[23]

---

[23] "Report of the Credit Life and Credit Accident and Health Insurance Subcommittee of the National Association of Insurance Commissioners," *Proceedings of the National Association of Insurance Commissioners,* June 7–11, 1954, p. 303.

The Subcommittee recommended the unearned gross premium as the proper method of reserves for consumer credit accident and health insurance paid on the single-premium basis. They further recommended that:

> Since all of the States have minimum reserve requirements applicable to this form of business, and the laws of the several states usually permit reasonable approximations, it would seem proper that the Departments of States, other than the State of domicile, accept the valuations made by the Departments of the domiciliary states.[24]

Companies writing consumer credit accident and health insurance or those writing consumer credit life insurance with a disability provision establish an additional reserve variously called a "claims reserve" or "disabled lives reserve" that is based upon a formula varying according to the monthly indemnity paid by the policy. The reserve is set up as soon as the notice of loss is received by the company. As claims are paid the reserve is reduced. One company makes payments either until the insured is no longer disabled or until the end of six months at which time an individual case-basis reserve is established. These claims are then periodically reviewed and the reserve reappraised.

To date no particularly important problems have arisen over the calculation and maintenance of consumer credit insurance reserves. Because the system is based upon the conservative approach currently being used in other lines of insurance, the reserves so developed appear to be adequate.

Acquisition Costs

Another component of the rate which must be given consideration is the compensation paid the lenders. A common practice among insurers of consumer credit life insurance on the group basis is to offer a premium adjustment or return to the lender-policyholder, variously termed a "retrospective rate," "experience refund," "premium refund," or, if paid by a mutual company, a "dividend." The payment is based upon the policyholder's experience, that is, the lender's experience, in a

---

[24] *Ibid.*

given fiscal period, usually a year. A typical calculation makes use of a rather complicated formula, which, in its simplest form, is as follows:

EXPERIENCE REFUND (OR DIVIDEND) = PREMIUMS − CLAIMS − IN-
SURER'S EXPENSE ALLOCATION − CONTRIBUTIONS TO INSURER'S CON-
TINGENCY RESERVE − "RISK SHARING" ELEMENT

Premiums and losses are easily available from insurance company records since separate accounts are kept for each policyholder. Expenses of underwriting a given lender, on the other hand, are derived from a formula which attempts to give proper recognition to both the fixed and variable elements in the expenses. The contingency reserve is generally based upon statutory reserve requirements and can be expected to vary slightly from state to state. The factor of "risk sharing" appears to be an attempt to provide the company with a reserve to handle extraordinary losses among lenders of a given class. As the lender's insured loan volume increases, the contribution to the "risk sharing" factor decreases because of the smaller likelihood of unusually large losses, lending recognition to the mathematical law which states the reliability of a given probability of loss increases as the number of exposure units (insured loans) increases. The premium refund is dependent upon the experience of the lender, and in some instances may also be dependent upon the experience of the entire group life department. In any event, the most important determinant of the amount of premium refund received by the lender is the mortality experience of a given lender's insured debtors.[25]

Several advantages accrue to the companies utilizing this system of retrospective rating. First, it results in assurance to the insurer that a good class of borrowers is covered because it establishes an incentive for the policyholder to insure only such classes of borrowers. The granting of coverage to a physically unfit person, for example, would probably result in a decreased premium refund. Because the experience refund is so highly dependent upon the loss ratio of a given lender, the

---

[25] See, for example, "Prudential Group Creditors Life Insurance," a brochure printed by The Prudential Press, March 1953, p. 6.

better its experience, the larger the refund, other things being equal.

A second advantage inherent in the system is that the risk[26] to the company is greatly reduced and, in a few cases, virtually eliminated. This occurs because the premiums of most companies are sufficiently "loaded" so as to be adequate to pay a premium refund even when the lender secures a somewhat below average class of borrowers. To the individual lender, adverse claim fluctuations would result in a decrease or non-receipt of a premium refund. Moreover, it is the insurer's right to increase the premium following a poor year's experience. It would thus seem that to the extent that the amount of experience refund is actually affected by chance fluctuations, a considerable amount of risk is borne by the lender rather than the insurer.[27]

A third major advantage of the retrospective rating system enjoyed by the insurance company is that it affords compensation to the lender. This makes sales more palatable to the policyholder in overcoming the objections of the lender who expects reimbursement of his expenses of administering the insurance program. Although not specifically designed to circumvent the statutes of those states prohibiting the payment of commission to lenders, the system does result in pecuniary return to the lender. Unlike a commission that is paid in advance, a premium refund is paid contingently at the end of a fiscal period. Both, however, are similar in that the amount of compensation is dependent to varying degrees upon the premium volume.

---

[26] Risk here is defined as uncertainty as to loss.

[27] This reduction of risk to the insurer was even more pronounced in those cases brought to light of lenders who operated in unregulated small-loan states under the ordinary method of insuring. A few cases of 85 per cent commission retentions were reported, which left approximately 15 per cent for the insurer. However, because most of the administrative functions, including the absolute control of loss payments, are performed by the lender-agent, one might well have asked if the insurance company under such a system has anything at risk. An opponent of the system expressed his belief that the lender, in fact, became the insurer or risk bearer, and that the 15 per cent retained by the insurance company was payment for the use of the company's name and license.

As will subsequently be noted, this system has been virtually eliminated by state statute or administrative rulings and today is only historically significant.

Although the semantics differ, the effect of either the commission or the experience refund is the same—compensation to the lender.

Let us consider the effect of these advantages that accrue to the insurers in relation to which of the parties, lender or borrower, pays the premium. There should be no less incentive for the lender to select carefully those of his borrowers that he insures no matter who pays the premium, since, in either case, an experience refund, if merited, is paid to the lender as policyholder. On the other hand it is quite conceivable that the probability of loss to the insurer may well vary between two lenders in a given class where one pays the entire premium for the borrower and the other where the premium is paid by the borrower. In the former, all borrowers would be covered, giving the insurer an average probability of loss. In the latter case, with the borrower paying the premium, and because the coverage is then voluntary, a greater amount of selection against the company can be anticipated because of the existing tendency of the less desirable classes of borrowers to purchase insurance more readily than an average or above-average individual. It is interesting to note in this respect that, in the company considered to be the largest writer of group consumer credit life insurance, about two thirds of all insured lenders made no charge to their customers for the coverage.[28] It is in the area of compensation to the lender in the form of experience refunds, however, that particularly important consideration must be given to which of the parties pays the premiums.

Where the entire cost of the insurance is paid by the lender, at no extra cost to the borrower, the fact that a lender receives an experience refund makes little or no difference to the individual borrower and the lender should then be entitled to any refunds paid.[29] Consider, however, the case where the bor-

---

[28] A statement attributed to E. B. Whittaker of the Prudential Insurance Company of America and quoted in the *Topeka Daily Capital*, February 17, 1955.

[29] This would be less true of course where the lender raises his interest or discount rate to enable him to "give" this insurance to the borrower.

rower pays the entire cost of the coverage. The consumer credit group life insurance contract provides for a premium refund based upon the previously cited factors to be paid by the insurer to the policyholder, that is, the lender, either in cash or as a reduction in premiums at the option of the policyholder.[30] There seems to be little doubt that, because of this option to the lender, it is possible, where premiums are paid solely by borrowers, that the lender will retain the fruits of favorable experience in the form of cash premium refunds. To the extent that such refunds are in excess of the lender's costs of administration, they are in effect an additional source of profit to the lender and have an effect similar to the commissions paid lenders under the ordinary method of insuring. This does not mean to condemn the retrospective rating system as such, but merely to point out that a potential for abuse is inherent in the mechanism.[31]

It might well be argued that the benefit properly belongs to those assureds (certificate holders) during the period for which the experience refund was calculated. If such a thesis is accepted, the practical problem arises of returning the proper share of the refunds to each assured. To do this, consideration must be given to calculating the proper pro-rata share of the refund due to each certificate holder on the basis of amount of insurance in force and/or the length of time insured. An additional problem would be encountered in attempting to return such calculated shares to each assured. Difficulty can be expected since many of the assureds who were borrowers during the time the refund was calculated would probably not be current debtors at the time the refund was being distributed. Thus it would involve more than crediting an existing account as might be done with those assureds who were still debtors of the same lender. When the costs of determining the proper share

---

[30] One large mutual company allows the additional option of leaving the dividend to accumulate at interest with the company.

[31] All literature written to date has merely described the process. To my knowledge no one has written of the potential abuse inherent in the mechanism, although most company officials interviewed have recognized its existence and subjection to abuse, both potential and real.

due each assured are considered, as well as the actual costs of returning this share to the assured, it becomes apparent that these expenses alone might well consume much, or perhaps all, of the experience refund.

Several insurance companies give recognition to the fact that lenders receive and retain the cash refunds rather than pass them on in the form of a decrease in rates to its debtors. These companies require that a substantial portion of the premium be paid by the lender, thus justifying the retention, at least to the extent of the lender's contribution.

One suggestion worth further study is the establishment of a fund or separate account by the lender-policyholder which would be credited with all premium refunds from the group consumer credit life insurance contract. Becuase of the emphasis given mortality experience in the calculation of the premium refund, it is possible that in a year of adverse claim experience no refunds to the policyholder might be made. The account or reserve could then be debited so that the charge to the borrowers would remain the same despite the currently poor experience of the group. When premium refunds are again received, the account or reserve could be replenished.

Recognizing the fact that this method contains some inequities to former insured borrowers, the plan does have the merit of surmounting the previous objection of possible excessive unjust enrichment to the lender policyholder, while at the same time affording a practical, inexpensive method of allowing insured borrowers to participate in premium refunds.

It is difficult to obtain data regarding the size of premium refunds because these payments may obviously be used competitively among insurance companies. That the net cost,[32] within certain limits, varies inversely with the premium volume of the lender is known and illustrated in Table XVII. Presented in tabular form are the estimated gross costs during the first policy year and also estimated cost for renewal years after dividends have become effective. It appears that the actual net costs have not varied materially from those estimated.

---

[32] Net cost here equals gross premiums less experience refunds or dividends.

TABLE XVII

Estimated Cost of a Twelve-Month Loan Allocated
as a Specific Charge for $100 of Initial Loan for
Various Amounts of Insurance in Force

(1) Total Amount of Insurance in Force	(2) First Policy Year	(3) Renewal Years	(4) Amount of Experience Refund	(5) Experience Refund as Percentage of Premium Gross
$100,000	$0.49	$0.45	$0.04	8.2%
$250,000 to $1,000,000	0.49	0.40	0.09	18.4
$1,000,000 or more	0.49	0.35	0.14	28.6

Source: The first three columns based upon "Prudential Group Creditors Life Insurance," a brochure published by The Prudential Press, March 1953, p. 7. The latter two are calculated.

Column 5 illustrates the percentage of premium expected to be refunded in renewal years. It will be noted that the experience refunds become larger as the lender's premium volume increases. Furthermore this refund is considerably less than the 40–55 per cent minimum commissions being paid to lenders under the ordinary method of insuring, but are nevertheless quite substantial dollarwise if it is assumed that the group method is used principally to insure larger accounts.

One large insurer of group consumer credit life insurance was reported paying aggregate dividends of approximately 31 per cent based on an eleven-year average of approximately $750,000 of outstanding loans.[33] Another study by a fairly small writer of group consumer credit life insurance[34] reported an average dividend for five years of experience for all of its policies to be 30.2 per cent. My study of insurers doing 58 per cent of the business indicated group consumer credit insurance dividends averaged 19.4 per cent of gross premiums.

Having some characteristics of both the "retrospective rating" plan and straight percentage commissions is the "contingent commission" system of compensating lender-agents. Here the earned premiums for each agent are calculated. From

---

[33] Jacobson, *op. cit.,* p. 27.

[34] "Creditors Group Life Insurance," State Farm Life Insurance Company, Bloomington, Illinois. Details of this study are cited in Appendix G.

them is deducted a percentage of such earned premiums and is called the company's gross retention. Also deducted are the net incurred losses and loss adjustment expenses arising from the business of each agent. The remainder represents the amount of commission payable. The gross retention varies among companies and depends mainly upon the individual agent's premium volume and the lender's plan of operation in administering the consumer credit insurance program. This system of compensation has not attained the wide use as has the system of retrospective rating. It is not expected to increase in popularity because it appears to violate certain state statutes and has thus been regarded with suspect by regulatory officials.

The role of the lender as the representative of the insurer has already been discussed. It was argued that the lender does in fact incur expenses of various kinds in making consumer credit insurance available. For a lender utilizing the ordinary method of insuring, it was found difficult to justify commissions of 40 to 55 per cent of premiums and unconscionable to accept those of 85 per cent. This is not intended as a condemnation of lenders who are forced either by law or company underwriting rules into offering consumer credit insurance on the ordinary basis, or not at all. It does mean, however, that the action of the American Life Convention and Life Insurance Association of America insofar as they attempt to force a limitation on the size of commissions paid by insurers to the lenders is to be commended.[35] Consideration should also be given to the operation of "reverse competition" in which commissions become a competitive tool among ordinary insurers and to a tendency toward offering successively larger commissions in an attempt to gain a larger share of the insurance market which exists to an unknown degree.

Several persons associated with ordinary insurance companies and wishing to remain anonymous have expressed their opinion that commissions were "high" and that some were probably "excessive." On the other hand, they found themselves indi-

---

[35] Cited earlier in Chapter IV.

vidually unable to reduce their commission scale without suffering a considerable loss of business to the company which maintained its higher scale of commissions.

It would seem that an acceptable method of accomplishing such a reduction and subsequent stabilization of commissions would be through voluntary means. The best attempt to date at organizing consumer credit insurers has been the Consumer Credit Insurance Association previously discussed. However, primarily because of the fear of losing accounts to its competitor, each individual insurer is reluctant to take the initiative in reducing commissions. Aslo, the Association's membership numbers but twenty-three companies. If all members were to agree to make voluntary reductions, nonmember insurers might possibly acquire accounts of the Association's members due to such compensation reductions. As will presently be seen,[36] the Consumer Credit Insurance Association has recently become the proponent of a Model Bill which would limit lender compensation by statute, thus enforcing some uniformity of lender compensation.

It might well be asked if the experience refunds under the group plan of consumer credit insurance and the commissions paid under the ordinary method closely reflect the actual costs of administration by the lender. Because of the elusive nature of the many "costs" involved in handling an insurance program by the lender, aspersions as to the validity of any given set of cost figures tend to arise.[37] Questions as to how to handle a lender's fixed expenses for purposes of such a survey have frequently been posed. One person might believe that part of the costs of rent, for example, should be charged to such a survey; another may believe that such a charge should not be included since the charge is paid by the lender regardless of the conduct of a consumer credit insurance program on the same premises. Then too, there is the practical deterrent to such a study being made to determine the administrative costs of pro-

---

[36] See Chapter IX.

[37] See statement of Edward Dunbar before the National Association of Insurance Commissioners, St. Louis, Missouri, May 15, 1956.

viding consumer credit insurance when the expense of such projects is considered. As a result, few valid comprehensive studies have been made.

Recently the Household Finance Corporation, one of the largest consumer finance companies in the United States, completed a survey of 89 of its branch offices which furnished group consumer credit life insurance to its customers. The results were based upon estimates supplied by each office manager. The conclusions of importance reflecting the annual cost of administering this company's program were as follows:[38]

TOTAL COST PER YEAR

Cost Per Loan
Per loan made	9.9¢
Per $100 loaned	2.9¢

Cost Per Year
Per loan outstanding	12.7¢
Per $100 outstanding	4.7¢

It should be noted that the results of this survey apply only to group consumer credit life insurance. We have already seen that the administration of ordinary insurance involves considerably more detail and should therefore prove to be more costly to administer. Then too, this study was made by just one type of the many classes of lenders, namely a consumer finance company operating a chain of offices nationally. Studies employing a similar methodology can be expected to produce different results among various classes of lenders if not among various consumer finance companies. Also, consideration should be given to the fact that this insurance protection is made available by the Household Finance Corporation at "no extra charge," the premium being paid entirely by the finance company. As a result, the amount of selling time involved would almost certainly be less than where coverage was purchased by a borrower at an extra charge, thus necessitating additional selling time and effort by the lender. Finally, it should be pointed out that the study was administered by Household's personnel

---

[38] "Cost of Administering HFC Insurance Program," the results of a survey made by the Household Finance Corporation, November 4, 1955.

and not by an independent firm of cost analysts. These constitute but some of the reasons for believing the application of the conclusions of this study to all lenders offering consumer credit insurance would be misleading.[39]

The Beneficial Management Corporation recently sponsored a study relating to the lender's cost of providing ordinary consumer credit life insurance to its borrowers. Unlike the Household Finance Corporation, Beneficial Management passes the charge on to the borrower in most states in which it operates. To gather data, a group of four lending offices were surveyed. These offices were a large office operated by a chain, a small office operated by a chain, a medium-sized office operated by an independent lender, and a small office operated by an independent lender. The companies chosen were the Beneficial Finance Company, Commonwealth Loan Company, and Missouri Loan Company, all of Kansas City, Missouri, and the Home Loan Company, Excelsior Springs, Missouri. They appear in the survey as the B.F. Co., C.L. Co., M.L. Co. and H.F. Co., respectively. Allocation of cost was based upon time studies of the various employees involved in the administration of the insurance program. Included in the allocation were the operating expenses and occupancy expenses. The important conclusions reached were the following:[40]

The cost per $100 of insured loans granted is shown for each office. This cost was obtained by dividing the total cost of handling Credit Life Insurance in each office, as follows:

	B.F. Co.	C.L. Co.	M.L. Co.	H.F. Co.	*Average*
Amount Loaned	$1,435,900	$242,200	$500,000	$290,700	$2,468,800
Total Cost	4,047.20	1,796.40	2,609.21	503.81	8,956.62
Cost per $100.00	0.28	0.74	0.52	0.17	0.37

[39] A study by the Commercial Credit Corporation of its loans made in Pennsylvania recently revealed the cost of administration of consumer credit insurance to this company at about 5 cents per $100. The details of this study were not available and it was thus felt its use in the body of this text would be open to question. For further details see *The National Underwriter,* December 2 and December 16, 1955.

[40] "Analysis of the Cost of Handling Credit Life Insurance," a study made for the Beneficial Management Corporation by Driscoll, Millet & Company, Analysts in bank management, Philadelphia, folio 3.

Commenting upon the results of this study, a company spokesman stated:

> The survey indicates that the actual out-of-pocket cost of selling a policy of credit life insurance to a borrower in a regulated small loan office is 37¢ per $100.00 of coverage per year. The fact that this figure is so close to the average and customary 40¢ is made even more significant by the considerable differences in cost between the offices studied.[41]

The results of this study would seem to support the validity of the joint American Life Convention–Life Insurance Association of America proposal to limit ordinary consumer credit life insurance commissions to 40 cents per year per $100 of initial indebtedness as representing a fair level of compensation, and the contention previously made that lenders do incur costs in the administration of the consumer credit insurance program.[42]

It is difficult to criticize the work of the independent analysts who conducted the Beneficial Management Corporation survey because the study indicates the meticulous devotion to detail with which few but cost accountants would be interested. Commenting on the results of an earlier study of this type, an insurance company executive of wide experience stated: "Through a system of time studies it could undoubtedly be found that the corner drug store was losing money by selling chewing gum at 1¢ a stick. I sincerely doubt that even with such information available the drug store would discontinue the sale of the gum."[43] Similarly, it is doubtful that a decrease in commission below 40 cents per $100 would result in fewer lenders offering consumer credit insurance coverage. Finally, it must be remembered that this study pertains only to small-loan companies in a regulated state and would probably be different in other

---

[41] Edward A. Dunbar, Associate Counsel of the Beneficial Management Corporation, in a letter to the members of the Sub-Committee on Credit Life and Credit Accident and Health Insurance of the Life Committee of the National Association of Insurance Commissioners, May 15, 1956, p. 3.

[42] A similar study sponsored by the Beneficial Management Corporation recently completed by Driscoll, Millet & Company indicated the cost of consumer credit life insurance on the group basis to be approximately 22 cents per $100 of insured loans.

[43] At his request, the gentleman remains anonymous.

states. These costs undoubtedly would vary from state to state among other classes of lending institutions, such as commercial banks, industrial banks, credit unions, and retailers.

The question of compensation to national banks handling consumer credit insurance prompted a formal opinion from the Comptroller of the Currency. In it he recognizes that the banks do have an insurable interest in the lives of their borrowers and should be allowed to purchase group or ordinary policies of life insurance to the extent of the unpaid balance.

Regarding the commission on such policies, the Comptroller states:

> A national bank located in a town of more than 5000 should not receive any part of the premium charged the borrower, by way of commissions, dividends, refunds of premium, or otherwise, *other than amounts sufficient to cover the actual cost to the bank of furnishing this service including clerical and stenographic expenses incurred in preparing reports, etc., made to the insurance company.*[44]

The office of the Comptroller of Currency has refused to state a specific percentage limitation or formula which might be used to determine whether a bank is meeting the requirement just quoted. This matter of determining banks' administrative cost of handling the insurance program appears to be subjective, resting entirely with the particular bank examiner in charge of an audit. It is usually at that time the question is considered. The examiner's judgment is tempered by the volume of the bank's consumer credit insurance and loan volume and the efficiency of such an operation.[45]

It must be conceded that the cost of administering a consumer credit insurance program by the lender will vary among different classes of lending institutions depending upon the volume of lending operations and insured loans. It thus becomes evident that no single commission could be applied to all types of lenders, indeed to lenders of a single class, that

---

[44] "Digest of Opinions of the Office of the Comptroller of the Currency Relating to Operations and Powers of National Banks," September, 1950 Supplement, Office of the Comptroller of Currency, Washington, D.C., Par. 9420A.

[45] This information was obtained by correspondence with the Office of the Comptroller of Currency, Washington, D.C.

would represent the actual costs to each lender of providing consumer credit insurance. If this idea were to be applied to Beneficial Management Corporation's study, it is seen that the loan offices designated C.L. Co. and M.L. Co. are "losing money" in the amount of 34 and 12 cents per $100 of insurance issued, respectively, based upon the American Life Convention–Life Insurance Association of America proposal to limit compensation under consumer credit life insurance to 40 cents per $100 of insurance. At the same time, it will be noted that two offices in this study are "making money." The office designated B.F. Co. is realizing an additional 12 cents, while the H.F. Co. is realizing 33 cents on the basis of a proposed 40 cent commission.

In a previous chapter the benefits gained by the lender who makes consumer credit insurance available to its clients were considered. Included in these advantages were the greatly increased chances for an advantage over its competitors, a possible increase in goodwill and the additional security of having the loan insured against the debtor's death or disability. That these benefits are actually realized is not generally in dispute and were, in some cases, suggested by lenders as reasons for having decided to provide this additional service to its customers.

The tendency to discuss actual out-of-pocket costs of administering the program without taking into consideration benefits similar to those just cited, which may be realized by lenders providing their clients with consumer credit insurance protection, results in but a partial exposition of the problem of costs at best. Consideration should be given not only to the additional cost of providing this customer service, but also to the increase in the lender's total revenue resulting from the inauguration of the insurance program. Another approach would be to say that not only should a comparison of *costs* of operation be made before and after the inception of consumer credit insurance, but also between the *total revenues* realized before and after the provision for insurance coverage.

If this coverage were sold (and purchased) on the basis of

its potential to increase the creditor's income from his lending operations and not as a profitable supplementary business, many of the abuses in this field might soon disappear. If the lender were convinced of this approach, that is, that consumer credit insurance represents a valuable additional service to his customers, that, if offered on reasonable terms, gives him a competitive edge over other lenders, he would attempt to secure the best and lowest cost coverage available.

A suggested alternative to the present system of compensation to the lenders under a program of consumer credit insurance is the fixed amount per policy which is unrelated to its size. The concept of the so-called "flat fee" is predicated upon the idea that the lender's cost of selling such policies is unrelated to their size and that, other things being equal, acquisition of a policy covering a $500 loan, for example, requires no more selling effort or dollar outlay by the lender than does one of $100. If this is true, the advocates of this system argue, than the commissions which are currently on a percentage basis can be set at an absolute amount which would more closely reflect the lender's costs of administering the insurance program. To a small degree, the life insurance industry as a whole recognizes the fact that commissions should not go up proportionately with the size of the policy. The "jumbo" life insurance policies previously discussed generally pay lower percentage commissions than do policies below $10,000. It was previously noted that commissions on regular group life policies tend to decrease percentagewise as the size of the policy increases.[46]

Probably the greatest appeal of the "flat fee" system is in its claim of limiting lender's commissions to the reasonable (not necessarily the actual) costs of administration to the exclusion of excessive and questionable profits.

---

[46] This discussion is not intended to suggest that an agent selling regular insurance on an individual policy basis should be compensated on a "flat fee" basis. The majority of agents would point out, and rightly so, that, in general, the higher the cost of the policy being sold, the greater will be the resistance and selling effort needed to make the sale. The present system recognizes this and compensates accordingly.

As far as is known, such a system has never been used, so that its attributes have yet to be proven. One main criticism has been leveled against the "flat fee." That is the fear of unwarranted loan refinancings or pyramiding of policies in an attempt by the lender to sell as many policies as possible to a given borrower, thus maximizing receipt of commissions. Since cases of pyramiding and excessive refinancing have been noted,[47] this fear is founded on more than mere speculation.

An additional objection to the "flat fee" system is the practical one of getting the lenders to accept what will probably amount to a decrease in commissions. Despite these objections, a considerable number of advocates of this plan exists. Since the system has strong arguments in its favor and because it has never been disproved, arguments of the proponents of this system should be heard.

Expenses

The remaining important component of the rate to be discussed is the over-all expense of providing this coverage. The only statistical basis of this discussion is my own study previously cited and explained in Appendix F. The data taken from this study, and presented in Table XVIII, indicate expense ratios by line of coverage for insurers operating in Wisconsin. The inclusion of commissions in this ratio has been generally accepted and is done here.[48]

The expense ratio for ordinary consumer credit life insurance is noted to be in excess of 70 per cent, while the same coverage on a group basis records a ratio of 15.2 per cent. This latter figure is an understatement of the expense ratio for group coverage if it is agreed that premium refunds and dividends are, in effect, a form of compensation to the lender. In such a case, they should be added to the expense ratio of 15.2 per

---

[47] "The Tie-In Sale of Credit Insurance in Connection With Small Loans and Other Transactions," a report of the Subcommittee on Antitrust and Monopoly Legislation of the Committee on the Judiciary, U.S. Senate (83rd Cong., 2nd Sess.) (Washington, D.C.: U.S. Government Printing Office, 1955), p. 9.

[48] See a discussion of this subject by Riegel-Miller in *Insurance Principles and Practices* (New York: Prentice-Hall Inc., 1947), pp. 151–52.

cent. The study referred to in Appendix F showed such premium returns to be about 19.4 per cent of earned premiums which, when totaled, amount to 34.6 per cent. Thus, the expense of writing consumer credit life insurance on the group plan appears to be about one half of that written on the ordinary basis.

The figures relating to consumer credit accident and health insurance are surprising in view of the fact that the process of administering this line of consumer credit insurance is more detailed and time consuming than for life insurance. It was

TABLE XVIII

EXPENSE RATIOS FOR VARIOUS TYPES OF CONSUMER CREDIT INSURANCE
(Represents the Business of 50 Companies for 1955)

	Expenses	Com-missions	Expense Ratios
Group Life Insurance (58% of total premiums)	8.6%	6.6%	15.2%
Ordinary Level Term	24.0	50.4	74.4
Ordinary Decreasing Term (61% of business in force)	24.6	46.6	71.2
Group A & H	16.1	27.9	44.0
Ordinary A & H (25% of total premiums, estimated)	18.6	31.2	49.8

Source: Appendix F, Table XXIX

therefore expected that the expense ratios would be considerably higher than the ratios for life insurance coverages.

It is quite clear from a review of Table XVIII that the major components of the rate for consumer credit insurance are the compensation paid to lenders and the costs of administration, collectively termed expenses. It is extremely desirable that insurers writing this coverage review their systems of rates in an attempt to reduce their expense ratios rather than argue for their maintenance at present levels.

Rather than resorting to questionable comparisons with other forms of insurance to prove the reasonableness of the present rates, the industry would accomplish much more by exhibiting a willingness to freely exchange experience.

Chapter VII

CLAIMS ADMINISTRATION

INTRODUCTION

One of the simpler operations comprising the consumer credit insurance mechanism is the administration of claims. The lender usually receives the notice of death or disability and distributes the proper forms to the claimant. With consumer credit life insurance, the insured's survivors are asked to submit either a Proof of Death or coroner's death certificate. Claimants under a consumer credit accident and health policy usually return Proofs of Loss and an Attending Physician's Statement and may also be asked to submit an employer's statement regarding the insured's period of disability. If the company admits liability under either policy, a draft is sent to the lender as beneficiary and is applied toward the reduction or elimination of the insured's outstanding balance.

FILING CLAIMS

The initiative for payment of a death claim under consumer credit life insurance ordinarily comes from the surviving spouse, parents, relatives, or administrators of the estate. In a few instances, where the lender is a personal friend of the deceased, the claim may originate with the lender. Claims cannot be expected to be made where the survivors are not aware of the existence of such coverage. Because the major concern of most borrowers is to obtain the loan, it is possible that a mere oral explanation, if given, relating to the insurance coverage, is easily forgotten, if ever fully understood. Consequently, it is the strong feeling of a growing number of state officials, lenders, and insurance executives that the delivery of evidence of insurance should be prescribed by law. This is particularly true when the lender makes an additional charge for such coverage. At least one state has found that promulgation of a rule requiring evidence of insurance to be given the borrower resulted in a 500 per cent increase in claims paid by the insurers operating within that state.[1]

It is not contended here that the issuance of such evidence will result in payment of all death claims due insured borrowers. Inadequate examination of a deceased's possessions, for example, may fail to disclose the availability of such coverage. Lost policies and certificates may account for other failures to claim benefits. This problem is not unique in that it may well occur when the deceased was covered by any other type of insurance, evidence of which was never discovered. These situations do not lessen the need for evidence of insurance, however.

Most borrowers today are sold a "package" consisting of a loan, insurance, and charges for each. Without a certificate describing the nature of the coverage, at least in general terms, it is doubtful that the borrower will remain aware of the existence or nature of the insurance for which he has paid.

CONSUMER CREDIT LIFE INSURANCE CLAIMS ADMINISTRATION

Because the proof of loss (death) is much simpler for life insurance than for disability insurance, the amount of specific information requested by the insurance company is held to a minimum. Under group consumer credit life insurance, the information usually required is the name and address of the borrower, the master policy number, the date the loan was executed, the amount of the original indebtedness, the amount repaid, and the unpaid balance remaining at the time of death. Some companies require the lender to forward original promissory notes or account cards with proof of loss to the home

---

[1] "Credit Life, A. & H. Practices, Theories Sharply Challenged," *The National Underwriter,* December 11, 1952, p. 19.

or branch office to further verify the existence of the loan.

Claim forms and procedures for companies operating under the ordinary method of doing business are more elaborate than under the group method. Because these companies issue both decreasing- and level-term life, the latter policy must provide for a beneficiary. This second beneficiary is entitled to the difference between the insurance in force at the time of the insured's death and the amount needed to pay the insured's loan balance.

CONSUMER CREDIT ACCIDENT AND HEALTH INSURANCE CLAIMS ADMINISTRATION

It is normally a simple matter to ascertain whether a person is dead or alive. Even a layman is usually capable of establishing such a loss. On the other hand, it may be extremely difficult to determine whether a person is disabled and to what extent. The problems of adjustment faced by consumer credit accident and health insurers are thus more involved than those faced by consumer credit life insurers. Under the monthly indemnity type of accident and health insurance policy, not only is the date of inception of liability important, but also the date of termination must be considered since payments are made on a prorata basis for the actual number of days of total disability. Because the layman is unable to accurately determine disability, the opinion of a professional is required. A statement by a licensed physician describing the nature and extent of disability as well as a prognosis of the disabled borrower's condition is included in registering the initial claim.

A policy of this type tends to cause considerable friction between all parties concerned, particularly where the nature or duration of the disability is in question. This is one reason why many insurers will not consider the sale of consumer credit accident and health insurance of the monthly indemnity variety.[2]

---

[2] Another reason why many companies object to the sale of this coverage and refuse to write it is because they feel the expenses connected with its sale

Despite the potential for differences of opinion that may arise in the adjustment of consumer credit accident and health losses, state regulatory officials generally agree that they do not receive an undue number of complaints regarding the payment of claims from insured debtors or survivors.

Where the disability claim is initially filed with the insurer, the doctor's diagnosis is considered in the company's decision to accept or reject liability on a claim. If the initial claim information creates a doubt or additional questions, a supplementary medical report may be requested. If liability is admitted, drafts are issued periodically once the required waiting period has elapsed. Periodic credit reports are then frequently secured to establish the continuance of the insured's disability.

VARIATION OF DUTIES AMONG LENDERS

The lender's role in the administration of claims varies considerably among insurance companies. Common functions that may be performed are the issuance and forwarding of completed claim forms to the insurer and the notification of the borrower or borrower's estate that the account has been credited or canceled. Several companies allow very large lenders to draw a draft payable to the maker, subject to the approval of the insurer in the event of the borrower's death.

A few companies formerly allowed the lender complete charge of the payment of claims. When the authority to accept or reject a claim was combined with a system of retrospective rating or contingent commissions, which were calcu-

---

are too great in relation to the benefits paid. See, for example, a statement by Edmund B. Whittaker, vice-president of The Prudential Insurance Company of America, before the Senate Judiciary Committee of the State of Kansas, February 15, 1955. At that time Mr. Whittaker, in speaking of consumer credit accident and health insurance, stated: "It seems to me that this type of insurance does not make sense. In my opinion the insurance mechanism, which has certain fixed expenses, should not be used to cover losses which the individual can be expected to carry on his own, and I suppose everybody in this room carries automobile insurance with a $50 deductible so that he does not waste his insurance money incurring claim expenses to pay $5 claims for denting a fender."

lated primarily upon the loss ratio of the lender and which varied inversely with this ratio, the potential for abuses must invariably become a reality. The lender thus has little incentive to pay claims; he has much more to gain by denying them. Fortunately such systems in which the lender has complete charge of claim payments have virtually been eliminated and are merely of historical importance.

ABUSES

As might be expected, consumer credit insurance is subjected to fraudulent claims just as any other form of insurance. Companies are faced with illegal claims perpetrated by all parties concerned, including the lender, borrower, and physician.

To illustrate with examples, one company, upon receipt of a claims form under a group life contract, decided to investigate further. It was subsequently discovered that the lender had used the name of a person listed on a tombstone in a neighboring graveyard. This "ghost account" was carried in the deceased's name, and since the claim was payable to the lender, it is unlikely that the fraud would ever have been detected had it not been for the "sixth sense" of a home office claims adjuster.

One example will serve to illustrate conspiracy on the part of both physician and borrower. In this particular instance, a Midwestern debtor became eligible for consumer credit accident and health insurance by virtue of his purchase of a new automobile, the policy being issued by the finance company. After a very few payments on the car, the insured became "ill" and made claim under his policy. The attending physician recommended a complete cessation of work and prescribed a trip to Florida. It was not until too late that the insurer discovered the claimant was not really disabled and that the physician, who was actually the insured's brother, had not only made the trip to Florida possible, but the free and clear ownership of a new car as well.

It appears that the administration of consumer credit accident and health insurance claims does involve more detail than consumer credit life insurance in any form. However, because of the minimum of exclusions in these contracts compared to other forms of life and accident and health coverage, the job of adjustment is considerably lightened.

MAGNITUDE OF CLAIMS PAYMENTS

The relative simplicity of the process of claims administration should not be allowed to detract from its importance. Table XIX indicates the volume of claims paid each year from the inception of consumer credit life insurance to the present. It is difficult to relate these figures to the peace of mind realized by the insured debtor during his lifetime and the satisfaction received by the survivors when the accounts are marked "paid in full."

TABLE XIX

CONSUMER CREDIT LIFE INSURANCE BENEFITS PAID

(000 Omitted)

Year	Ordinary	Group	Total	Year	Ordinary	Group	Total
1917	$...	$...	$...	1937	$ 160	$ 690	$ 850
1918	6	...	6	1938	210	960	1,170
1919	18	...	18	1939	230	1,100	1,330
1920	20	...	20	1940	280	1,500	1,780
1921	24	...	24	1941	340	1,800	2,140
1922	31	...	31	1942	330	1,800	2,130
1923	32	...	32	1943	250	1,400	1,650
1924	36	...	36	1944	250	1,200	1,450
1925	61	...	61	1945	310	1,300	1,610
1926	74	1	75	1946	500	1,800	2,300
1927	120	3	123	947	890	3,100	3,990
1928	130	17	147	1948	1,400	5,000	6,400
1929	170	70	240	1949	1,800	6,700	8,500
1930	200	130	330	1950	2,300	11,000	13,300
1931	180	230	410	1951	3,200	15,000	18,200
1932	200	270	470	1952	4,400	19,000	23,400
1933	240	260	500	1953	5,400	27,000	32,400
1934	120	300	420	1954	6,600	33,000	39,600
1935	130	310	440	1955	7,000	45,000	52,000
1936	140	390	530				

Source: Division of Statistics and Research, Institute of Life Insurance, New York.

Chapter VIII

POLICY PROVISIONS

INTRODUCTION

As do most other forms of life and disability insurance, consumer credit life and accident and health insurance policies vary among jurisdictions, insurers, and lender-beneficiaries. Thus a group creditor's life insurance policy issued to a sales finance company in Kentucky by the ABC Credit Life Insurance Company may differ markedly from one issued by the XYZ Mutual Life Insurance Company to a bank in New York City. Because no standard policy has yet been developed or accepted, the insurers may and do vary the form of the policy issued from time to time to maintain a degree of flexibility in their operations as well as to comply with changing state regulations. When it is remembered that significant differences are evident in the operations of various kinds of lenders for which specific adaptations of policies must be made, it is clear that a discussion of "a" single policy would not be inclusive, while an explanation of all policies issued would be impractical.

Despite the many differences that exist among the policies, there are a sufficient number of similarities to give the reader a general indication of their contents. It is the purpose of this chapter to discuss these similarities in both group and ordinary policies and attempt to give the reader a general idea of their terms.

GROUP CONSUMER CREDIT LIFE INSURANCE

As has previously been noted, group consumer credit life insurance accounts for the greatest share of the premiums in this line. It is therefore proper that attention be first directed to an examination of this important coverage.

Insuring Agreement

The group consumer credit life insurance master policy promises that, upon due proof of death of the insured debtor, payment will be made to the creditor in the amount for which the debtor was insured at the time of death. The creditor, then, plays the dual role of policyholder and beneficiary. Most master policies require that the proceeds received by the creditor be applied toward the discharge of the insured's indebtedness.

Because the majority of the group policies in this line are on the decreasing-term basis, the insurance in force on the individual debtor's life remains equal to, or sometimes less than, the outstanding balance of the loan.[1] As a consequence, there is no mention of a second beneficiary in the policy since the contract never provides more insurance in force than what is owed to the creditor.

Eligible Debtors

To be an assured under a group consumer credit insurance policy, a debtor must be an individual and not a partnership, association, or corporation. Some companies also consider ineligible a debtor who at the inception of the loan is on active duty in the armed forces of any country at war. This latter qualification has been of relatively minor importance because of the absence of a "hot" war in most recent years, resulting in a waiving of this requirement by most insurers.

Qualifications as to type of indebtedness are also generally listed in the policy. For example, many group policies require that eligible loans be of the installment variety and repayable

---

[1] The amount of insurance in force on the life of any single debtor may be less than the outstanding balance of his loan because the loan may exceed: (*a*) the underwriting limitation stated in the policy which is considered the insurer's judgment of the maximum permissible coverage to be granted to any one debtor of a given lender, or (*b*) the maximum amount of insurance on the lives of any individual debtor as prescribed by state statutes.

within thirty-six months. This provision is usually left blank in the policy until such time as the insurance company decides upon the classes of loans that it feels are eligible. These classes are then typed into the blank form or added by endorsement.[2]

Inception of Coverage

Each eligible debtor usually becomes automatically insured as of the effective date of the master policy when the premiums are paid entirely by the lender. When the premiums are shared by the debtor, most policies require that all persons becoming debtors of the lender-policyholder after the effective date of the master policy become assureds so as to prevent antiselection against the insurance company. Under a group policy requiring 100 per cent participation, a debtor who is eligible for coverage but who is unwilling to pay for the insurance is then covered by the payment of the premium by the lender. If the lender fails to insure the required number of persons, he is put on notice that no new debtors may be insured. Also, new debtors are not eligible for insurance if the master policy is about to terminate.

Termination of the Coverage

Coverage on the life of the individual debtor may be terminated in several ways. In the event that the debtor repays his loan prior to its original maturity date, or if the loan runs for the agreed length of time, the insurance expires with the discharge of the indebtedness. In no event may the insurance remain in force after the loan has been repaid. Termination of the master policy also terminates the coverage to all isured debtors. In the event that the indebtedness is transferred to another creditor the insurance must be canceled. Another reason for the termination is excessive delinquency in repayment of the loan. Although little uniformity exists as to the number of delinquent payments that would render an insured ineligible for coverage, most policies require that the protection must

---

[2] The usual types of qualifying debtors are discussed in Chapter V.

cease when the number stipulated in the policy is exceeded. The variation noted in the number of delinquent payments was found to be between one and six months. When this occurs, the creditor then has the option of continuing the debtor's payments for up to six months beyond the date the loan would have matured. For the loan covered by this insurance, the protection terminates when the security has been repossessed or is the subject of a court judgment.

Tendering of the Premiums by the Policyholder

All premiums due are to be paid to the insurance company's authorized representatives or to the home or branch office. As mentioned previously, the trend toward diversification and expansion results in an increasing number of functions being assumed by the branch offices.

Computation and Payment of Premiums

Most insurance companies operating on the group consumer credit life insurance basis use the $0.75 per $1,000 per month rate applied to the outstanding insurable loan balance. This has proved to be the most popular method of calculating premiums, most probably because of its simplicity of operation. However, most companies also provide alternative methods of calculation. For example, a few allow computation based upon the "Schedule of Monthly Premium Rates per $1,000 of Insurance," which is based upon the actual ages of the insured borrowers.[3] Obviously, this method would entail a greater amount of clerical detail than the outstanding balance method, so that its use is currently limited. In a few instances advance premiums under the group method are accepted. The policy may provide for any method mutually agreed upon between the insurance company and the lender-policyholder.

The premium based upon the outstanding balance method, although paid monthly, may also be paid quarterly, semian-

---

[3] See Chapter VI, Table XIV for a typical schedule.

nually, and annually. Most companies retain the right to change the rate prospectively at the end of the policy year if the experience of the group so dictates.

A grace period of thirty-one days is provided to the policyholder for the payment of premiums. If the payment is not received within this additionally allotted time, the policy is terminated and the lender becomes liable for the payment of this coverage. In the event that the creditor requests cancellation at an earlier date, the premiums due are a prorata portion for the period commencing with the date the premium became due and terminating on the date requested by the policyholder.

Misstatement of Age

A common provision states that, in the event the premium calculation is dependent upon the age of the individual borrower, any misstatements of age will be equitably adjusted. In some cases the creditor may be called upon to pay an additional premium that should have been paid to the insurer if the true age of the debtor had been known. Because of the greater use of the outstanding balance method of premium calculation, this provision is seldom operative, as this method does not deal directly with the insured's age.

Information to Be Furnished the Company

The policies allow the insurance company access to all records of the lender which pertain to consumer credit insurance. The insurer may thus make certain that only eligible debtors and classes of loans are being insured and also may see that the lender is meeting underwriting requirements as to minimum numbers and percentages of debtors insured.

Certain other information may be requested as provided in the policy. One company, for example, requires the right to secure information relating to new debtors becoming insured, installments in default, changes in the amount of insurance in force, and termination of insurance by the debtors.

Evidence of Insurance to Debtors

A few companies require that lenders give some evidence of insurance to their insured debtors in the form of certificates which briefly describe the protection afforded. The majority of companies have established no such requirement. It appears that, when a charge is made for the insurance, the debtor should certainly be provided with evidence of that purchase so that claims might be collected without further question of the claimant's right to do so.

Premium Refunds and Dividends

Most group contracts of consumer credit life insurance provide that a premium refund shall accrue to the lender-policyholder based upon the experience of the company and the individual lender-policyholder as determined by the insurer's current formula. Mutual insurers call this refund a dividend. This refund or dividend may be paid in cash to the creditor or applied toward the payment of any premium at the policyholder's option. One mutual company allows the policyholder to leave the dividend with the company at a stipulated rate of interest.

GENERAL CONTRACT PROVISIONS

Incontestability

Most group consumer credit life insurance contracts become incontestable, except for nonpayment of premiums, if the policy has been in force for a given period of time, such as one or two years. The merit of this provision seems rather dubious since the contract is annually renewable by either party.

Entire Contract

The policy and application constitute the entire contract between the parties. No modification of the policy can be made unless such an amendment signed by both parties is attached to the policy as an endorsement.

Termination of the Master Policy

The creditor may terminate the policy by giving written notice of his desire to do so to the insurance company. The effective date of the cancellation is the date requested by the creditor.

The insurance company may cancel the master policy by giving the creditor written notice 31 days in advance that it may decline to insure additional debtors if the number of newly insured debtors does not meet the company's underwriting standards. Insurers seem to cancel master policies most frequently when the policyholder's losses are excessive and/or fraudulent claims persist.

Certificates of Insurance

As previously mentioned, the majority of group consumer credit life insurers do not require evidence of insurance to be given insured debtors. However, companies that do require it furnish each creditor-policyholder with a supply of certificates generally following the format of the company's regular policies. The certificate is usually a much more brief description of the insurance in force on the life of the insured debtor than that contained in a regular group life certificate issued to an employee, for example. It commonly contains the name of the creditor to whom the proceeds are to be paid and identifies the master policy which the creditor holds and the insurance company underwriting the coverage. It further provides that, upon due proof of death, payment will be made to the creditor on the insured's behalf up to the limit stated in the policy or the amount of the outstanding indebtedness at the time of death, whichever is less.

Also listed are the conditions under which the insurance terminates to the insured debtor. Typical reasons listed are the discharge of the indebtedness, transfer of the indebtedness to another creditor, default of the debt, and termination of the master policy.

Unlike regular group life insurance, the certificates issued to debtors under a group consumer credit life insurance policy do not contain a provision for converting to another form of insurance once the insured leaves the group. No group consumer credit life insurance policies issued today contain such a provision.

ORDINARY CONSUMER CREDIT LIFE INSURANCE

Information Usually Required

The information most generally requested for the individual consumer credit life insurance contract consists of the name, address, and age of the insured. It will be remembered that the insured here is the individual debtor and not the lender. Also required is the effective date of the policy (which is the commencement date of the loan), the initial amount of the loan (which is the initial amount of insurance in force), the amount of the premium paid for the policy, the term of the policy (which is the term of the loan), the name of the creditor-beneficiary (sometimes termed the first beneficiary), and, when applicable, the name of the second beneficiary.[4]

Insuring Agreement

The insurer promises upon the receipt of due proof of death of the insured to pay the creditor, generally designated as an irrevocable beneficiary, the amount of insurance then in force on the life of the deceased debtor as the creditor's interests may appear. A second beneficiary is also designated in the contract in the event that the amount of the insurance in force at the time of the debtor's death is in excess of the first beneficiary's interest. The second beneficiary is sometimes a specifically named person, or, if the policy so provides, is the estate of the deceased.

Amount of Insurance

Under group consumer credit life insurance, it was noted that the amount of insurance in force on the life of an indi-

---

[4] A few such policies contain a "facility of payment clause," which provides for payment of the face to the person equitably entitled to the proceeds and chosen by the insurance company.

vidual debtor was always equal to, or less than, the current amount of his indebtedness.[5] Under ordinary consumer credit life insurance, however, it may happen that the amount of insurance in force could equal or be greater than the outstanding indebtedness. This results from the method of computing the amount of insurance in force and the practice of allowing the policy to remain in force after the loan has been repaid. To calculate the amount of insurance in force at a given time, the initial amount of insurance in force is progressively reduced by an equal amount at the end of each successive policy month. This successive reduction of the face amount is determined by dividing the initial amount of insurance in force by the number of months in the original term of the policy. In the event that the loan is repaid ahead of schedule, and unless the insured requests cancellation, the ordinary policy may remain in force for the remainder of the original loan period. Thus, for example, an initial loan of $120 taken out on January 1 and repayable in twelve monthly installments would carry an initial amount of insurance of $120. On February 1, the amount of indebtedness would be $110, as would the insurance in force. If the loan were repaid at the end of March, the insurance in force on April 1 would be $90 and in the event of death would go entirely to a second beneficiary, since the lender no longer has an interest in the proceeds of the insurance. This would account for the designation of the second beneficiary who becomes the recipient of the insurance in force if the debt is repaid.

Under the level-term plan, there may or may not be a benefit to a second beneficiary, although the former is more probable. If the loan is of the installment variety and it is being repaid as scheduled, a benefit can be expected by a second beneficiary, since, with the exception of the first month, the insurance in force will always exceed the outstanding installment loan balance.

---

[5] An exception to this would be group consumer credit life insurance written on the level-term plan. As far as is known, the volume of this form of coverage is an insignificant portion of the total group consumer credit life insurance premiums.

If the loan is of the noninstallment variety, the second beneficiary may or may not recover any proceeds of the policy, depending on the nature of the loan and the schedule of its repayments.

Payment of the Premium

The policy states that payment of the premium is payable at the home office of the company or to any agent of the insurer. In practice the amount of the premium is usually added to the debtor's loan and then forwarded to the company as an advance single premium. Unlike regular forms of ordinary life insurance, no reduction of premium is made for payment in advance.

Incontestability

The policies are generally incontestable from the date of issuance, except for the nonpayment of premiums.[6]

Exclusions

Most policies of ordinary consumer credit life insurance have no exclusions. One company does exclude suicides by the insureds within two years from the date of the inception of the policy. In this case the company is required to return the premiums paid, the policy reserve, or make payment to the creditor as his interests may appear, whichever is greater. Thus, in terms of exclusions of coverage, the ordinary policy appears to be even more liberal than the group policy, which contains a minimum of exclusions.

Reserve

The reserve basis is customarily stated in the policy, with all companies using the Commissioner's Standard Ordinary Mortality Table. The various interest assumptions utilized are 2, 2.5, and 3 per cent.

---

[6] Several companies make the policy incontestable after it has been in force for two years.

Condition of the Insured at the Time of Issuance

A statement to the effect that the company assumes no obligation toward the debtor unless he is alive at the time of the issuance of the policy is included in several ordinary insurance policies.

Other Common Provisions

Most contracts contain provisions regarding misstatement of age that are handled in a manner similar to those already discussed under group insurance.

Because most ordinary consumer credit life insurance policies are issued by stock insurance companies without provision for "premium refunds," they are said to be nonparticipating. They are also considered nonrenewable since the insured is unable to renew an expired policy merely through the payment of another premium, nor can the company renew the policy unless the insured again becomes an eligible debtor, and then only to the extent of the indebtedness.

ORDINARY CONSUMER CREDIT ACCIDENT AND HEALTH INSURANCE

Before beginning a detailed discussion of the provisions in the ordinary consumer credit accident and health insurance policy, it should be noted that perhaps the greatest differences among consumer credit policies are found among those issued by companies writing this coverage. Not only are the policy provisions much less uniform but also a variety of lengths of waiting periods are incorporated into the policies. At the same time, however, a sufficient number of similarities exist to merit a general discussion of their provisions.

Information Required

Usually required in order to effect coverage are the insured's name, address, and age, policy number, effective and expiration date of the policy (or the term of the policy or loan), the monthly indemnity afforded by the policy, the premium paid for the coverage, the name of the creditor to whom benefits are made payable, and the signature of the licensed agent.

Insuring Agreement

The company promises to indemnify the insured who becomes totally disabled, so that he is unable to perform each and every duty pertaining to his occupation, by accidental means or as a direct and independent result of sickness contracted within the policy term, if such is treated regularly by a legally licensed physician.[7]

It will be noted that this provision reflects an attempt to exclude pre-existing conditions, that is, those sicknesses leading to disabilities that were contracted and diagnosed before the policy was issued. Exclusion of pre-existing conditions is generally accepted in all lines of accident and health insurance as one method of keeping down the cost of the coverage.[8]

All consumer credit accident and health insurance policies require that the insured be disabled for at least three days before payment can be made. The length of the waiting period varies from three to thirty-one days. If the insured is still totally disabled after the specified waiting period has elapsed, payments on his behalf are made. These payments may be made back to the first day of disability, as under the Retroactive Plan, or may commence only after the waiting period has elapsed and are then made from the end of the waiting period to the termination of disability or the end of the policy period, whichever is less. The latter plan is called the Elimination Plan because it makes no payments during the waiting period in any event.

Determination of Benefits Paid

Payments on behalf of the insured are made by the insurance company to the creditor based upon the monthly indem-

---

[7] The physician must be someone other than the named insured.

[8] One large multiple-line stock insurer has recently begun issuing an ordinary accident and health policy that provides payments for disabilities *including* those pre-existing the inception of the policy. Begun on an experimental basis, the outcome should prove interesting.

nity amount stated in the policy. This amount is equal to the monthly repayment of the insured debtor's loan. One-thirtieth of this amount for each day of disability is paid the insured once the waiting period has passed.

Exclusions (Exceptions)

The greatest differences among these policies are found in the exclusions. Of the following list of noted exclusions, a few companies offer this coverage with as few as two exclusions, whereas others include all of them. Exclusions noted were disabilities caused by childbirth, pregnancy, miscarriage, and abortion; injuries or diseases contracted outside the United States, Territory of Hawaii, Alaska, Canada, and Mexico; war or act of war; and accident and sickness contracted while in the military or naval services of any country at war.

Standard and Additional Provisions

All consumer credit accident and health policies contain a number of standard and optional or additional provisions. There is no uniformity as to the number of such provisions or type of such provisions included. In many cases, both the standard and optional or additional provisions are irrelevant. These policies are nonparticipating, nonrenewable, and nonconvertible.

Consumer credit life insurance, particularly the ordinary policies, is relatively easily understood and liberal as to the conditions under which death payments are made. The ordinary consumer credit accident and health insurance policy is more involved in its wording and administration. This is to be expected since, whereas the loss under the life policy is more easily determined, that under the accident and health policy is subject to a greater degree of subjectivity on the part of the claimant and claims administrators.

In conclusion, it should be emphasized that the description of consumer credit insurance in this chapter is of a relatively general nature. Because of the multiplicity of creditor-debtor situations that lend themselves eligible to consumer credit protection, each master policy group certificate and ordinary policy should be consulted for its specific terms and coverage.

To many borrowers, the conditions under which they or their survivors may collect are readily forgotten, if ever completely understood. As a result, the expression "Read your policy" remains sound advice to insured debtors.

Chapter IX

REGULATION

INTRODUCTION

Since its inception in 1917, consumer credit insurance has generally been subjected to the same laws as those governing other forms of life and accident and health insurance. As a result, until recently the degree of regulation has been no more stringent for consumer credit insurance than it has for other forms of insurance with respect to company formation, methods and practices, maintenance of reserves, filing of policies and rates, dissolution, and the like. However, because of the uniqueness of this coverage, which was mentioned previously, and its misuse by an unscrupulous few in ways to be described, legislators, administrators, trade organizations, insurance executives, and critics have recently become aware of the need for supplementary regulation.

THE NAIC SUBCOMMITTEE REPORT OF JUNE 7, 1954

Several states have recently inaugurated applicable legislation and administrative rules in an attempt to deal with some of the problems arising specifically from the sale of consumer credit insurance. However, the body which has probably given most thought and study to the subject has been the National Association of Insurance Commissioners (NAIC), a voluntary, co-operative organization of state insurance officials whose recommendations, although advisory only, have been responsible for a substantial amount of insurance regulation. The first Association committee to grapple exclusively with the problem was the Credit Life and Credit Accident and Health Subcommittee, hereafter referred to as the Subcommittee. During its four-year study of the problem, the Subcommittee was deluged with hundreds of pages of written material, was subjected to long and persistent oratory by opposing factions, and listened to many witnesses in open sessions. A very significant result of all these efforts was the report of the Subcommittee dated June 7, 1954, adopted by the Association as a whole. This report contained recommended Principles and Rules and Regulations to be given consideration by each insurance commissioner in his appraisal and approach to the consumer credit insurance problems within his state. It is generally agreed by those connected with the administration of consumer credit insurance that the adopted Principles and Rules and Regulations, if followed by the individual states, would result in the abatement of many, if not most, of the abuses in the consumer credit insurance field.

Study of the problems of consumer credit insurance regulation by the NAIC was initiated mainly by the abuses that had come to light and a subsequent demand for their elimination. It appears that the Rules and Regulations represent the Subcommittee's best attempt at eradication of abuses and have become the unofficial guiding principles in many states. It is proper therefore to examine not only the proposed Rules and Regulations to become acquainted with these abuses, but also the nature of the proposed remedies.

Excessive Insurance

The first major abuse noted was the sale by lenders of excessive amounts of insurance in relation to the size of a loan. To illustrate the general type of problem faced, one example that might be termed typical of the many encountered is discussed here. In this case a three-month $50 insured loan carried a premium of $9.50 for consumer credit life and accident and health insurance. The premium, although correctly calculated according to filed rates, actually represented a charge for a $100 one-year life policy and $150 accident and health policy issued for a term of four months. Had these contracts been issued for a three-month period to coincide with the length of the loan period, the proper premium calculated on the basis of the same filed rates would have been $2.75.[1]

Such an overload is clearly in violation of the consumer credit insurance concept, because the intent of the coverage has always been to insure a borrower or purchaser of goods in connection with a specific credit or loan transaction. When excessive insurance is forced upon the borrower, the fundamental concept of insuring only to the extent of the indebtedness is abandoned and the action becomes a serious prostitution of a basically sound concept.[2]

To combat oversale of insurance, the Subcommittee recommended the following measures in its report dated June 7, 1954:

The amount of credit life insurance written under one or more policies shall not exceed by more than $5.00 the original face amount of the specific contracts of indebtedness in connection with which it is written, provided however, that where the indebtedness is repayable in installments the amount of insurance shall never exceed the approximate unpaid balance of the loan.

The total indemnities provided under the terms of credit accident and health coverage shall not exceed by more than $5.00 the amount of the initial indebtedness.

The term of such coverages shall not extend more than fifteen (15) days beyond the term of the indebtedness except where extended without additional cost to the insured borrower or purchaser.

---

[1] See "Abuses Arising from the Sale of Credit Life and Credit Accident and Health Insurance in Connection With Small Loans—From the Viewpoint of a State Administrative Official," an address by the Honorable J. Edwin Larson, State Insurance Commissioner of Florida and currently chairman of the National Association of Insurance Commissioners' Subcommittee on Credit Life and Credit Accident and Health Insurance, delivered at Washington University, St. Louis, Missouri, April 27, 1956.

[2] One consumer credit insurance executive believes: "Whenever insurance is sold in amounts in excess of the indebtedness, the insurance is no longer consumer credit insurance." See Arthur J. Cade, "The Fundamental Issues of Consumer Credit Insurance," The Insurance Law Journal, February, 1955, p. 79.

This concept cannot be accepted here, however, because the definition of consumer credit insurance used requires only that the insurance cover the death or disability of a borrower whose non-real estate loan is of 36 months' duration or less.

The effect of these Rules is to prevent overinsurance by limiting the amount of life insurance to within $5.00 of the original indebtedness and the total payments under the accident and health coverage in the same manner. Furthermore, by limiting the term of the policy to a length approximately equal to the term of the loan, another potential method of selling excess insurance is eliminated.

Pyramiding

The second major abuse brought to the attention of the Subcommittee was that of pyramiding of coverages. Because a great number of loans of all types are refinanced before reaching maturity, it was found that some lenders would issue policies of consumer credit insurance without canceling the current policies, thus causing pyramiding of insurance and coverage in amounts far in excess of the indebtedness. Instances were noted where the creditor required the debtor to renew his loan for the sole purpose of issuing new insurance and gaining additional commissions. Where debtors subject to such practices have several policies in force, the amount of insurance will again be in excess of the loan and contrary to the consumer credit insurance concept of insuring a credit transaction in an amount approximately equal to the debt. To remedy this abuse the Subcommittee proposed:

If through prepayment, renewal or refinancing, the indebtedness is discharged prior to the scheduled maturity date, cancellation of the credit insurance then in force shall be mandatory. In the event of cancellation, the return premium shall be promptly paid to the person entitled thereto. The formula to be used in computing the amount of the return premium shall be filed with and approved by the Commissioner of Insurance. The policy form shall contain a termination clause in accordance with the foregoing provision. The responsibility for the enforcement of these conditions shall be upon the agent and company alike and failure on the part of the agent to enforce the provisions of this section shall be cause for the cancellation of such agent's license.

The Subcommittee evidently felt that cancellation of the policy should be mandatory upon prepayment, renewal, or refinancing of the loan. The Consumer Credit Insurance Association, however, proposed to make such cancellation optional because it felt that "many of the individuals who enjoy the benefits of credit insurance protection are convinced of its merits and do desire to retain the right to maintain such insurance in force for their own protection and the protection of their families even though the indebtedness may have been liquidated prior to its scheduled maturity date."[3]

Although no specific discussion of this point by the Association was recorded in their *Proceedings,* it appears that adoption of such a principle would again lead to the abandonment of the concept that the length of insurance protection should be approximately equal to the period of the loan, since in this case the protection may exist without the indebtedness. In addition, the potential for antiselection against the insurer seems obvious. For example, an uninsurable risk for regular life insurance purposes, with full knowledge of this option, might secure a loan and consumer credit life insurance. He might then repay the loan at a very early date and, because of the policy option, retain the life insurance in force for the entire length of the original loan period. With such an option there is nothing to prevent an uninsurable risk who qualifies for a loan covered by consumer credit insurance from using the loan as a subterfuge in obtaining and continuing insurance in force which under ordinary circumstances he could not acquire. The danger in such a plan is that the insurance, rather than the loan, becomes most important to the borrower. Where this occurs in consumer credit insurance, adverse selection is the natural result.

Recently, interested groups have begun advocating regulations that would allow an insured debtor to have no more than one consumer credit insurance policy in force at one time. Under this system, no new policy could be issued unless all

---

[3] "Statement by the Consumer Credit Insurance Association," *Proceedings of the National Association of Insurance Commissioners,* Vol. II, June 7–11, 1954, p. 307.

prior policies were terminated or canceled. The idea does have merit, particularly as a device to eliminate the pyramiding of policies.

The Subcommittee's Regulations cited previously also require the insurer to file cancellation methods and tables with the Commissioner. It was previously noted that there was little uniformity regarding cancellation of consumer credit insurance policies and that this led frequently to ill will and misunderstanding by insureds. Serious thought should therefore be given to standardizing the method of cancellation as well as to the table itself.

It will be noted that the responsibility for the payment of the return premium is placed with both the company and the agent. During its deliberations, the Subcommittee was frequently irritated with the shifting of blame for abuses between the agent and insurer. Indeed this very act of shunning responsibility was termed an abuse by the chairman of the Subcommittee.[4]

Overcharging

A third major abuse found by the Subcommittee was that of overcharging for insurance. Instances were discovered where the lenders charged the borrowers amounts in excess of the actual premiums. Such action in most states is contrary to existing laws which provide that only those rates filed with state insurance departments may be used. However, the difficulty with consumer credit insurance was that the borrower in many instances had no knowledge of the amount of premium for which he was being charged and in some cases had no knowledge of the existence of insurance protection.

The Subcommittee attempted to remedy this situation in all states by providing that: "The premium rates for Credit Life and Credit Accident and Health Insurance shall be filed with the Commissioner of Insurance."

For group consumer credit insurance, the Subcommittee

---

[4] Larson, *op. cit.*

stated: "Where an identifiable charge for group credit insurance is made to insured borrowers or purchasers such charge shall be consistent with the premium provided for in the group policy issued to the creditor."

It will be noted that the first-cited Regulation provides merely that the rates be filed and not approved. This stems from the opposition by the entire life and accident and health insurance industry which maintains, that insurance regulation should not include the regulation of rates by the state but should be left to the most efficient regulator—competition.

The paragraph in the Rules and Regulations pertaining to group consumer credit insurance was thought necessary because of the noted tendency of some lenders operating under the group plan to charge higher rates to borrowers than were actually being collected by the insurer from the lender-policyholder. For example, the lender might charge a borrower $1.00 per $100 under a group plan in which the premium stated in the master policy is but $0.75 per $1,000 on the outstanding loan balance.

On April 20, 1956, Insurance Commissioner Larson of Florida promulgated Rules and Regulations for that state which paralleled those adopted by the NAIC.[5] In a subsequent bulletin to insurers writing consumer credit in Florida, the Commissioner clarified the interpretation of the word "consistent" used as a modifier of group premiums. Because Commissioner Larson served in the capacity of both member and chairman of the Credit Life and Credit Accident and Health Subcommittee, the Florida interpretation may be used as a guide to the meaning of the word "consistent" as contained in the NAIC Rules just cited. In attempting to clarify the situation, the Department bulletin stated:

By *consistent* this Department understands a variation of two and one-half cents per thousand dollars of original indebtedness. For example:

---

[5] "Credit Life and Credit Accident and Health Insurance Rules and Regulations," Bulletin No. 172, Office of the Insurance Commissioner, State of Florida, April 20, 1956.

a) A filed rate of 60¢ per $1,000 of outstanding balances per month to the policyholder means a rate of 39¢ per $1,000 of original indebtedness per month to the borrower. There is no need for adjustment in this case.

b) A filed rate of 75¢ per $1,000 of outstanding balances per month to the policyholder means a rate of 47.75¢ per $1,000 of original indebtedness per month to the borrower. The two and one-half cent adjustment permits the lender to charge the borrower 50¢ per $1,000 of the original indebtedness per month without violation of the regulation on overcharging.[6]

The question of interpreting the word "consistent" apparently was raised by the insurers on behalf of their policyholders who found calculations using numbers ending in "O" and "5" easier to work with.

Insurance Commissioner Thurman of Kentucky, in a bulletin dated September 25, 1956, declared that a charge was consistent with the premium stated in the policy if "the aggregate of all such identifiable charges to all debtors of the same class . . . is not greater than the total premium cost of the insurance to the creditor for such debtors." It is expected that other states will promulgate similar rulings to eliminate the abuse of inconsistent premium charges.

Evidence of Insurance

Along with the provision that only the filed rate may be charged, the Subcommittee stated:

A. All Credit Insurance sold shall be evidenced by a policy, certificate or statement of insurance which shall be delivered to the insured borrower or purchaser.

B. Said policy, certificate or statement shall describe the amount and term of the coverage, the amount of the premium and a description of the coverage including any exceptions, limitations or restrictions.

C. Said policy, certificate or statement shall be delivered to the insured borrower or purchaser at the time the indebtedness is incurred except as hereinafter provided.

---

[6] "Credit Life and Credit Accident and Health Insurance Rules and Regulations," Bulletin No. 172, Supplement A, Office of the Insurance Commissioner, State of Florida, June 4, 1956.

D. If said policy, certificate, or statement is not delivered to the insured borrower or purchaser at the time the indebtedness is incurred, a copy of the application for such policy or certificate shall set forth the amount of the premium, the amount and term of the coverage provided, and a brief description thereof, which shall be delivered to the purchaser at the time of such application. Upon approval of such application and within thirty (30) days of the date upon which the indebtedness is incurred, the insurance company shall cause to be delivered to the insured borrower or purchaser the policy or certificate. Said application shall serve as a binder and the coverage provided shall become effective as of the date the indebtedness is incurred.

E. If the policy, certificate or statement is not delivered to the insured borrower or purchaser at the time the indebtedness is incurred, and if no application is taken, then the insured borrower or purchaser shall be furnished at the time the indebtedness is incurred a statement setting forth a brief description of the coverage provided. Said statement may be made a part of the contract of indebtedness. Said statement shall serve as a binder and the coverage provided shall become effective as of the date the indebtedness is incurred.

F. All policies, certificates, binders or statements of insurance, applications, endorsements, riders and other forms constituting a part of the contract or contracts of insurance with the insured borrower or purchaser shall be filed with or approved by the Commissioner of Insurance of the state in which the policy is issued.

Because knowledge by the insured of the existence of coverage frequently is acquired entirely from the information contained in a policy or certificate of insurance, the need for such evidence cannot be too strongly emphasized. Delivery of such evidence to the insured, in addition to informing him of the existence of such coverage and a statement of the premium charged, is of the utmost importance in maintaining the integrity of the business. Unless insured borrowers who contribute toward the payment of consumer credit insurance are given evidence of their purchase, the value of such coverage is open to serious doubt.

Nonpayment of Claims

Another abuse encountered by the Subcommittee closely allied with those just discussed was the nonpayment of claims. There were several contributing factors. In some cases the borrower had no evidence of the insurance with which to press his claim. In other cases, debtors with evidence of insurance were denied their claims when the entire responsibility and authority for settling claims was solely in the hands of the lender. As one commissioner stated: "Under such circumstances, if the creditor's compensation was in any way related to loss experience, there existed an obvious temptation to deny as many claims as possible."[7] To resolve this problem the Subcommittee recommended:

> No company shall execute any contract or agreement with any person, firm or corporation which permits such persons, firm or corporation to retain any portion of the premium for payment of losses incurred or to be incurred under policies or certificates of insurance issued by said company.
>
> All claims shall be promptly reported to the insurance company or its designated claim agent or representative by the agent, and the company shall maintain adequate claim files.
>
> All claims shall be settled strictly in accordance with policy terms.
>
> All claims shall be paid either by draft drawn upon the company or by checks of the company to the order of the claimant to whom payment of the claim is due pursuant to the policy provisions, or upon direction of such claimant to one specified. In the case of Credit Life Insurance, separate payments shall be made to the creditor beneficiary and to the named second beneficiary if any, as their interest may appear. If the policy contains no provision for the designation of a second beneficiary, then it shall contain a facility of payment clause authorizing the company to pay any insurance in excess of the unpaid balance of the indebtedness to the estate, wife, husband, children, or other blood relative, or other person equitably entitled thereto as determined by the company.
>
> No plan or arrangement shall be used whereby any person, firm or corporation other than the company or its designated claim agent or representative shall be authorized to settle or adjust claims. Agents, brokers, or persons affiliated with a creditor may not be designated as claim agents or representatives for the insurance company in adjusting claims. Provided, that a group creditor policy holder may, by arrangement with the Group insurer, draw drafts or checks in payment of claims due to the creditor-policy holder subject to audit and review by the insurance company.

---

[7] Larson, *op. cit.*

Fortunately, claims administration vested solely in the hands of the creditor is virtually nonexistent today.

Coercion

Charges and proof that coercion of the borrower has been exercised by lenders in an effort to force the purchase of consumer credit insurance have been found mainly in states having no legislation or ineffective laws and/or poor enforcement of existing statutes. It was previously seen that coercion is difficult to prove because it assumes a variety of forms and usually involves two parties in conversation. Most states have so-called "anticoercion" laws which are attempts at preventing the lender from forcing the borrower into obtaining insurance from persons and/or insurers specifically designated by the lender. In practice these laws have been rather ineffective because of the difficulty of proving the existence of coercion.

Originally, lenders were allowed to require the borrower to purchase insurance on mortgaged property. Many lenders currently require the borrower to purchase consumer credit insurance as additional security and a condition precedent to a loan. Where the laws allow the creditor to require insurance, the debtor has the right to offer an existing policy or may secure required coverage from an agent and company of his choice. Whether the creditor establishes the insurance requirement for security reasons or to take advantage of the opportunity to increase income through commissions on the sale of this coverage, or both, is difficult to determine in most cases. In any event it has been pointed out that lenders handling consumer credit insurance are being reimbursed for their administrative costs, and it is suspected that in many cases the commissions paid the lender-agent result in additional income and profit to the lender over and above these costs.[8]

---

[8] It is interesting to note that at least one state consumer finance association publicly speaks of "profits" from the sale of consumer credit insurance. In a statement before the Subcommittee of the Indiana Legislative Advisory Commission, the Indiana Consumer Finance Association, Inc., at Indianapolis, on March 15, 1956, described the operation of their consumer credit insurance program and stated: "The lender collects the cost of such insurance from the

That the courts recognize and permit the use of consumer credit insurance as security and a condition precedent to a loan has been fairly well established[9] and is illustrated by a recent Kansas decision in which the court said:

> The law seems to be well settled that in determining whether or not a transaction is usurious, the Court will disregard the form of the transaction and look to the substance and effect of it. If, in fact, the collection of insurance premiums is a subterfuge for the collection of additional interest in excess of that allowed by law, it must be condemned. The requirement of credit insurance as a prerequisite to a loan is not in itself illegal, and under proper circumstances the courts have many times held that the requirement of such insurance is a proper security device.[10]

Recognizing the prominence of such decisions, the Subcommittee advocated: "Where insurance is required as additional security, the debtor shall have the right to furnish as security an existing policy or to procure the necessary coverage through any insurer authorized to transact business within the state."

This Regulation is an attempt to lessen the possibility of coercion by giving the debtor the right to submit existing coverage or acquire new protection from any licensed insurer to meet the lender's security requirement. A feasible but little-used alternative for the borrower is to assign new or existing regular life insurance policies having cash values to the lender to satisfy his requirement.

Unlicensed Agents

The sale of consumer credit insurance by unlicensed and irresponsible individuals was another problem faced by the

---

borrower usually in the form of one lump payment by each borrower at the time the loan is made. *The profit to the lender* from the use of this insurance occurs when the amounts collected from the borrower exceed the amounts actually paid out for the insurance plus dividends as the lender may receive as the policyholder." (Italics added.)

[9] For a good discussion of this problem see Willard Van Slyck, Jr., "Insurance Security for Loans—Historical Development of Court-Made Law," *The Journal of the Bar Association of the State of Kansas,* Vol. XXIII, No. 3, February, 1955, p. 239.

[10] See the letter opinion of the Court dated January 4, 1955, in the case of the *State of Kansas* ex rel. *Harold R. Fatzor, Attorney General, Plaintiff,* v. *P. H. Molitor d/b/a New Way Company, et al, Defendants* (No. 89407-A).

Subcommittee. It was dealt with by requiring that "all policies be issued through licensed agents."

This problem has not appeared to be of major importance in most states because of the existence of laws which provide that only licensed agents may procure insurance. As more states inaugurate laws requiring written examinations of new agents, such legislation will undoubtedly result in better-qualified agents. However, in states where such laws are unreasonable, they may have the adverse effect of an increase in "bootlegging" or unlawful sale of insurance by unlicensed agents who either do not wish to prepare for such examinations or are unable to pass them. A solution to this might be the licensing of agents on a limited basis, enabling them to sell one or more special lines, such as consumer credit insurance, without having to qualify for a general license involving the knowledge of all coverages.

The Level of Rates

The Subcommittee, faced with the controversial issue of rates and compensation of agents, took no immediate action in the matter. However, in December of 1956, before a newly created committee of the NAIC, the question of regulation of the consumer credit insurance industry was again discussed, this time with considerable emphasis on the rate structure "including loss ratios and other component elements."[11] Of significant importance was the subject of compensation to the creditor. There appears to be a growing feeling among Insurance Commissioners that the current rates for consumer credit insurance are excessive and that the amount of compensation paid to lenders is the major contributing factor.

As a possible method of affecting such reductions, the Consumer Credit Insurance Association recently proposed a Model Bill to the NAIC, which, in addition to incorporating many of the Regulations previously agreed upon as feasible by the body, also included a provision to "place a limit on the compensation

---

[11] Report of the Committee on Insurance Covering All Installment Sales and Loans of the National Association of Insurance Commissioners, meeting of December 5, 1956, Miami Beach, Florida.

which may be received by the creditor or its affiliate, associate or subsidiary, or a director, officer or employee of any of them, expressed in dollars and cents, and be similar to the proposal made in a joint statement heretofore submitted to the N.A.I.C. by the A.L.C. and L.I.A.A."[12]

The proposal by the Consumer Credit Insurance Association appears to be a sensible method of effecting such reductions for several reasons. In the first place, the lender is bound to resist any attempt at reducing his income from insurance commissions. If an individual insurer attempts to reduce lender compensation, it may well result in the loss of that account to the insurance company. Secondly, although an attempt to reduce lender compensation through voluntary means is generally preferable to government control, it may smack of possible illegality relating to price-fixing agreements. As a result, regulation of this important component of the rate seems to be the only feasible solution proposed to date. It is hoped that such a reduction will be forthcoming soon to enable consumer credit insureds to enjoy these reduced rates with a minimum of delay. In the meantime, the subject of consumer credit insurance rates will continue to occupy an important place on the NAIC's agenda.

Because the legislative machinery of government operates slowly, the impact of these Rules and Regulations is still to be felt in the majority of states and only time will testify as to their effectiveness. This does not mean to imply, however, that the states have remained legislatively idle in anticipation of the NAIC's findings.

STATE REGULATION

Insurance Regulation

Recently a growing number of states have demonstrated an interest in the regulation of consumer credit insurance to a greater degree than in the past, but among those states taking

---

[12] "Proposed Model Bill of the Consumer Credit Insurance Association," submitted to the Committee on Insurance Covering All Installment Sales and Loans at the meeting of the National Association of Insurance Commissioners, Miami Beach, Florida, December, 1956.

The joint proposal of the A.L.C. and the L.I.A.A. was cited in Chapter IV.

TABLE XX

State Regulation of the Sale of Consumer Credit Insurance by Small-Loan Licensees

	Have Some Form of Permissive Legislation	Laws Prohibit Sale of Cons. Credit Ins. If Additional Charge Is Made to Borrower	Regulations Provide Dollar Limits Borrower May Pay for Ins.	Limit Life Ins. to Unpaid Balance and to Term of Loan	Limit Periodic Benefit under Accident & Health to Periodic Installment Due on Loan	Require Refund Where Loan is Renewed	Legislation or Regulation Prohibits Profit from Sale of Insurance	Legislation Or Regulation Allows Profit from Sale of Ins.
Alabama								
Arizona	x							x
Arkansas								
California		x	x					
Colorado	x			x	x	x		x
Connecticut								
Delaware								
District of Columbia								
Florida			x				x	
Georgia	x		x			x		x
Idaho								
Illinois								
Indiana								
Iowa								
Kansas	x			x	x	x		x
Kentucky								
Louisiana	x		x					x
Maine								
Maryland	x					x	x	
Massachusetts	x							
Michigan								
Minnesota								
Mississippi								
Missouri	x					x		x
Montana								
Nebraska	x			x	x	x		x
Nevada		x						
New Hampshire								
New Jersey								
New Mexico								
New York								
North Carolina								
North Dakota								
Ohio		x						
Oklahoma								
Oregon	x		x					
Pennsylvania	x							
Rhode Island								
South Carolina	x			x	x	x		x
South Dakota	x							
Tennessee								
Texas								
Utah								
Vermont	x					x	x	
Virginia							x	
Washington								
West Virginia			x					
Wisconsin								
Wyoming	x							

Source: Adapted from "The Regulation of the Sale of Credit Life, Health and Accident Insurance by Licensed Lenders," a statement by Edward A. Dunbar, Associate Counsel Beneficial Management Corporation, at the Third Annual Consumer Credit Conference, Washington University, at St. Louis, Missouri, April 27, 1956.

such action, few have approached the comprehensive nature of the Rules and Regulations just described. Regulations in Kansas and Kentucky, for example, are similar to the NAIC's Model Rules and Regulations. Approximately 32 states, however, have promulgated no special regulations for consumer credit insurance. State regulation in this area has assumed five basic forms. They are statutory, administrative, and judicial law, attorney generals' opinions, and regulation by state banking departments. Each of these must give consideration to the various types of lenders because these five basic forms of regulation would apply in different ways to each type of lender. Because of this multiplicity of regulation, categorization of the regulation in all states is difficult, while standardization of regulation is nearly impossible. As the Subcommittee aptly stated: "Although uniformity is desirable, because of the varying statutes, it is practically impossible to enact rules and regulations which will fit the particular problems of each jurisdiction."

To demonstrate the heterogeneous nature of existing regulation, reference may be made to Table XX, which indicates to a limited degree the present status of regulation of consumer credit insurance sold by small-loan lenders. Attention is called to the limited number of categories noted. The reason for this is the difficulty of selecting a category that does not contain too many exceptions. It must also be remembered that Table XX pertains only to small-loan lenders.

Table XXI, compiled by James B. Jacobson, is an attempt to categorize the statutes applying to group consumer credit life insurance. It should be noted that this latter table applies only to state statutes and does not attempt to consider other forms of regulation. Moreover, both tables are expected presently to become outdated because of the increasing trend toward regulation of consumer credit insurers and their representatives. The principal reason for reviewing existing regulation is to emphasize the wide divergency of approaches among the various jurisdictions.[18]

---

[18] The following significant developments in group consumer credit life insurance have taken place or are pending: Arizona now has a contributory group

For example, Georgia makes a specific reference in its statutes to consumer credit insurance while Florida, a contiguous state, does not, the latter state using administrative rules promulgated by the Commissioner of Insurance. Both states set specific maximum premiums to be paid by borrowers for consumer credit life insurance, but Georgia allows a profit to be made from the sale of this coverage while Florida does not.

Not only is the regulatory picture not uniform, but it is also uncertain and confused in a few states. For example, although there are eight states listed in Table XX in which legislation or other forms of regulation allow the lender to make a profit on the sale of consumer credit insurance and four states which do not permit it, the remaining thirty-six states constitute an area of doubt. Moreover, a few states specifically define an insurance premium as a "charge." When so defined, a lender charging the legal maximum rate of interest under the Small Loan Law and passing the premium for consumer credit insurance on to the borrower may violate either the maximum rate of interest established by statute or be construed to be in violation of the "other business" provision. These latter statutes were attempts at barring collateral transactions used by some borrowers to evade the legal maximums prescribed by statute.

Banking Regulation

An additional method of regulating consumer credit insurers is through the regulation of agents or policyholders in the person of the lender. This jurisdiction assumes various forms. Considerable initiative, for example, has been displayed by many banking departments in insisting upon full disclosure of charges made to borrowers. Such insistence generally results in an itemization indicating the amounts and types of insurance that were sold to the borrower.

---

statute with a $5,000 maximum; Arkansas, Florida and Idaho have raised the group maximum to $10,000; Colorado has increased the group maximum to $10,000 this year but the bill awaits the Governor's signature; Indiana and Nebraska have a pending amendment to raise the maximum amount to $10,000; Ohio has a pending amendment to permit contributory group life.

Because major changes in the statutes are occurring as this book goes to press, the reader is cautioned against relying too heavily upon the information in this chapter as reflecting the current status of the law in a given state.

TABLE XXI

Group Consumer Credit Life Insurance State Statute Summary

State	Group Creditors Insurance Permitted	Eligible Creditors*	Maximum Individual Amount	Maximum Duration	Premium Must Be Paid By*	Less Than 100% Participation Permitted	Must Individual Certificates Be Issued
Alabama	Yes-No law						
Arizona	Yes	Fi, V	$ 5,000	No limit	Dr or Cr[a]	Yes[b]	No
Arkansas	Yes	Fi, V	5,000	No limit	Dr or Cr[a]	Yes[b]	No
California	Yes	Fi, V, A	10,000	32 years	Dr or Cr[c]	Yes[d]	No
Credit Union	Yes	Credit Union	10,000	20 years	Dr or Cr	Yes[d]	No
Colorado	Yes	Fi, V	10,000	No limit	Dr or Cr[a]	Yes[b]	No
Connecticut	Yes[e]	Fi, V	10,000	No limit	Dr or Cr[a]	Yes[b]	No
Delaware	Yes-No law						
District of Columbia	Yes	Fi, V	5,000	No limit	Dr or Cr[a]	Yes[b]	No
Florida	Yes	Fi, V	5,000	No limit	Dr or Cr[a]	Yes[b]	Yes
Georgia	Yes-No law						Yes[g]
Idaho	Yes	Fi, V	5,000	No limit	Dr or Cr[a]	Yes[b]	No
Illinois	Yes	Fi, V, A	10,000	10 years	Cr[f]	No[f]	No

* Key: Fi—financial institutions; V—vendor; A—assignee (creditor to whom original creditor transfers the indebtedness); Dr—debtor; Cr—creditor.

[a] Law provides that premium shall be remitted by policyholder.

[b] Must insure all debtors or all of any class determined by conditions pertaining to indebtedness, except those for whom evidence of insurability is unsatisfactory; where debtor contributes, must insure at least 75 per cent.

[c] Premium paid by or through creditor.

[d] Law is vague, but permitted in actual practice.

[e] Company may write group life insurance as defined by insurance commissioner. Commissioner has accepted Model Bill definition. Sec. 295-24a, Insurance Commissioner Administrative Regulations, March 29, 1954 increases maximum to $10,000.

[f] Law provides that premium must be payable by the creditor, and that policy must cover all members of a group of persons who become borrowers.

State							
Indiana	Yes	Fi, V	5,000	No limit	Dr or Cr[a]	Yes[b]	No
Iowa	Yes	Fi, V	10,000	No limit	Dr or Cr[a]	Yes[b]	Yes
Kansas	Yes	Fi, V	5,000	No limit	Dr or Cr[a]	Yes[b]	Yes
Kentucky	Yes	Fi, V	No maximum	No limit	Dr or Cr[a]	Yes[b]	No
Louisiana	Yes	Fi, V, A	10,000	No limit	Dr or Cr[a]	Probably[a]	No
Maine	Yes	Fi, V	5,000	No limit	Dr or Cr[a]	Yes[b]	No
Maryland	Yes—No law						
Massachusetts	Yes	Fi, V, A	10,000	10 years	Dr or Cr[h]	Yes[i]	No
Michigan	Yes	Fi, V, A	5,000[j] 10,000[k]	3 years	Dr or Cr	Yes[l]	Yes
Minnesota	Yes—No law						
Mississippi	Yes—No law						
Missouri	Yes—No law						
Montana	Yes—No law						
Nebraska	Yes	Fi, V	5,000	No limit	Dr or Cr[a]	Yes[b]	No
Nevada	No[r]						
New Hampshire	Yes	Fi, V	10,000	No limit	Dr or Cr[a]	Yes[b]	No
New Jersey	Yes	Fi, V, A	10,000	No limit	Dr or Cr[a]	Yes[b]	Yes
New Mexico	Yes—No law						
New York	Yes	Fi, V, A	10,000	20 years	Dr or Cr[a]	Yes[b]	Yes[n]
North Carolina	Yes	Fi, V	5,000	No limit	Dr or Cr[a]	Yes[b]	Yes[o]
North Dakota	Yes—No law						
Ohio	Yes	Fi, V, A	10,000	10 years	Cr[p]	No[p]	No
Oklahoma	Yes	Fi, V	5,000	No limit	Dr or Cr[a]	Yes[b]	No
Oregon	Yes—No law						

[a] Law is vague, but optional policy probably could be issued.

[h] Law does not provide who is to pay premium.

[i] Law does not specifically require insurance on all members of a group.

[j] If 50 or more, but less than 100, new entrants yearly.

[k] If 100 or more new entrants yearly.

[l] Debtors have option to reject the insurance where they are paying part or all of the premium.

[m] Sec. 2(b) of S.205, Laws of 1953, provides that if any charge for insurance is included under any conditional sales contract for the sale of a vehicle, a certificate of insurance shall be issued to the buyer within 30 days.

TABLE XXI—*Continued*
GROUP CONSUMER CREDIT LIFE INSURANCE STATE STATUTE SUMMARY

State	Group Creditors Insurance Permitted	Eligible Creditors*	Maximum Individual Amount	Maximum Duration	Premium Must Be Paid By*	Less Than 100% Participation Permitted	Must Individual Certificates Be Issued
Pennsylvania	Yes	Fi, V	5,000	No limit	Dr or Cr[a]	Yes[b]	No
Rhode Island	Yes-No law	Fi, V	Original loan	No limit	Dr or Cr[a]	Yes[b]	No
South Carolina	Yes						
South Dakota	Yes-No law						
Tennessee	Yes-No law						
Texas	Yes	Fi, V	10,000	No limit	Dr or Cr[a]	Yes[d]	No
Utah	Yes-No law						Yes[q]
Vermont	Yes	Fi, V	5,000	No limit	Dr or Cr[a]	Yes[b]	No
Virginia	Yes	Fi, V, A	10,000	10 years	Dr or Cr[a]	Yes[b]	No
Washington	Yes	Fi, V	5,000	No limit	Dr or Cr[a]	Yes[b]	No
West Virginia	Yes	Fi, V	5,000	No limit	Dr or Cr[a]	Yes[b]	Yes
Wisconsin	Yes	Fi, V	10,000	No limit	Dr or Cr[a]	Yes[b]	No
Wyoming	Yes-No law						

[n] Regulation 27 provides that if the purchaser of financed personal property or a borrower as part of the loan transaction directly contributes toward the cost of life insurance, a statement of insurance must be issued to him.

[o] Rules of September 1, 1950 provide that certificate must be issued. Rules apply "when in connection with the making of a loan of any type an insurance agent at the same time offers for sale a policy." Although directed at individual credit life insurance, would probably apply to group creditors insurance as well.

[p] Law requires that creditor pay premiums, and that policy must cover all members of a group of persons who become borrowers.

[q] Section of 15-2a of Utah Code provides that if any charge for insurance is included under any conditional sales contract for the sale of personal property, a certificate of insurance shall be issued to the buyer within 30 days.

[r] Insurance Department Ruling 54-1, March 12, 1954, based on Opinion 318, Department of Attorney General, February 26, 1954.

[s] Sec. VIII of Insurance Commissioner Regulations adopted November 3, 1953, as amended February 15, 1954.

Source: James B. Jacobson, *An Analysis of Group Creditors Insurance* (M.B.A. thesis, University of Southern California, 1955), published by The Prudential Insurance Company of America.

Where audits are made of the lender's operations by state banking departments, such things as the amount and charge made for consumer credit insurance may be checked as well as the method of cancellation and the amount of premium returned to the borrower where a loan is repaid or refinanced. The thoroughness of such examinations is generally an individual matter among state departments but serves to illustrate another area of regulation.

Such "dual regulation" by state banking and insurance departments was recognized by the Subcommittee when it concluded:

> Throughout the deliberations of this subcommittee, it has become apparent that it is impossible to separate the sale of insurance from the lending or credit transaction. As this field of insurance continues to grow, additional problems will no doubt arise due to the fact that the sale of insurance is interwoven with the credit transaction which cannot be controlled by regulations governing only the sale of insurance. We, therefore, feel that it is necessary that legislation be enacted to govern phases not controlled by regulations of the Insurance Department.

In an attempt to determine the status of state banks and their relationship to the sale of consumer credit life insurance, Professor Wallace P. Mors surveyed state banking departments. The results are compiled in Table XXII and indicate that the majority of those state reporting allow the banks under their jurisdiction to offer both group and ordinary consumer credit life insurance.[14] Eight out of twenty-seven states surveyed did not allow the creditor to retain as a commission a portion of the premium under the ordinary form of consumer credit life insurance. It appears that about a third of the states do not allow their banks to receive such commissions. At the same time, it should be mentioned that these same states also disallow receipt of commissions for other types of insurance as well.

A group of state regulatory officials in the field of small

---

[14] For a detailed and interesting discussion of the types of laws that might affect a decision to disallow commissions to state banks, see Wisconsin Attorney General's Opinion dated June 29, 1954 to G. M. Matthews, Commissioner of Banks, State Banking Department, Madison, Wisconsin.

loans took a position with respect to consumer credit insurance and its sale to borrowers only to modify their stand one year later. The National Association of Small Loan Supervisors went on record in September of 1949 against the tie-in sale of consumer credit insurance in conjunction with the placement of small loans. This is a position that might well have been expected inasmuch as the greatest number of abuses were

TABLE XXII

LEGAL STATUS OF STATE BANK ACTIVITIES WITH RESPECT TO CREDIT LIFE INSURANCE WRITTEN IN CONNECTION WITH INSTALLMENT CASH LOANS

Questions Asked in a Letter Dated 9/9/55 Are State Banks Permitted to:	Answers Received*				
			Laws Are	No Answer	
	Yes	No	Silent	Given	Total
Offer group consumer credit life	22	3	2	0	27
Pass all or part of the cost of group consumer credit life insurance on to borrowers	19	6	2	0	27
Offer individual consumer credit life insurance	17	7	2	1	27
Keep part of the premium charged for individual credit life insurance	15	8	2	2	27

* Replies received from 27 states.
Source: Wallace P. Mors, "Consumer Installment Credit Insurance," *The Insurance Law Journal*, May 1956, p. 299.

noted in connection with the unscrupulous few in the small-loan industry. In 1950, however, the same body adopted a resolution which stated: "It appears as though the legislature should definitely determine, in each instance, whether or not insurance is to be sold by small loan companies, setting out fully rights, limitations and restrictions."[15] At the present time, no such prohibitive legislation exists in any state.

[15] See Harold Johnson, "Nebraska Has no Loan Shark Problem Today," 19 Law and Contemporary Problems 42, (Winter, 1954), page 51.

Maximum Interest, Discount, and Usury Laws

State statutes affecting credit transactions and most directly related to the sale of consumer credit insurance are those relating to maximum interest, discount and usury laws. Because our system of state regulation permits the drafting of laws in accordance with the wishes of the mandate of each individual state, these laws and their interpretations have various effects on the legality and operation of the consumer credit insurance mechanism in different jurisdictions. For example, where the state interprets its maximum discount and interest laws to mean that the calculation of the maximum statutory rate of interest includes all charges made to the borrower, including the "charge" for consumer credit insurance, in the event that this combined figure exceeds the maximum rate as provided by law, the lender is then subject to prosecution. In a few states lenders are fearful or are in doubt about offering this coverage where the charge is passed on to the borrower because they, and sometimes the regulatory authorities as well, are not sure of the manner in which the courts will construe the nature of the consumer credit insurance premium. If, as just noted, it is construed as a "charge," the lender is then subject to the penalties under the law. To the extent that the state department having jurisdiction of the maximum interest and usury laws may have expressed its views on this subject in the form of rules and directives, consumer credit insurance is subjected to additional regulation.

Several states have legislation pertaining to the form, content, and use of the conditional sales contract. These laws usually specify that the charges for insurance are clearly stated and that the types of insurance are summarily described. Again, where audits are made of lenders by the states, these contracts may be checked and the disposition of the premiums may be traced. Such checking invariably involves the co-operation of the insurance department of that state for information such as the policy provisions and schedule of filed rates. It thus becomes apparent that the consumer credit insurance mechanism embraces the fields of both insurance and finance and thus merits the co-operation of the state officials charged with regulation in both these areas.

FEDERAL REGULATION

Federal Trade Commission

The Federal Government has traditionally exerted little or no influence in the regulation of insurance, although recently the Federal Trade Commission has seen fit to exercise its rights born of the South-Eastern Underwriters decision.[16] The recent indictments by the Federal Trade Commission of several accident and health insurers did not include any specific reference or charge against insurers of consumer credit insurance. Neither does the new advertising code developed by the commission for accident and health insurers directly concern the operations of consumer credit insurers. Nevertheless, the companies have come to realize that the Federal government's role is potentially significant.

Comptroller of the Currency

At the present time the Federal government is exerting an indirect influence over the regulation of consumer credit insurance through the office of the Comptroller of the Currency, which has jurisdiction over the operation of national banks. In an opinion previously cited, the Comptroller states that in cities with populations of 5,000 and over, national banks may receive compensation for the sale of consumer credit insurance only to the extent of their actual cost of administering such a program. This limitation assumes no dollar and cents maximum and varies among individual banks.

PRESENT STATUS

The abuses and suggested remedies that arose from the sale of consumer credit insurance have been reviewed. It is

---

[16] *United States* v. *South-Eastern Underwriters Association et al,* 322 U.S. 533 (1944).

evident that the National Association of Insurance Commissioners, through its Credit Life and Credit Accident and Health Insurance Subcommittee, has exposed most of the major problems and has proposed workable legislation and rulings which, if placed into effect, would probably eradicate current abuses to a substantial degree in most states.

Because legislation and administrative rulings affecting insurance and banking have generally developed independently, the status of consumer credit insurance, which invades both fields, is currently dynamic, heterogeneous, and confused. It is obvious that satisfactory regulation at the statutory and administrative level can be achieved only through increased cooperation of the state insurance and banking administrators, comprehensive rather than piecemeal legislation, and the cooperative, voluntary efforts of the consumer credit insurance industry.

Chapter X

SUMMARY AND CONCLUSIONS

The concept of insuring a short-term financial obligation against the death or disability of the debtor is not new or foreign to the insurance-minded American populace. The consumer credit insurance mechanism began in 1917 as a device to eliminate the difficulties experienced by cosigners and survivors following the death of the borrower in subsequent attempts of creditors to collect the balance of the debt. Not only has the availability of such insurance made it easier for the debtor to obtain a cosigner, but it has also given him a personal assurance that his passing would not bring an additional burden to his bereaved survivors. It is clear that debtors still desire such peace of mind.

In establishing an individual's insurance program, consideration must be given to the periodic changes which take place in needs. An accepted approach has been to increase insurance purchases at the approximate time new debts are assumed so that, in the event of death or disability, repayments of the debt are made. Because of the unique method of marketing consumer credit insurance, this coverage is made available to the debtor in amounts equal to newly incurred debt. It also allows the debtor to obtain the insurance at the very time the debt is assumed, thus adding to his insurance estate when it is needed most.

The creditor beneficiary under such policies is guaranteed that in the event of the debtor's death or disability the obligation will be assumed by the insurance company. Offering such a service to its borrowers, the lending institution obtains a substantial amount of goodwill because it is then unnecessary to subject cosigners and survivors to embarrassment and legal action if the borrower dies, or the borrower himself in case of his disability. Not only does this create good customer relations, but also reduces collection costs and losses due to such contingencies.

The feasibility of purchasing consumer credit insurance in small amounts might be questioned by students of insurance advocating the "large loss principle." Proponents of this concept believe that one should insure only for those losses that are potentially large in import but have a relatively small probability of occurrence. They believe that the intelligent buyer should give more attention to the severity of the loss rather than to its probability of occurrence. When viewed with this idea in mind, life insurance purchased to cover relatively small financial obligations might appear to be in disregard of this principle. At the same time it must be remembered that the term "large" is somewhat subjective and will vary according to one's station in life. Moreover, it has been established that the American people generally may be divided into two general classes: those who commonly use consumer credit, and those who do not. Members of the former group at any given time tend to have several kinds of debts outstanding in the form of cash loans, conditional sales contracts, retail credit accounts, and the like. To these individuals outstanding debt may assume major proportions and a potentially major financial obligation which may properly be classified as falling within the purview of the "large loss principle."

With consumer credit accident and health insurance, the "large loss principle" may be violated where the debtor purchases the usual policy of this type with a fourteen-day waiting period. An annual loan of $300 would require repayments of approximately $30 per month. The indemnity per day for each loan insured under a consumer credit accident and health policy would thus amount to approximately $1.00, a relatively small amount for most individuals. Furthermore, the major use of consumer credit on the installment basis has generally been ascribed to the middle-income group. Such individuals are usually able to meet their financial obligations after they have become disabled beyond the fourteen-day period for several reasons, among which might be mentioned accumulated sick leave, a time lag in the payment of wages and salaries, and a generally adequate supply of liquid savings. To such an individual a two-week disability is not generally considered a loss of large import.

It was noted that administration of a consumer credit accident and health claim arising from policies providing prorata payments of monthly indemnities for each day of disability beyond a waiting period involves a considerable amount of attention by the lender and insurance company because of the absence of a definitive loss. Furthermore, the frequency of disability of the insured for a period of say fourteen days may be expected to be much greater among borrowers disabled for thirty days, for example. Because the frequency of adjustment is higher among insureds under the fourteen-day plan, the costs of such a plan are substantially higher, this being principally due to the length of the waiting period.

Several insurers have evidenced a recognition of the need for coverage more clearly coming under the concept of the "large loss principle" by providing an accident and health policy with a waiting period of from thirty to ninety days after which the disability is treated as though it were permanent. Under this plan a single payment is made on the insured's behalf in the amount of his insured indebtedness outstanding. This plan has the advantage of providing a more realistic waiting period in recognition of present-day employee benefits and generally financially liquid positions of the middle-income groups. Also, the frequency of loss is lower as is the adjustment expense, the two resulting in a relatively low rate. Such coverage more readily meets with the insurance needs of the middle-income groups and the requisites of the "large loss principle" inasmuch as it insures against contingencies of considerable financial import which have a relatively small probability of occurrence.

It is interesting to note that none of the groups or associations appearing before public bodies has opposed the consumer credit insurance concept in principle. Disagreements have arisen, however, because of differences with respect to its operational aspects.

One of the most controversial issues is that of the right of the lender to receive compensation for the sale of consumer credit insurance and in what amounts. The National Association of Life Underwriters has consistently fought payment of any form of compensation to lender-agents and lender-policyholders in the form of commissions or premium refunds. This group has expressed the fear that where loans and insurance are made available by the same institution, the inevitable result is coercion of the borrower into purchasing insurance in conjunction with a loan whether or not it is required for security purposes. While it must be conceded that coercion has been noted in several states, this position minimizes the fact that, in addition to the majority of lenders being subjected to close regulation, the borrower in most instances has the choice of an alternative lender if coercion is exercised. Moreover, the integrity of the lender seems to be unduly discounted despite the fact that most states establish minimum character qualifications for licensed lenders.

Representatives of the Household Finance Corporation have expressed the belief that coercion is fostered by allowing the premium for consumer credit insurance to be passed on to the borrower as an additional "charge" over and above the amount permissible by law. According to this company's interpretation of the small-loan laws of several states, the application of a single rate of interest to the outstanding balance of the indebtedness is an "all-inclusive charge," anything additional being in violation of this principle. According to this view, the Model Small Loan Law drafted by the Russel Sage Foundation had the intent of eliminating all conceivable tie-in or collateral sales, once used as a subterfuge to circumvent the usury laws. Thus if the lender is allowed to conduct such collateral sales, besides questioning the legality of such practice, Household Finance Corporation representatives would agree that the permission of such transactions leads inevitably to coercion of the borrower.

Without becoming involved in the issue of legality of the

sale of consumer credit insurance where the premium is paid entirely by the borrower, and conceding that a few state laws do in fact specifically prohibit the collateral sale of insurance while other laws leave one in doubt as to the legality of such tie-in sales, the allegation of coercion of the borrower suffers from the same defects as those in the argument of the National Association of Life Underwriters cited previously. This view apparently fails to consider fully the caliber of present-day regulation of the lender, the oligopolistic rather than monopolistic nature of the small-loan market in most areas, the moral fiber of the lenders as well as the acumen of present-day debtors.

The amount of compensation paid to the lender has been, and remains, a question of great significance. Studies of compensation to lenders under the group method of consumer credit life insurance indicate the return to be reasonable. However, for ordinary consumer credit life insurance, the commissions paid the lender-agent run well above either the $0.40 per $100 of insurance limitation proposed by the life insurance industry through its trade organizations, the American Life Convention and the Life Insurance Association of America, as well as the Beneficial Management Corporation's recent study showing an average expense to small loan lenders of $0.37 per $100 of insurance. Based upon the life insurance industry proposal and Beneficial Management's study of four representative small-loan offices, present-day commissions on ordinary consumer credit life insurance appear to be excessive.

In any discussion of the problem of consumer credit insurance compensation, consideration must be given not only to the lender's expense in providing this coverage to its customers, but also to the additional income realized in making it available. Because benefits in several forms accrue to the lender in providing this coverage, the cost per $100 of insurance must be considered in light of total revenue increases.

If commissions for ordinary consumer credit life insurance are excessive, the rate, of which commissions are the major component, must also be high. Because high commissions contribute to a high expense ratio, the amount of premium dollar left for the payments of losses must necessarily be low. Such appears to be the case in at least a significant portion of the ordinary consumer credit life insurance business. While it is true that extremely low loss ratios are experienced in other forms of insurance, such as title and boiler and machinery insurance, a comparison of losses in these lines with ordinary consumer credit life insurance is highly questionable. The reason for the low loss ratios in the former group of coverages is the high cost of searching abstracts and inspecting premises. These items are charged to the company as general insurance expense and represent attempts at loss prevention, the success of which is partially measured by the low resulting loss ratios. The commission paid to a lender-agent under ordinary consumer credit insurance cannot possibly be construed as a payment for loss prevention. As long as commissions are maintained at their present levels, loss ratios will remain relatively low because, with such a substantial portion of the premium dollar going to the lender, there is a definite limit to the proportion of the premium dollar which can go toward the payment of losses to debtor insureds. To date no valid argument has been advanced that would justify the present level of commissions being paid to lenders. A proposed solution to this problem which seems to be gaining an increasing number of proponents is the regulation of lender compensation by the states, that is, regulation of an important component of the consumer credit insurance rate.

The term "reverse competition" was noted in connection with the tendency of consumer credit insurers to bid up the commission scales paid the lender in an attempt at securing more volume and thereby resulting in high and increasing insurance rates to the borrowing public. To what extent this practice is utilized is not known because negotiations of this type remain confidential. However, forces appear to be forming which tend, in effect, to retard the effects of "reverse competition." For example, because the lender offering consumer credit insurance performs a considerable amount of administrative work with respect to the insurance plan, all other things being equal, the insurer offering the more easily administered plan of coverage would be in a better competitive position. Another force would be a given insurer's ability to provide a flexible plan of insurance ideally suited to the needs of a particular lender and his customers. Finally, there are increasing indications that borrowers interested in consumer credit insurance are becoming more price conscious, thus bringing pressure to bear on lenders for low-cost coverage. If a lender selects a given consumer credit insurer's plan because of any of the reasons just cited, it is clear that the choice of this plan for reasons other than high commissions tends to mitigate the effects of "reverse competition." Progress along these lines is noted with interest since their continuance will probably have a leveling effect on lender compensation and may eventually provide needed additional and desirable competition.

It has frequently been suggested that, because group consumer credit life insurance is so much lower in cost than ordinary, lenders who offer the latter do not have their customers' best interests at heart and are commission hungry and shady, if not dishonest. Allusion has been made throughout this text to the instances of flagrant abuses of consumer credit insurance usually associated with a small minority of small-loan licensees. To say that *all* who sell ordinary consumer credit life insurance are guilty of one or all of these allegations is erroneous and unfair. Several valid reasons account for the lender's offering ordinary consumer credit insurance to his customers. For one reason, not all states permit the writing of this coverage on a group basis and some that do permit it specify special circumstances under which it may be written. In addition, several states fail to mention creditors as an eligible group under the group life definition laws. Where such is the case, and laws do not prohibit charging the premium for consumer credit insurance to the borrower, lenders may adopt the ordinary basis of insuring to avoid any potential legal entanglements. Also, in many instances insurers set up participation requirements for group consumer credit life insurance at a level beyond the reach of a number of small lenders, so that even if all creditors wished to offer this coverage on the group basis they would be unable to do so. For example, one insurer reportedly will not write small-loan lenders unless the lender has a minimum of $500,000 in loans outstanding, and then only if the premiums are paid entirely by the creditor. Such high minimum outstanding balance requirements are fortunately the exception rather than the rule, a more realistic figure being approximately $100,000 as the point at which a lender qualifies for consumer credit life insurance on the group basis.

Without condoning the operations of inefficient lenders, it seems clear that a borrower indebted to a small independent lender is generally no less in need of consumer credit insurance than one indebted to a large nationally operated chain. Because the former does not have the volume to qualify under many insurance company underwriting rules, the debtor should not be forced to go without consumer credit insurance protection. It would seem, therefore, that there are instances where lenders are using the ordinary method of insuring because of the unavailability of a practical alternative.

At the same time that recognition is made of the attributes of consumer credit life insurance written on the group basis, such as lower rates, commissions, and expenses, note should also be made of areas for its potential and, in some cases, real abuse. Because of its necessarily high participation requirements (in many cases 100 per cent), the lender-policyholder who passes on the premiums to the borrowers may be tempted to "pressure" customers into purchasing such coverage. The consequences of the lender's failure to secure the agreed participation may result in the termination of the master policy or in the lender's bearing the nonparticipant's portion of the premium.

Another area currently receiving the attention of an increasing number of regulatory officials is the amount of premium passed on to the debtor by the creditor. It will be remembered that the group consumer credit life master policy provides that the premium be paid by the creditor. This premium may be borne entirely by the lender or borrower, or shared in some predetermined proportion. Where the premium is borne by the borrower, it is very difficult for the insurer with his limited investigational authority to determine *who* is actually paying the premium, much less *how much*. Instances have been noted where the premium charged the borrower under a group consumer credit life insurance policy was in excess of the premium forwarded to the insurance company by the lender according to the terms of the master policy. In recognition of this potential abuse, the National Association of Insurance Commissioners, through its Subcommittee on Credit Life and Credit Accident and Health Insurance, has recommended that state laws require the premium charged the borrower be "consistent" with that made to the lender. It appears that such a regulation, properly enforced, would rectify this situation of overcharging.

In the field of regulation, the report of the Subcommittee of the National Association of Insurance Commissioners was mentioned, not only to illustrate the nature of the abuses surrounding the sale of consumer credit insurance, but also to indicate the nature of the proposed remedies. While offering no solution to the problem of excessive commissions, the Rules and Regulations contained in the Subcommittee's report can generally be expected to constitute satisfactory legislation against existing abuses. At the same time it should be emphasized that law without enforcement is worse than no law at all. The National Association of Insurance Commissioners has constructed a foundation upon which sound regulation can be built. Once the legislation is inaugurated, its success will depend upon the effective enforcement by the joint efforts of insurance and banking regulatory officials.

It is believed that support should be given to the National Association of Insurance Commissioners' Rules and Regulations as representing a major step in the protection of the consumer credit insurance–buying public and as assisting a basically sound insurance concept in attaining its rightful place in the insurance industry.

Chapter XI

POTENTIAL DEVELOPMENTS

It is clear that the greatest influence on the future of consumer credit insurance in the United States has been, and will continue to be, the level of consumer credit. It appears equally plain that the present system of purchasing goods on credit, particularly on the installment basis, will continue as part of the American way of living. At the present time the majority of students of finance believe the composition of consumer debt to be sound and forsee continued growth in this area,[1] with but few predicting a decline.[2] Consumer credit insurance executives readily admit that their industry's growth has resulted almost directly from the pronounced acceptance of consumer credit buying by the American public. At the same time, most believe that if consumer debt suddenly declined, their business would probably follow but not necessarily at the same rate. The principal reason for this is the industry's continued success in discovering new areas for the development of consumer credit insurance sales.[3]

Vendors of consumer credit insurance have markedly dem-

---

[1] See, for example, Ernst A. Dauer, "The Consumer Credit Situation," an address to the Robert Morris Associates, Dallas, Texas, November 14, 1955; Arthur R. Upgren, "Why Things Look Good Ahead," The Amos Tuck School of Business Administration, Dartmouth College, Hanover, New Hampshire, 1956; "Are We Mortgaging Our Future Too Much?", *Vital Speeches,* May, 1956, p. 431.

[2] See, for example, "The Coming Turn in Consumer Credit," *Fortune,* March 1956, p. 99.

[3] Another method of hedging against a downturn in consumer credit is the development of additional lines of coverage which are not expected to be affected by a decrease in consumer debt. Allied coverages, such as regular life and accident and health insurance, special accident policies, polio and dread disease policies, and the like are often chosen to supplement and diversify a specialty company's business.

onstrated a real ability to perceive new uses for their coverages. Originally conceived in terms of insurance on the life of an unsecured cash borrower, the concept has developed into the provision of both death and disability coverages to debtors involved in both cash and merchandise transactions covering a variety of lending institutions. It appears that the most recent successful area of sales emphasis has been at the retail level where purchasers of both durable and nondurable goods are insured.

A few progressive consumer credit insurers have recently begun a very extensive program of market research in an attempt to uncover new fields to develop. In many instances these programs are conducted on an experimental basis for a considerable period of time, sometimes at a loss, before they actually become self-supporting. Many of these programs require a substantial amount of time and investment. Such research is significant in two major respects. First, it is evidence that the principles of market research, so common in other fields of insurance and business, have pervaded the consumer credit insurance industry. The results of such research programs have usually added not only to the quality of the service offered to the public, but also to the stability of the insurance companies as well. Second, it is significant evidence that the consumer credit insurance industry is not just a "fly-by-night" operation as some of its critics intimate. Indeed, such programs indicate the industry's foresightedness and concern over the future.

For this coverage to remain competitive, serious consideration will have to be paid to increasing the efficiency of its administration. Because of the nature of consumer credit insurance and its volume operations, the continued modernization of its administration is essential to the maintenance of any individual company's competitive position. This is particularly applicable to the ordinary insurers because of the necessarily more detailed records needed for individual policyholders. Increasing use of electronic equipment for calculating, tabulating, billing, and record keeping is noted and expected to increase.

As the companies continue to increase their volume of sales, more statistical information will become available. Then, too, the increasingly larger participation within eligible groups diminishes the amount of antiselection. These factors influence the credibility of the statistical experience and allow a more intelligent appraisal of the industry's present position and will undoubtedly assist in future planning and research. It is highly desirable that the companies inaugurate a system whereby there is a free exchange of statistical data made available to all companies for their mutual advantage.

Consumer credit insurance contains within itself the necessary factors for sound growth. In summary, industry executives are convinced that the outlook for the American economy as a whole is promising, and they envisage continued growth of consumer credit insurance within an expanding economy. Made five years ago, the statement, "The future in this field is virtually unlimited,"[4] is reflective of the attitude of the entire consumer credit insurance industry today. When carefully considered, this optimism does not appear unwarranted. All indications point to an increasingly security-minded populous which accepts the existing system of time purchasing and the consumer credit insurance mechanism as an important adjunct.

---

[4] Ray Vicker, "Credit Insurance," *The Wall Street Journal,* Vol. XXXII, No. 124, March 13, 1952, p. 1.

Appendix A

DEFINITION AND PROVISIONS OF GROUP CONSUMER CREDIT INSURANCE TAKEN FROM THE GROUP LIFE INSURANCE DEFINITION AND STANDARD POLICY PROVISIONS ADOPTED BY THE NATIONAL ASSOCIATION OF INSURANCE COMMISSIONERS, JUNE 1946 AND REVISED DECEMBER 1948

(2) A policy issued to a creditor, who shall be deemed the policyholder, to insure debtors of the creditor, subject to the following requirements:

   a) The debtors eligible for insurance under the policy shall be all of the debtors of the creditor whose indebtedness is repayable in instalments, or all of any class or classes thereof determined by conditions pertaining to the indebtedness or to the purchase giving rise to the indebtedness. The policy may provide that the term "debtors" shall include the debtors of one or more subsidiary corporations, and the debtors of one or more affiliated corporations, proprietors or partnerships if the business of the policyholder and of such affiliated corporations, proprietors or partnerships is under common control through stock ownership, contract, or otherwise.

   b) The premium for the policy shall be paid by the policyholder, either from the creditor's funds, or from charges collected from the insured debtors, or from both. A policy on which part or all of the premium is to be derived from the collection from the insured debtors of identifiable charges not required of uninsured debtors shall not include, in the class or classes of debtors eligible for insurance, debtors under obligations outstanding at its date of issue without evidence of individual insurability unless at least 75% of the then eligible debtors elect to pay the required charges. A policy on which no part of the premium is to be derived from the collection of such identifiable charges must insure all eligible debtors, or all except any as to whom evidence of individual insurability is not satisfactory to the insurer.

   c) The policy may be issued only if the group of eligible debtors is then receiving new entrants at the rate of at least 100 persons yearly, or may reasonably be expected to receive at least 100 new entrants during the first policy year, and only if the policy reserves to the insurer the right to require evidence of individual insurability if less than 75% of the new entrants become insured.

d) The amount of insurance on the life of any debtor shall at no time exceed the amount owed by him which is repayable in instalments to the creditor, or $5,000, whichever is less.

e) The insurance shall be payable to the policyholder. Such payment shall reduce or extinguish the unpaid indebtedness of the debtor to the extent of such payment.

Appendix B

Life Insurance

Year	Admitted Assets	Net Reserve	Capital and Surplus	Insurance Written	Insurance in Force
1933	$ 581,191	$ 168,154	$ 300,000	$ 3,725,148	$ 7,757,076
1943	1,093,337	482,971	419,225	53,896,089	51,471,693
1949	3,382,807	1,244,828	1,358,908	274,871,424	302,718,052*
1950	4,515,956	1,744,474	1,567,147	433,578,541	471,748,696
1951	5,867,520	2,537,205	1,800,182	649,888,669	784,534,958
1952	8,155,416	2,962,078	2,705,636	815,330,172	958,939,174
1953	10,422,405	3,674,878	3,402,309	958,563,364	1,174,564,849
1954	13,216,179	3,920,108	4,056,902	1,200,686,020	1,441,205,016
1955	17,266,962	4,406,592	4,522,543	1,854,143,196	2,120,189,449

Accident and Health Insurance

Year	Net Premiums Written	Net Premiums Earned	(1) Loss Ratio	(2) Expense Ratio	(3) Underwriting Results
1950	$ 733,442	$ 386,236	44.2	50.7	−229,961
1951	179,490	536,240	38.0	201.2	−28,606
1952	572,889	354,537	30.3	97.1	−309,545
1953	674,516	448,257	34.3	42.5	8,077
1954	1,658,773	1,009,901	54.0	15.8	203,659
1955	1,743,104	1,194,230	73.4	19.8	−27,338

*Includes State Life Fund, 1949, $332,719.
(1) Losses and loss adjustment expenses incurred to earned premiums.
(2) Underwriting expenses incurred to written premiums.
(3) Before Federal Income Taxes.
Source: *Best's Life Reports* (New York: Alfred M. Best Co., Inc., 1956), p. 1067.

Appendix C

The Growth of Loan Protection Insurance in the
CUNA Mutual Insurance Society from 1940 to 1956
(Excluding Canadian Business)

Year	Number of Contracts	Insurance in Force	Number of Claims	Amount
1940	3,129	$ 70,000,000*	2,193	$ 340,796
1941	3,720	88,000,000*	2,722	448,528
1942	3,932	64,478,229	2,960	471,207
1943	3,959	53,246,151	2,640	395,394
1944	3,900	51,435,641	2,440	342,597
1945	3,907	54,117,341	2,399	358,484
1946	4,017	82,407,288	2,285	391,316
1947	4,341	126,835,936	2,602	505,419
1948	4,770	188,843,456	3,200	780,359
1949	5,382	261,017,864	4,037	1,136,825
1950	6,322	368,062,566	4,738	1,582,801
1951	7,191	422,137,984	5,950	2,055,359
1952	8,328	582,926,136	6,857	2,532,270
1953	9,966	826,332,496	8,287	3,448,268
1954	11,561	1,021,597,475	10,396	5,036,146
1955	12,866	1,296,684,276	11,490	5,921,331
1956	14,094	1,599,203,314	13,594	7,785,691

*In force estimated.

Source: Prepared at the author's request by the CUNA Mutual Insurance
Society, Madison, Wisconsin.

Appendix D

Company	Ordinary	Group	Both
Aetna Life, Conn.		x	
Alinco Life Ins. Co., Ind.	x		
All American Assur., La.		x	
Allied Bankers, Tex.		x	
American Bankers, Fla.			x
American General, Tex.		x	
American Guaranty, Tex.		x	
American Life, Ala.		x	
American Nat'l., Tex.		x	
American Republic, Iowa			x
American United, Ind.		x	
Andrew Jackson Life, Miss.		x	
Atlantic Nat'l., Ala.		x	
Atlas Life, Okla.		x	
Atlas Life, S.D.	x		
Audubon Life, La.		x	
Augwood L & A, S.C.		x	
Bankers Life, Iowa		x	
Bankers Nat'l., N.J.			x
Bankers Security, N.Y.			x
Bankers Service, Okla.	x		
Beacon Life, Okla.	x		
Beneficial Std., Calif.		x	
Benefit Assoc. of R.R. Employees, Ill.		x	
Brotherhood Mutual, Ind.		x	
Businessmen's Assur., Mo.		x	
Calif. Life			x
Calif.-Western States, Calif.		x	
Cavalier Life, Md.			x
Central American, Tex.			x
Central National, Nebr.			x
Central Plains, Kan.			x
Central States H & A, Nebr.			x
Citadel Life, N.C.			x
Citizens Nat'l., Ind.	x		
Coastal Plains, N.C.	x		
Coastal States, Ga.		x	
Colonial Life, N.J.		x	
Colorado Credit		x	
Columbia Gen., Tex.			x
Columbia Life, D.C.	x		
Columbian Nat'l., Mass.			x
Commercial & Ind., Tex.		x	
Commercial L & A, Tex.	x		
Commercial Security, Tex.			x
Commercial Travelers, Utah		x	
Commonwealth Life, Ky.		x	
Commonwealth Life, Okla.			x
Confederation Life, Can.		x	
Conn. General, Conn.		x	
Consolidated Bankers, Tex.		x	
Consolidated Gen., Tex.			x
Constitution Life, Calif.			x
Continental American, Del.		x	
Continental American, Miss.	x		
Continental American, Tex.			x
Continental Assur., Ill.		x	
Continental L & A, Idaho		x	
Cornbelt Life, Ill.	x		
Credit Life, Ohio			x
Crown Life, Can.		x	
Cuna Mutual, Wis.		x	
David Crockett, Tex.		x	
Dominion Life, Can.		x	
East Coast Life, N.C.		x	

Company	Types of Credit Business			Company	Types of Credit Business		
	Ordinary	Group	Both		Ordinary	Group	Both
Eastern Life of N.Y.		x		Independence Life, N.C.	x		
Educators Investment, Tex.		x		Industrial Life, Tex.			x
Employees Security, Tex.		x		International Fidelity, Tex.			x
Employers Life, Ala.		x		International Service, Tex.			x
Equitable Life, N.Y.		x		Interstate L & A, Tenn.		x	
Eureka Life, Tex.		x		Interstate Life, N.J.		x	
Family Security, S.C.		x		Interstate Life, Tex.	x		
Federal Life & Cas., Mich.		x		Jackson Life, Tenn.		x	
Fidelity Bankers, Va.			x	John Hancock, Mass.		x	
Fidelity L & I Mutual, Mich.			x	Kentucky Home Mutual		x	
Fidelity Life, Tex.			x	Lafayette Life, Ind.		x	
Financial L & C, S.C.		x		Leo Nat'l., La.		x	
First Pyramid Life, Ark.	x			Legal Std. Life, Tex.	x		
First Security, Tex.		x		Liberty Life, S.C.		x	
Forest Lawn Life, Calif.		x		Life & Casualty, Tenn.			x
General American Life, Mo.		x		Life Ins. Co. of Ala.		x	
General Assur., Ga.		x		Life Ins. Co. of America, Wis.	x		
Globe L & A, Okla.		x		Life Ins. Co. of N.C.	x		
Gov't Employees, D.C.			x	Life Ins. Co. of Tex.		x	
Great Amer. Reserve, Tex.			x	Life Ins. Corp. of America, Utah	x		
Great Atlantic, Fla.	x			Life of Virginia		x	
Great Charter, Tex.		x		Life Underwriters, La.		x	
Great Lakes, Ill.		x		Lincoln Nat'l., Ind.		x	
Great-West Life, Can.		x		Loyal American, Ala.		x	
Great Western, Okla.			x	Manhattan Life, N.Y.		x	
Group Health Mutual, Minn.		x		Mass. Mutual		x	
Guarantee Reserve, Colo.		x		Metropolitan, N.Y.		x	
Guaranty Life, Tex.		x		Michigan Life		x	
Guaranty Union, Calif.		x		Midland Empire, Kan.		x	
Gulf Life, Fla.		x		Mid-States Life, Fla.	x		
Haven Life, Fla.		x		Minnesota Mutual		x	
Home L & A, Tex.			x	Missouri Ins.		x	
Home Life, N.Y.		x		Mission Life, Tex.	x		
Home Security Life, N.C.	x			Monarch Life, Mass.		x	
Homesteaders Life, Iowa		x		Mutual Life, N.Y.		x	
Home State Life, Okla.			x	Mutual Service, Minn.		x	
Hoosier Farm Bureau Life, Ind.		x		Nat'l. Fidelity, Mo.		x	
Houston American, Tex.			x	Nat'l. Home Life, Mo.		x	
Independence L & A, Ky.	x			Nationwide, Ohio		x	
				New England Mutual, Mass.		x	
				New York Life		x	
				North Amer. L & C, Minn.			x
				North American, Ill.		x	
				North American Acc., Ill.		x	

Company	Ordinary	Group	Both	Company	Ordinary	Group	Both
North American Reassur., N.Y.	x			Security L & T, N.C.			x
North Central, Minn.			x	Security Mutual, N.Y.		x	
Northwestern Life, Wash.		x		Security Mutual, Nebr.		x	
Northwestern Nat'l., Minn.		x		Southern Life, Ga.		x	
Occidental Life, Calif.		x		Southland Life, Tex.		x	
Ohio Nat'l.		x		Standard Life, Ind.			x
Oil Industries, Tex.		x		Standard Life, Miss.		x	
Oklahoma Benefit	x			Standard L & A, Okla.			x
Old American, Mo.		x		State Capital, N.C.			x
Old Dominion, Va.		x		State Farm, Ill.		x	
Old Republic Credit, Ill.			x	State Life, S.C.	x		
Old Security, Mo.			x	State Mutual, Mass.		x	
Olympic Nat'l., Wash.		x		State Mutual, Ga.		x	
Pacific Mutual, Calif.		x		State National, Mo.	x		
Pan American, La.		x		Stuyvesant Life, Pa.			x
Patriot Life, N.Y.			x	Sunland Life, Tex.		x	
Peninsular Life, Fla.		x		Sun Life, Can.		x	
Peoples Life, Ind.		x		Sun Life of Amer., Md.		x	
Philadelphia United, Pa.		x		Superior Life, S.C.		x	
Piedmont Life, Ga.		x		Tennessee Life, Tex.		x	
Piedmont Mut. L & A, S.C.	x			Texas Reserve, Tex.		x	
Pierce Ins. Co., Calif.		x		Time Life, Tex.	x		
Pilot Life, N.C.		x		Travelers, Conn.		x	
Pioneer American, Tex.		x		Union Cas. & Life, N.Y.		x	
Pioneer L & C, Ala.		x		Union Central, Ohio		x	
Plymouth Life, Tex.		x		Union Labor, N.Y.		x	
Progressive, Ga.		x		Union Mutual, Maine			x
Protective, Ala.		x		Union Security, Ga.	x		
Protective Life, Nebr.			x	Union Standard, Tex.	x		
Provident L & A, Tenn.		x		United Benefit, Nebr.			x
Prudential Life, N.J.		x		United Fidelity, Tex.		x	
Public Life Ins. Co. of America, Fla.	x			United L & A, N.H.		x	
Public Savings, S.C.	x			United States, N.Y.		x	
Pyramid Life, N.C.		x		Universal Security, Tex.	x		
Ranchers Life, Tex.			x	Valley Life, Tex.		x	
Reliance Mut., Ill.			x	Volunteer States, Tenn.		x	
Republic Nat'l., Tex.	x			Vulcan L & A, Ala.		x	
Resolute Credit, R.I.		x		Washington Nat'l., Ill.		x	
Richmond Life, Va.		x		Webster Life, Iowa		x	
Rushmore Mutual, S.C.		x		West Coast, Calif.		x	
Sabina-Neches, Tex.	x			Western General, Tex.			x
Security Benefit, Kan.		x		Western Nat'l., Tex.			x
Security L & A, Colo.		x		Wisconsin Life, Wis.	x		
				Wisconsin Nat'l., Wis.	x		
				Woodman L & A, Nebr.			x
				World Insurance, Nebr.			x

Source: Institute of Life Insurance.

ORIGINAL TERM OF LOAN OR INSURANCE	1	2	3	4	5	6	7	8	9	10	11	12	13	14	15
1	0														
2	33.33	0													
3	50.00	16.67	0												
4	60.00	30.00	10.00	0											
5	66.67	40.00	20.00	6.67	0										
6	71.43	47.62	28.57	14.29	4.76	0									
7	75.00	53.57	35.71	21.43	10.71	3.57	0								
8	77.78	58.33	41.67	27.78	16.67	8.33	2.78	0							
9	80.00	62.22	46.67	33.33	22.22	13.33	6.67	2.22	0						
10	81.82	65.45	50.91	38.18	27.27	18.18	10.91	5.45	1.82	0					
11	83.33	68.18	54.55	42.42	31.82	22.73	15.15	9.09	4.55	1.52	0				
12	84.62	70.51	57.69	46.15	35.90	26.92	19.23	12.82	7.69	3.85	1.28	0			
13	85.71	72.53	60.44	49.45	39.56	30.77	23.08	16.48	10.99	6.59	3.30	1.10	0		
14	86.67	74.29	62.86	52.38	42.86	34.29	26.67	20.00	14.29	9.52	5.71	2.86	.95	0	
15	87.50	75.83	65.00	55.00	45.83	37.50	30.00	23.33	17.50	12.50	8.33	5.00	2.50	.83	0
16	88.24	77.21	66.91	57.35	48.53	40.44	33.09	26.47	20.59	15.44	11.03	7.35	4.41	2.21	.74
17	88.89	78.43	68.63	59.48	50.98	43.14	35.95	29.41	23.53	18.30	13.73	9.80	6.54	3.92	1.96
18	89.47	79.53	70.18	61.40	53.22	45.61	38.60	32.16	26.32	21.05	16.37	12.28	8.77	5.85	3.51
19	90.00	80.53	71.58	63.16	55.26	47.89	41.05	34.74	28.95	23.68	18.95	14.74	11.05	7.89	5.26
20	90.48	81.43	72.86	64.76	57.14	50.00	43.33	37.14	31.43	26.19	21.43	17.14	13.33	10.00	7.14
21	90.91	82.25	74.03	66.23	58.87	51.95	45.45	39.39	33.77	28.57	23.81	19.48	15.58	12.12	9.09
22	91.30	83.00	75.10	67.59	60.47	53.75	47.43	41.50	35.97	30.83	26.09	21.74	17.79	14.23	11.07
23	91.67	83.70	76.09	68.84	61.96	55.43	49.28	43.48	38.04	32.97	28.26	23.91	19.93	16.30	13.04
24	92.00	84.33	77.00	70.00	63.33	57.00	51.00	45.33	40.00	35.00	30.33	26.00	22.00	18.33	15.00
25	92.31	84.92	77.85	71.08	64.62	58.46	52.62	47.08	41.85	36.92	32.31	28.00	24.00	20.31	16.92
26	92.59	85.47	78.63	72.08	65.81	59.83	54.13	48.72	43.59	38.75	34.19	29.91	25.93	22.22	18.80
27	92.86	85.98	79.37	73.02	66.93	61.11	55.56	50.26	45.24	40.48	35.98	31.75	27.78	24.07	20.63
28	93.10	86.45	80.05	73.89	67.98	62.32	56.90	51.72	46.80	42.12	37.68	33.50	29.56	25.85	22.41
29	93.33	86.90	80.69	74.71	68.97	63.45	58.16	53.10	48.28	43.68	39.31	35.17	31.26	27.59	24.14
30	93.55	87.31	81.29	75.48	69.89	64.52	59.35	54.41	49.68	45.16	40.86	36.77	32.90	29.25	25.81
31	93.75	87.70	81.85	76.21	70.77	65.52	60.48	55.65	51.01	46.57	42.34	38.31	34.48	30.85	27.42
32	93.94	88.07	82.39	76.89	71.59	66.48	61.55	56.82	52.27	47.92	43.75	39.77	35.98	32.39	28.98
33	94.12	88.41	82.89	77.54	72.37	67.38	62.57	57.93	53.48	49.20	45.10	41.18	37.43	33.87	30.48
34	94.29	88.74	83.36	78.15	73.11	68.24	63.53	58.99	54.62	50.42	46.39	42.52	38.82	35.29	31.93
35	94.44	89.05	83.81	78.73	73.81	69.05	64.44	60.00	55.71	51.59	47.62	43.81	40.16	36.67	33.33
36	94.59	89.34	84.23	79.28	74.47	69.82	65.32	60.96	56.76	52.70	48.80	45.05	41.44	37.99	34.68
	1	2	3	4	5	6	7	8	9	10	11	12	13	14	15

NUMBER OF MONTHS

Source: J. Reuben Darr, "Refund of Installment Loan Charges and Consumer Credit Insurance Premiums" (New York: Bankers Security Life Insurance Society).

PERCENTAGE REFUND CHART

Based on "Sum of the Digits" commonly known as the "Rule of 78."

1. Percentage of refund of unused interest or discount due borrower on prepayment, refinancing or recasting of installment loan.

2. Percentage of refund premium due insured when a single premium decreasing term life insurance policy is canceled prior to original date of expiration.

HOW TO USE THIS CHART

1. Locate the original term of the loan or insurance in months in the vertical column on the left.

2. Locate the number of months the loan or insurance has already run in either the oblique line at the top or the horizontal line at the bottom.

3. Where the column and the line intersect is the percentage of interest, discount or premium to be refunded.

OR INSURANCE HAS RUN

19	20	21	22	23	24	25	26	27	28	29	30	31	32	33	34	35	36
.48	0																
4.30	.43	0															
2.37	1.19	.40	0														
3.62	2.17	1.09	.36	0													
5.00	3.33	2.00	1.00	.33	0												
5.46	4.62	3 08	1.85	.92	.31	0											
7.98	5.98	4.27	2.85	1.71	.85	.28	0										
9.52	7.41	5.56	3.97	2.65	1.59	.79	.26	0									
1.08	8.87	6.90	5.17	3.69	2.46	1.48	.74	.25	0								
.64	10.34	8.28	6 44	4.83	3.45	2.30	1.38	.69	.23	0							
.19	11.83	9.68	7.74	6.02	4.52	3.23	2.15	1.29	.65	.22	0						
5.73	13.31	11.09	9.07	7 26	5.65	4.23	3.02	2 02	1.21	.60	.20	0					
7.23	14.77	12.50	10.42	8.52	6 82	5.30	3.98	2.84	1.89	1.14	.57	.19	0				
8.72	16.22	13.90	11.76	9.80	8.02	6.42	4.99	3.74	2.67	1.78	1.07	.53	.18	0			
.17	17.65	15.29	13.11	11.09	9.24	7.56	6.05	4.71	3.53	2.52	1.68	1.01	.50	.17	0		
.59	19.05	16.67	14.44	12.38	10 48	8.73	7.14	5.71	4.44	3.33	2.38	1.59	.95	.48	.16	0	
.97	20.42	18.02	15.77	13.66	11.71	9.91	8.26	6.76	5.41	4.20	3.15	2.25	1.50	.90	.45	.15	0
19	20	21	22	23	24	25	26	27	28	29	30	31	32	33	34	35	36

SURANCE HAS RUN

NUMBER OF MONTHS

ORIGINAL TERM OF INSURANCE	1	2	3	4	5	6	7	8	9	10	11	12	13	14	15	16
1	0															
2	50.00	0														
3	66.67	33.33	0													
4	75.00	50.00	25.00	0												
5	80.00	60.00	40.00	20.00	0											
6	83.33	66.66	50.00	33.33	16.67	0										
7	85.71	71.43	57.14	42.86	28.57	14.29	0									
8	87.50	75.00	62.50	50.00	37.50	25.00	12.50	0								
9	88.89	77.78	66.67	55.56	44.44	33.33	22.22	11.11	0							
10	90.00	80.00	70.00	60.00	50.00	40.00	30.00	20.00	10.00	0						
11	90.90	81.81	72.72	63.63	54.54	45.45	36.36	27.27	18.18	9.09	0					
12	91.66	83.33	75.00	66.66	58.33	50.00	41.67	33.33	25.00	16.67	8.33	0				
13	92.30	84.61	76.92	69.23	61.54	53.84	46.15	38.46	30.77	23.08	15.38	7.69	0			
14	92.85	85.70	78.56	71.42	64.28	57.14	50.00	42.85	35.71	28.57	21.43	14.28	7.14	0		
15	93.32	86.66	80.00	73.33	66.66	60.00	53.33	46.66	40.00	33.33	26.66	20.00	13.33	6.67	0	
16	93.75	87.50	81.25	75.00	68.75	62.50	56.25	50.00	43.75	37.50	31.25	25.00	18.75	12.50	6.25	
17	94.11	88.23	82.35	76.47	70.58	64.70	58.82	52.94	47.06	41.17	35.29	29.41	23.53	17.65	11.76	5.8
18	94.44	88.88	83.33	77.77	72.22	66.66	61.11	55.55	50.00	44.44	38.89	33.33	27.78	22.22	16.67	11.1
19	94.73	89.47	84.21	78.95	73.68	68.42	63.16	57.89	52.63	47.37	42.10	36.84	31.58	26.32	21.05	15.7
20	95.00	90.00	85.00	80.00	75.00	70.00	65.00	60.00	55.00	50.00	45.00	40.00	35.00	30.00	25.00	20.0
21	95.22	90.46	85.70	80.94	76.18	71.42	66.65	61.89	57.13	52.37	47.61	42.85	38.09	33.33	28.57	23.8
22	95.45	90.90	86.36	81.81	77.27	72.72	68.18	63.63	59.09	54.54	50.00	45.45	40.91	36.36	31.82	27.2
23	95.63	91.29	86.94	82.59	78.25	73.90	69.55	65.21	60.86	56.51	52.16	47.82	43.47	39.12	34.78	30.4
24	95.82	91.65	87.49	83.32	79.15	74.99	70.82	66.66	62.49	58.32	54.16	49.99	45.83	41.66	37.49	33.3
25	96.00	92.00	88.00	84.00	80.00	76.00	72.00	68.00	64.00	60.00	56.00	52.00	48.00	44.00	40.00	36.0
26	96.15	92.30	88.46	84.61	80.77	76.92	73.07	69.23	65.38	61.54	57.69	53.84	50.00	46.15	42.31	38.4
27	96.28	92.58	88.87	85.17	81.47	77.76	74.06	70.36	66.65	62.95	59.25	55.55	51.84	48.14	44.44	40.7
28	96.42	92.85	89.28	85.70	82.13	78.56	74.99	71.42	67.85	64.28	60.71	57.14	53.57	49.99	46.42	42.8
29	96.54	93.10	89.65	86.20	82.75	79.30	75.86	72.41	68.96	65.51	62.06	58.62	55.17	51.72	48.27	44.8
30	96.66	93.32	89.99	86.66	83.33	79.99	76.66	73.33	69.99	66.66	63.33	59.99	56.66	53.33	50.00	46.6
31	96.75	93.53	90.30	87.08	83.85	80.63	77.40	74.18	70.95	67.73	64.50	61.28	58.05	54.83	51.60	48.3
32	96.88	93.75	90.63	87.50	84.38	81.25	78.13	75.00	71.88	68.75	65.63	62.50	59.38	56.25	53.13	50.0
33	96.96	93.93	90.90	87.87	84.84	81.81	78.78	75.75	72.72	69.69	66.66	63.63	60.60	57.57	54.54	51.5
34	97.05	94.11	91.17	88.23	85.29	82.35	79.41	76.47	73.53	70.58	67.64	64.70	61.76	58.82	55.88	52.9
35	97.14	94.28	91.42	88.57	85.71	82.85	80.00	77.14	74.28	71.43	68.57	65.71	62.85	60.00	57.14	54.2
36	97.20	94.42	91.64	88.86	86.09	83.31	80.53	77.76	74.98	72.20	69.43	66.65	63.87	61.09	58.32	55.5
	1	2	3	4	5	6	7	8	9	10	11	12	13	14	15	16

NUMBER OF MONTHS

Source: J. Reuben Darr, "Refund of Installment Loan Charges and Consumer Credit Insurance Premiums" (New York: Bankers Security Life Insurance Society).

PERCENTAGE REFUND CHART

Pro-rata basis

Percentage of refund premium due insured when a single premium level term life or single premium accident and health insurance policy is cancelled prior to original date of expiration.

HOW TO USE THIS CHART

1. Locate the original term of the insurance in months in the vertical column on the left.
2. Locate the number of months the insurance has already run in either the oblique line at the top or the horizontal line at the bottom.
3. Where the column and the line intersect is the percentage of insurance premium to be refunded.

...SURANCE HAS RUN (oblique heading)

	19	20	21	22	23	24	25	26	27	28	29	30	31	32	33	34	35	36
0																		
?6	0																	
?0	5.00	0																
?8	9.52	4.76	0															
?8	13.64	9.09	4.55	0														
?4	17.39	13.04	8.69	4.35	0													
?0	20.83	16.66	12.50	8.33	4.17	0												
?0	24.00	20.00	16.00	12.00	8.00	4.00	0											
?7	26.92	23.08	19.23	15.38	11.54	7.69	3.85	0										
?3	29.62	25.92	22.22	18.52	14.81	11.11	7.41	3.70	0									
?1	32.14	28.57	25.00	21.43	17.86	14.28	10.71	7.14	3.57	0								
?3	34.48	31.03	27.58	24.14	20.69	17.24	13.79	10.34	6.90	3.45	0							
?0	36.66	33.33	30.00	26.66	23.33	20.00	16.67	13.33	10.00	6.67	3.33	0						
?3	38.70	35.48	32.25	29.03	25.80	22.58	19.35	16.13	12.90	9.68	6.45	3.23	0					
?5	40.63	37.50	34.38	31.25	28.13	25.00	21.88	18.75	15.63	12.50	9.38	6.25	3.13	0				
?5	42.42	39.39	36.36	33.33	30.30	27.27	24.24	21.21	18.18	15.15	12.12	9.09	6.06	3.03	0			
?6	44.12	41.17	38.23	35.29	32.35	29.41	26.47	23.53	20.59	17.65	14.71	11.76	8.82	5.88	2.94	0		
?7	45.71	42.86	40.00	37.14	34.28	31.43	28.57	25.71	22.86	20.00	17.14	14.29	11.43	8.57	5.71	2.86	0	
?9	47.21	44.43	41.66	38.88	36.10	33.32	30.55	27.77	24.99	22.22	19.44	16.66	13.89	11.11	8.33	5.55	2.78	0
	19	20	21	22	23	24	25	26	27	28	29	30	31	32	33	34	35	36

...SURANCE HAS RUN

Appendix F

A STUDY OF CONSUMER CREDIT INSURANCE EXPERIENCE OF
COMPANIES LICENSED AND DOING BUSINESS IN WISCONSIN
(Business of 1955)

The primary reason for making this study is the lack of statistical experience currently existing in the consumer credit insurance field. Although much talk has been heard recently concerning the level of consumer credit insurance rates, very little statistical evidence has been offered, either by those who maintain that rates are reasonable, or by those who suggest that they are excessive. Chapter VI cites several statistical studies reported by insurers and lenders relative to mortality experience of their insureds. Because these studies represent almost the total experience available to the public, they are indeed very valuable. At the same time they are limited to an extent as to lack of credibility from which valid conclusions might be drawn. Until very recently, experience available from reports filed with state insurance departments did not segregate consumer credit insurance business from regular lines so that even regulatory officials were not fully cognizant of underwriting results.

The source of statistical information for this study was the new "Credit Life and Accident and Health Insurance Exhibit" which, beginning May 1, 1956, was required to be filed with state insurance departments by all consumer credit insurers. The Exhibit represents the first attempt at segregating consumer credit insurance experience from other lines into a meaningful presentation of important statistical data.

All Exhibits submitted to the Wisconsin State Insurance Department were included in this study. These exhibits totaled 50 from the 188 companies known to be writing any and all forms of consumer credit insurance during the calendar year 1955.

Out of the 188 companies, 151 were known to be writing group consumer credit life insurance;[1] 42 of these companies are licensed and reported business to the Wisconsin Insurance Department. Although representing 28 per cent of all group consumer credit life insurance companies, based upon premium volume, these companies

---

[1] As reported by the Institute of Life Insurance.

182

wrote approximately 58 per cent of the total consumer credit life insurance on the group basis.[2]

Eleven of the sixty-five companies known to be writing ordinary consumer credit life insurance reported to the Wisconsin Insurance Department. Based upon total ordinary consumer credit life insurance in force for 1955, the total in-force volume of $1,459,613 reported by these eleven companies accounted for approximately 61 per cent of the ordinary business in force.[3]

Fourteen companies reported consumer credit accident and health business on a group basis to the Wisconsin Insurance Department and eleven reported writing this coverage on the ordinary basis. Gross premiums totaled $9,982,279 for all consumer credit accident and health insurance written in Wisconsin. It is estimated that total nation-wide premium volume for this line for 1955 was $40,000,000.[4] This would mean approximately 25 per cent of the total consumer credit accident and health business was reported to the Wisconsin Department of Insurance and included in this study.

The data submitted are nationwide premiums on the accrual basis, which is identical to the incurred basis. The "Credit Life and Accident and Health Insurance Exhibit" is prepared on the same basis as the Annual Statement insofar as reinsurance is concerned. Reinsurance accepted is included in premium writings, while reinsurance ceded is deducted. Two companies had a relatively insignificant volume reported on a direct basis. Tables XXIII, XXIV, and XXV, are facsimiles of work sheets used to gather the data for consumer credit group life, ordinary level-term, and decreasing-term life, and ordinary and group accident and health experience. These tables indicate the names of the companies surveyed and their individual underwriting results with respect to nationwide consumer credit insurance business in 1955. The net nationwide premium volume by types of insurance reported

---

[2] The Institute of Life Insurance reports that group consumer credit life insurance accounted for $108,000,000 in premiums for 1955; this study included $62,795,425 in group consumer credit life insurance premiums.

[3] The Institute of Life Insurance reports that at the end of 1955 total ordinary consumer credit life insurance in force was $2,379,000,000.

[4] This amount was estimated by an executive of a consumer credit insurance company.

TABLE XXIII

CONSUMER CREDIT LIFE AND ACCIDENT AND HEALTH INSURANCE EXPERIENCE OF
COMPANIES DOING BUSINESS IN WISCONSIN FOR THE YEAR 1955
GROUP CONSUMER CREDIT LIFE INSURANCE

	(1)	(2)	(3)	(4)
Company	Gross Premiums	Losses	Loss Expense	Commissions
Aetna Life Ins. Co.	$ 1,050,570	$ 813,063		$ 24,486
American United Life	404			26
Bankers Life Co.	14,402	8,001		1,477
Benefit Assn. of R.R. Employees	16,661	12,136		1,466
Business Men's Assur. Co.	37,655	24,470	$ 652	1,213
Connecticut General Life	1,571,987	715,967	7,366	22,293
Continental Assur. Co.	2,765,835	1,015,071	4,171	454,293
Credit Life Ins. Co.	1,025,088	455,118		79,161
CUNA Mutual Ins. Soc.	10,019,476	6,891,447		
Equitable Life Assurance Soc.	370,427	262,466	2,440	12,876
Federal Life Ins. Co.	517	132		65
Federal Life & Cas. Ins. Co.	576,395	117,291	5,970	78,999
Group Health Mutual Inc.	567	112		22
John Hancock Mutual Life	969,396	454,504		27,430
Lafayette Life Ins. Co.	1,345	69		108
Mass. Mutual Life	131,671	96,192		6,123
Metropolitan Life Ins. Co.	886,876	325,187	2,955	119,586
Monarch Life Ins. Co.	2,305	2,873		107
Mutual Life Ins. Co. of N.Y.	30,424	6,617		3,813
Mutual Service Life Ins. Co.	2,310	756	15	862
New England Mutual Life	34,125	12,768		5,129
New York Life	1,066,585	893,830		43,373
North American Life & Cas.	115,489	37,466		23,479
North American Life Ins. Co.	657			164
North Central Life	17,386	16,500		
Northwestern National Life	73,377	51,644	287	11,569
Occidental Life Ins. Co.	1,937,977	961,014	4,805	17,190
Old Republic Life Ins. Co.	11,235,580	4,344,076	15,317	2,844,824
Paul Revere Life Ins. Co.	146			36
Pacific Mutual Life Ins. Co.	123,441	57,720	1,045	5,967
Provident Life & Accident	1,184	1,366		54
Prudential Ins. Co. of America	26,413,768	17,358,900	112,866	266,447
Security Mutual Life Ins.	52,853	40,775	832	5,723
State Mutual Life Assur. Co.	24,265	11,537		4,962
Travellers Ins. Co.	1,154,117	713,763		28,304
Union Casualty & Life Ins. Co.	26,497	30,402		1,136
Union Central Life Ins. Co.	319,632	178,196		23,671
Union Labor Life Ins. Co.	13,819	18,205	34	
United Benefit Life Ins. Co.	15,447	5,961		1,103
United States Life Ins. Co.	236,029	76,205		6,605
Washington National Ins. Co.	448,644	301,987		20,054
Woodmen Accident & Life Co.	10,096	5,632		245
Total	$62,795,425	$36,319,419 (57.8%)	$1,58,755 (0.3%)	$4,144,441 (6.6%)

(5)	(6)	(7)	(8)	(9)	(10)	(11)	(12)
General Insurance Expense	Taxes, Licenses, and Fees	Reserve Increase	Misc.	Total Col. 2–8 Incl.	Net Gain Before Dividends and Retro Crs.	Dividends and Retro Crs.	Net Gain After Dividends and Retro Crs.
$ 34,825	$ 18,359	$ 5,800	$	$ 896,533	$ 154,036	$ 123,340	$ 30,697
3,587	135	6		3,755	−3,351		−3,351
965	346	240		11,029	3,373	2,385	988
950	367	1,981		16,899	−238	2,349	−2,587
1,586	868	125	$ 5,952	34,865	2,790	4,242	−1,452
69,963	36,173	194,408		1,046,170	525,817	245,038	280,779
89,622	64,018	158,837		1,786,013	979,822	371,517	608,305
175,399	28,511	129,335		867,524	157,564		157,564
895,850	125,807	135,945		8,049,049	1,970,427	1,969,275	1,152
12,570	6,842	−6,785		290,399	80,028	77,000	3,028
76	18	28		319	198		198
109,196	16,260	222,785	7,001	564,502	11,893		11,893
57	17	31		239	328		328
47,697	18,255	39,301	7,297	594,484	374,912	323,840	51,072
100		926		1,202	143		143
8,712	2,998	1,120	43	115,187	16,484	9,354	7,130
82,886	16,021	177,070		723,705	163,171	233,630	−70,459
52	41			3,073	−767	51	−818
17,406	608	20,250		48,695	−18,271	5,204	−23,475
284	46			1,964	347		347
7,706	761			26,364	7,761	7,741	20
139,289	19,551	8,329		1,104,372	−37,787	145,288	−183,075
41,294	3,702	−313		105,628	9,861	2,727	7,134
	13	745		922	−265		−265
853	571	203		18,126	−741	2,552	−3,292
3,265	1,486	5,474		73,724	−347		−347
95,719	34,741	122,089		1,235,559	702,418	580,309	122,109
598,627	461,757	2,041,196		10,305,798	929,782	405,979	523,803
281	3	30		351	−204		−204
12,706	1,172	−3,854		75,356	48,085	33,026	15,059
41	33			1,495	−310		−310
925,947	642,627	469,841	61,435	19,838,064	6,575,704	7,088,420	−512,716
4,492	1,096	−13,282		39,636	13,217	9,016	4,201
3,161	651	−58		20,253	4,011	933	3,078
98,103	19,254	29,006		888,430	265,687	237,265	28,422
1,630	540	162		33,545	−7,048	1,021	−8,069
46,382	6,798	410		255,457	64,175	97,372	−33,197
648	351	2		19,239	−5,420	4,632	−10,052
441	209	−679		7,036	8,411	892	7,519
30,003	9,140	3,250		125,203	110,826	80,974	29,851
39,309	14,125	−58,807		316,668	131,975	118,706	13,269
2,337	384	1,263		9,860	236	2,032	−1,796
$3,604,017	$1,554,655	$3,686,410	$81,728	$49,556,692	$13,238,733	$12,186,110	$1,052,624
(5.7%)	(2.5%)	(5.9%)	(0.1%)		(21.1%)	(19.4%)	(1.7%)

TABLE XXIV

CONSUMER CREDIT LIFE AND ACCIDENT AND HEALTH EXPERIENCE
COMPANIES DOING BUSINESS IN WISCONSIN FOR THE YEAR 1955
ORDINARY BASIS

Ordinary Level-Term Life	(1) Gross Premiums	(2) Less Return Premiums on Canceled Pol.	(3) Col. 1 Mi-nus Col. 2	(4) Losses	(5) Loss Expense	(6) Com-missions
Continental Assur. Co.	$ 136,942		$ 136,942	$ 27,697	$ 114	$ 82,162
Credit Life Ins. Co.	1,889,626	$ 560,628	1,328,998	280,034		554,301
Independence Life & Accident	2,493	79	2,414	592	59	1,207
North Amer. Life and Cas.	12,911	2,054	10,857	1,366		5,799
North Central Life Ins. Co.	445,808	24,965	420,843	86,491		198,699
Old Republic Life Ins. Co.	2,410,715	223,170	2,187,545	526,414	1,890	1,217,815
Total	$ 4,898,495	810,896	$4,087,599	$ 922,594 (22.6%)	$2,063	$2,059,983 (50.4%)

Ordinary Decreasing-Term Life

	Gross Premiums	Less Return Premiums on Canceled Pol.	Col. 1 Mi-nus Col. 2	Losses	Loss Expense	Com-missions
Connecticut General Life	$ 4,963		$ 4,963			
Continental Assur. Co.	68,402		68,402	$ 13,892	$ 57	$ 41,041
Credit Life Ins. Co.	5,042,361	$ 771,600	4,270,760	990,236	228	1,741,755
Independence Life & Accident	15,063	476	14,587	3,576	358	7,294
Life Ins. Co. of America	218,553	8,660	209,893	8,258		10,523
North American Accident Ins.	165	41	124			37
North Amer. Life & Cas. Co.	35,529	3,471	32,058	6,044		16,413
North Central Life	465,064	26,973	438,090	48,332		206,809
Old Republic Life	4,595,813	677,355	3,918,458	1,208,218	4,339	2,151,082
United Benefit Life	20	4,243	−4,223	4,959		−1,988
Wisconsin National Life	11,388	2,263	9,125			
Total	$10,457,321	$1,495,082	$8,962,237	$2,283,515 (25.5%)	$4,982	$4,172,966 (46.6%)

to the Wisconsin Insurance Department and included in this study is as follows:

Consumer Credit Life Insurance

Group basis		$62,795,425
Ordinary basis		
Level term	$4,087,599	
Decreasing term	8,962,237	
Total ordinary consumer credit life		$13,049,836
Total consumer credit life insurance		$75,845,261

Consumer Credit Accident and Health Insurance

Group basis		$ 4,790,222
Ordinary basis		5,192,057
Total consumer credit A & H insurance		$ 9,982,279
Total consumer credit insurance on a net premium basis		$85,827,540

Losses, loss expense, general insurance expenses, taxes, licenses and fees, reserve increase (and decrease), net gain before dividends and retrospective credits and net gain after dividends and retrospective credits were calculated as a percentage of net premiums. Ratios de-

(7) Gen. Ins. Exp.	(8) Taxes, Licenses, and Fees	(9) Reserve Increase	(10) Total Col. 4–9 Incl.	(11) Net Gain Before Dividends and Retr. Crs.	(12) Dividends and Retr. Crs.	(13) Net Gain After Dividends and Retr. Crs.	(14) Amt. Of Ins. In Force 12–31–55
$ 4,437	$ 3,170	$ −1,665	$ 115,919	$ 21,024		$ 21,024	$ 6,752,763
257,403	35,460	67,580	1,194,777	134,221		134,221	81,085,173
422	59	432	2,772	−357		−357	118,197
2,503	348		10,016	841		841	800,242
63,165	13,632	34,425	396,412	24,431	$22,313	2,118	17,909,735
508,248	89,543	−261,784	2,082,126	105,419		105,419	207,142,128
$ 836,178	$142,212	$ −161,012	$3,802,022	$ 285,579	$22,313	$ 263,266	$ 313,808,238
(20.5%)	(3.5%)	(−3.9%)		(6.9%)		(6.4%)	
$ 264	$ 116	$ 311	$ 691	$ 4,272		$ 4,272	$ 257,950
2,216	1,581	2,347	61,137	7,266		7,266	3,147,310
832,189	113,973	189,590	3,867,971	402,789		402,789	250,906,993
2,552	357	2,610	16,747	−2,159		−2,159	715,406
19,415	336	70,542	109,074	100,819		100,819	10,214,748
17	6	−110	−50	174		174	4,406
7,391	1,027	88	30,964	1,094		1,094	1,200,362
65,743	14,208	59,927	395,019	43,071	$23,224	19,848	17,585,845
968,929	170,706	−1,087,742	3,415,531	502,927		502,927	860,697,051
		−20,896	−17,925	13,703		13,703	514,304
1,368	630	2,757	4,775	4,370		4,370	
$1,900,084	$302,940	$780,570	$7,883,934	$1,078,326	$23,224	$1,055,103	$1,145,244,375
(21.2%)	(3.4%)	(− 8.7%)		(12.0%)			

veloped from these figures for consumer credit life insurance are shown in table XXVI. From this table it will be noted that the loss ratios for group, ordinary level term, and ordinary decreasing term were 57.8, 22.6, and 25.5 per cent respectively.[5]

Ratios developed on a similar basis from these Exhibits for consumer credit accident and health insurance are contained in Table XXVII.

By combining loss expense, general insurance expense, taxes, licenses and fees, and miscellaneous expenses into a single category, expense, and by combining the consumer credit life experience with

---

[5] A study in 1954 conducted by the Consumer Credit Division of the Wisconsin State Banking Department on consumer credit life insurance sold by small-loan licensees was made on the basis of written premiums to paid losses. The total net premium volume included in this study was $620,493 and was broken down between licensees operating under Wisconsin Statutes 115.07 and 115.09. The loss ratios developed were 24.04 and 22.41 per cent respectively.

For a further description of this study, see the "Annual Report on the Operations of Small Loan Companies, Discount Companies, Foreign Exchange Companies, Community Currency Exchange and Collection Agencies for 1954," State Banking Department of Wisconsin, p. 7.

TABLE XXV

CONSUMER CREDIT LIFE AND ACCIDENT AND HEALTH EXPERIENCE
COMPANIES DOING BUSINESS IN WISCONSIN FOR THE YEAR 1955
ACCIDENT AND HEALTH

	(1)	(2)	(3)	(4)	(5)	(6)
Group Accident and Health	*Gross Premiums*	*Less Return Premiums on Canceled Pol.*	*Col. 1 Minus Col. 2*	*Losses*	*Loss Expense*	*Com-missions*
Amer. Cas. Co. of Read. Pa.	$ 494,768		$ 494,768	$ 86,733	$ 510	$ 241,818
Continental Casualty Co.	1,807,452		1,807,452	388,360	43,216	1,087,069
Credit Life Ins. Co.	110,375		110,375	28,055		33,420
Federal Life & Casualty	494,327		494,327	93,166	4,739	89,664
LaFayette Life	2,672		2,672	153		801
Monarch Life	2,254		2,254	862		28
North American Life & Cas.	37,422		37,422	6,989		4,596
North Central Life	2,839		2,839	371		172
Occidental Life Ins. Co.	675		675	242	5	113
Old Republic Life Ins. Co.	1,807,631		1,807,631	771,535	7,678	−121,703
Transportation Ins. Co.	881		881		4	264
Union Cas, & Life Ins. Co.	1,104		1,104	713	104	38
U.S. Life Ins. Co. of N.Y.	1,732		1,732	1,866		−139
Woodmen Accident & Life	26,090		26,090	9,932	605	805
Total	$4,790,222		$4,790,222	$1,388,977	$56,861	$1,336,944
				(29.0%)	(1.2%)	(27.9%)

Ordinary Accident and Health

Central National Ins. Co.	$ 198,034	$ 19,217	$ 178,817	$ 32,087	$−1,207	$ 111,497
Continental Cas. Co.	1,312,769	120,819	1,191,949	238,557	21,806	435,979
Credit Life Ins. Co.	2,612,369	497,659	2,114,710	748,918	1,304	855,292
Federal Life & Cas.	97,033	12,656	84,377	21,431	1,090	945
North Amer. Accident Ins. Co.	658		658	344		230
North Amer. Life & Cas. Co.	8,094	4,685	3,408	5,553		1,709
North Central Life Ins. Co.	160,639	9,976	150,663	23,523		63,934
Old Republic Life	745,579	181,546	564,033	80,626	10,026	−130,488
Transportation Ins. Co.	5,862	324	5,538	317	60	2,358
U.S. Life Ins. Co. of N.Y.	49,491	1,087	48,404	18,123	427	15,478
Wis. Nat. Life Ins. Co.	1,529	186	1,343			
Total	$5,192,057	$848,155	$4,343,900	$1,169,479	$33,506	$1,356,934
				(26.9%)	(0.8%)	(31.2%)

TABLE XXVI

CONSUMER CREDIT LIFE INSURANCE RATIOS OF COMPANIES DOING BUSINESS IN
WISCONSIN
(Based on Net Earned Premiums)

		Ordinary	
	Group	*Level Term*	*Decreasing Term*
Losses	57.8%	22.6%	25.5%
Loss expenses	0.3	. . .	. . .
Commissions	6.6	50.4	46.6
General insurance expense	5.7	20.5	21.2
Taxes, licenses, and fees	2.5	3.5	3.4
Reserve increase	5.9	−3.9	−8.7
Miscellaneous	0.1	. . .	. . .
Net gain before dividends and retrospective credits	21.1	6.9	12.0
	100.0%	100.0%	100.0%

(7)	(8)	(9)	(10)	(11)	(12)	(13)	(14)
Gen. Ins. Exp.	Taxes, Licenses, and Fees	Reserve Increase	Misc.	Total Col. 4–10 Incl.	Net Gain Before Dividends and Retr. Crs.	Dividends and Retr. Crs.	Net Gain After Dividends And Retr. Crs.
$ 15,889	$ 9,877	$ 10,036		$ 364,863	$ 129,905		$ 129,905
255,836	32,844	29,640		1,836,964	−29,512		−29,512
1,348	2,769	61,219		126,810	−16,434		−16,434
93,997	13,940	213,285	$6,487	515,279	−20,952		−20,952
300		2,381		3,635	−963		−963
197	58	2,124		3,269	−1,016	$ 167	−1,182
11,138	1,267	11,613		35,602	1,820		1,820
162	57	129		892	1,947		1,947
205	22	−109		477	198		198
196,895	66,241	239,131		1,159,777	647,854	638,306	9,548
26	103	761		1,159	−278		−278
260	25	−1,511		−372	1,476		1,476
70	35	262		2,095	−362		−362
3,461	608			15,411	10,680	5,812	4,868
$579,784	$127,846	$ 568,961	$6,487	$4,065,861	$ 724,363	$644,285	$ 80,079
(12.1%)	(2.7%)	(11.9%)	(.1%)		(15.1%)		(1.7%)
$ 4,955	$ 4,108	$ 22,228		$ 173,668	$ 5,148		$ 5,148
129,094	16,573	399,729		1,241,738	−49,789		−49,789
178,240	58,283	569,790		2,411,827	−297,117		−297,117
15,809	2,386	6,915	$ 683	49,261	35,116		35,116
				574	84		84
751	115	−8,384		−255	3,664		3,664
17,109	3,035	38,767		146,369	4,295		4,295
257,100	76,614	299,215		593,092	−29,059		−29,059
353	245	3,437		6,770	−1,232		−1,232
6,510	1,139	30,772		72,449	−24,045		−24,045
201	336	508		1,045	298		298
$610,122	$162,834	$1,362,977	683	$4,696,538	$−352,637		$−352,637
(14.0%)	(3.8%)	(31.4%)			(−8.1%)		(−8.1%)

TABLE XXVII

Consumer Credit Accident and Health Insurance Ratios of Companies Doing Business in Wisconsin

	Group	Ordinary
Losses	29.0%	26.9%
Loss expense	1.2	0.8
Commissions	27.9	31.2
General insurance expense	12.1	14.0
Taxes, licenses, and fees	2.7	3.8
Reserve increase	11.9	31.4
Miscellaneous	0.1	. . .
Net gain before dividends and retrospective credits	15.1	−8.1
	100.0%	100.0%

that of consumer credit accident and health into a single exhibit, results are produced as embodied in Table XXVIII.

By removing expenses and commissions from the data, expense ratios by line are calculated as in Table XXIX.

TABLE XXVIII

CONSOLIDATED EXPERIENCE, CONSUMER CREDIT LIFE AND ACCIDENT AND HEALTH INSURANCE OF COMPANIES DOING BUSINESS IN WISCONSIN

	Group Life	Ord. Level Term	Ord. Decr. Term	Group A&H	Ord. A&H
Losses	57.8%	22.6%	25.5%	29.0%	26.9%
Expenses	8.6	24.0	24.6	16.1	18.6
Reserve increase	5.9	−3.9	−8.7	11.9	31.4
Commissions	6.6	50.4	46.6	27.9	31.2
Retrospective credits	19.4	0.5	0.2	13.4	. . .
Gain	1.7	6.4	11.8	1.7	−8.1
	100.0%	100.0%	100.0%	100.0%	100.0%

TABLE XXIX

CONSUMER CREDIT INSURANCE EXPENSE RATIOS, BY LINE, OF COMPANIES DOING BUSINESS IN WISCONSIN

	Expenses	Com- missions	Total Expense Ratios
Group life insurance (58% of total premiums)	8.6%	6.6%	15.2%
Ordinary level term	24.0	50.4	74.4
Ordinary decreasing term (61% of business in force)	24.6	46.6	71.2
Group A&H	16.1	27.9	44.0
Ordinary A&H (25% of total premiums, estimated)	18.6	31.2	49.8

CONCLUSIONS APPLICABLE TO THIS STUDY

1. Reference to Table XXVIII will indicate that the loss payment ratio calculated as a percentage of premiums for consumer credit life insurance on the group basis is about twice that of coverage written on the ordinary basis.[6] The ratios of 57.8 per cent for the group coverage

---

[6] Although it is technically incorrect to speak of loss ratios in life insurance, the term is retained here for both life and accident and health insurance for purposes of consistency.

as compared with 22.6 and 25.5 per cent for ordinary level and decreasing term respectively were developed from a rate of approximately $0.49 per $100 of insurance for group and $1.00 per $100 for ordinary. Thus it is evident that the consumer credit life insurers operating on the group basis return approximately $0.28 in loss payments *for each $0.49 in premiums,* while insurers operating on the ordinary basis return approximately $0.23 to $0.26 *for each $1.00 in premiums.*

2. Table XXVIII indicates that loss ratios for group and ordinary consumer credit accident and health insurance are fairly comparable, the former recording a 29.0 per cent ratio and the latter a 26.9 per cent ratio. The present policy of the New York State Insurance Department regarding the reasonableness of a loss ratio for this line of coverage is as follows: "Credit accident and health policies do not afford substantially full coverage in a limited area and therefore should produce a loss ratio of *at least 50 per cent* even if the single or annual premium is less than $10."[7] (Italics added.)

It appears that the companies reporting to the Wisconsin Insurance Department did not comply with this minimum.

3. Percentagewise, commissions on ordinary consumer credit life insurance were approximately six to seven times greater than under the group plan. Table XXVIII indicates commissions of 50.4 and 46.6 per cent for level-term and decreasing-term life insurance respectively and 6.6 per cent for group. It should be mentioned that, insofar as these figures include contingent commissions, it might be argued that such contingent compensation should not be included since it is a retroactive payment based upon a given group's mortality. On the other hand these payments, although dependent upon subsequently developed experience of the insureds of a particular agent—the insured borrowers of a lender-agent—are nevertheless properly classified as acquisition cost and therefore should be included in the category of commissions.

The substantial differences in commissions paid to writers of group insurance as compared to writers of ordinary insurance should be further considered in relation to the operational aspects of each type of coverage. Group consumer credit life insurance generally supports the American agency system by utilizing existing channels of acquisition. Commissioned agents are insurance company representatives and are not connected in any way with the lending institution. Compensation to such agents has been found to average 6.6 per cent of group premiums, as per Table XXVIII. Lenders subscribing to a group plan

---

[7] Max J. Schwartz, *Examination of Insurance Companies,* a series of lectures delivered before the examiners of the New York State Insurance Department, Albany, New York, 1955, Vol. 6, p. 447.

receive premium refunds or dividends if their experience warrants it. This study indicates that 19.4 per cent of premiums are returned to lender-policyholders. It is true that a dividend cannot be considered an expense of doing business since it is formulated *after* expenses have been determined. However, the *effect* of such returns, which accrue to the lender's benefit, is similar to the compensation paid to a lender-agent under ordinary consumer credit insurance in that both are forms of reimbursement for the lender's administrative expenses. It might well be argued that to establish a common basis of comparison between group and ordinary consumer credit insurance, premium refunds and dividends, that is, retrospective credits to commissions, should properly be added. If this were done, consumer credit insurance written on the group basis would then register a 26 per cent acquisition cost (19.4 per cent in retrospective credits plus 6.6 per cent in commissions), compared to 50.4 and 46.6 per cent for ordinary consumer credit life insurance written on the level-term and decreasing-term plan respectively. The result is that acquisition costs for coverage on the ordinary basis then become about twice those for the group plan.

4. Differences between commissions for group consumer credit accident and health insurance written on the ordinary basis, 27.9 and 31.2 per cent respectively, are relatively insignificant. However, if retrospective credits are added to commissions and if the reasoning and method used to establish acquisition costs are accepted as in conclusion 3, group consumer credit accident and health would register a cost of 41.3 per cent (27.9 per cent in commissions plus 13.4 per cent for retrospective credits) and coverage written on the ordinary basis would produce a 31.2 per cent acquisition cost.

5. Expenses (excluding acquisition costs) of companies offering group consumer credit life insurance are about one-third of the expenses of companies operating on the ordinary plan. This is to be expected because of the necessarily higher expenses of writing this coverage on the ordinary basis due to the more detailed records and other costs incurred by ordinary insurers.

6. Expenses (excluding acquisition costs) on group consumer credit accident and health insurance are within 2.5 percentage points of the expenses of companies writing on the ordinary basis. Because of this insignificant difference, it would appear that there is very little difference between the group and the ordinary basis in the efficiency of administration of this coverage.

7. Companies operating under the group consumer credit life insurance plan realized a 1.7 per cent gain after dividends and premium refunds, while the ordinary insurers operating under the level-term and decreasing-term method averaged 6.4 and 11.8 per cent respec-

tively. These latter figures are not too meaningful since no consideration is given to investment income from this business.

8. Insurers operating under the group and ordinary method of insuring consumer credit accident and health recorded a 7.7 and −8.1 per cent profit and loss respectively. At the same time, the largest reserve increase was noted under ordinary consumer credit accident and health insurance. The loss may thus be partially attributed to the large reserve increase, which in turn has probably resulted from a significant increase in new business.

9. Table XXIX indicates the development of a total expense ratio of 74.4 per cent on level term and 71.2 per cent on decreasing term for ordinary consumer credit life insurance. It must be concluded that such expense ratios are excessive and attributable mainly to the current high level of commissions. Both the study by the Beneficial Management Corporation cited in Chapter VI and the joint American Life Convention–Life Insurance Association of America proposal referred to in Chapter IV concluded that reasonable maximum compensation to lender-agents should be $0.40 per $100 of insurance.

10. In summary, it appears that the group method of consumer credit life insurance affords a more efficient method of providing coverage than does the ordinary method. This is borne out statistically by the higher returns to insureds in the form of losses, the lower expenses and profit ratios, and the decidedly lower premium rates for group insurance. It further appears that the loss ratios for ordinary *and* group consumer credit accident and health coverage are lower than those prescribed by insurance regulatory officials.

Although expenses are necessarily higher under the ordinary method of insuring, it appears quite conclusive that the major contributing factor is the current high level of commissions paid to lenders.

Appendix G

RESULTS OF A STUDY OF GROUP CONSUMER CREDIT LIFE INSURANCE
CONDUCTED BY THE STATE FARM LIFE INSURANCE COMPANY

We have recently summarized our Creditor's Group Life experience
from our re-entry 1950 to the policy anniversary date in 1955. For
expenses we have used (1) 2 per cent of total premiums for premium
tax, (2) actual commissions paid, (3) actual claims paid, (4) actual
dividends paid, (5) $51 per policy year plus 2 per cent of total pre-
miums for administrative expense.

Sixty-three policies have completed one or more years for a total of
173 complete policy years.

For All Policy Years Completed as of 12–31–55

		Per cent of Premium
Premiums collected	$344,824.40	100.0
Less claims	156,994.82	45.5
	$187,829.58	
Less total expense*	40,933.67	11.9
	$146,895.91	
Less dividends	104,141.06	30.2
Contribution to surplus	$ 42,754.85	12.4

* Includes premium taxes, commissions, administrative
expense.

For Last Completed Policy Year (Ending in 1955)

		Per cent of Premium
Premiums collected	$144,901.34	100.0
Less claims	68,920.11	47.6
	$ 75,981.23	
Less total expense*	16,498.41	11.4
	$ 59,482.82	
Less dividends	45,689.45	31.5
Contribution to surplus	$ 13,793.37	9.5

* Includes premium taxes, commissions, administrative
expense.

No contingency reserve of any sort has been provided for in arriving
at the contribution-to-surplus figure.

194

On 18 of the 63 cases we have a *negative* contribution to surplus. Many cases are not supporting themselves but require funds from the group as a whole to pay expenses and minimum dividends. Two of the cases account for 51.8 per cent ($22,139.54) of the contribution to surplus (an average of $2767.44 per policy year). These two cases plus the next four largest contributions, contributed 81.4 per cent ($34,-795.09) of the contribution to surplus (an average of $1,512.83 per policy year). The other 57 cases made an average contribution of $53.07 per policy year to surplus. All cases except the highest two contributed an average of $124.94 per policy year to surplus.

Bibliography

GENERAL

BERGENGREN, ROY F. *Crusade.* New York: Exposition Press, 1952.

Best's Life Insurance Reports. New York: Alfred M. Best Co., Inc., 1956.

BOYD, MELVIN T., and STEFFEY, FRED H. "North Carolina Acts to Curb Small Loan Abuses," *Personal Finance Law Quarterly Report,* Vol. 9, No. 4 (Fall, 1955), p. 107.

BRIDGE, HARRY P. *Practical Advertising.* New York: Rinehart and Co., 1949.

BRYSON, DEAN F. "Oregon Enacts Consumer Finance Act," *Personal Finance Law Quarterly Report,* Vol. 9, No. 2 (Spring, 1955), p. 36.

BUCK, HAROLD. "Credit Life, Health and Accident Insurance: Functions and Operations," *Insurance Law Journal* (June, 1953).

BULEY, R. C. *The American Life Convention.* New York: Appleton-Century-Crofts, Inc., 1953.

CADE, ARTHUR J. "The Fundamental Issues of Consumer Credit Insurance," *The Insurance Law Journal* (February, 1955), p. 76.

"Cade Warns Credit Insurance in Danger of Over-Regulation," *National Underwriter* (March 12, 1954), p. 20.

CHRISTY, ROBERT H. "Credit Life, Health and Accident Insurance and the Small Loan Industry in Indiana," *Insurance Law Journal* (July, 1954), p. 465.

CONFERENCE DIRECTORY. The Health and Accident Underwriter Conference, Chicago.

CONSUMER CREDIT INSURANCE ASSOCIATION. "Articles of Incorporation." Chicago.

———. "Fact Sheet on Consumer Credit Insurance," Chicago, July, 1953.

———. "How Consumer Credit Insurance Protects You and Your Family," Chicago.

———. "What About Consumer Credit Insurance," Chicago, 15 pages.

COX, REAVIS. The Economics of Installment Buying. New York: The Ronald Press Co., 1948.

"Credit A & S Rates Reduced in Texas," *National Underwriter* (May 4, 1956).

"Credit Assn. Hails Code," *National Underwriter* (August 21, 1953), p. 11.

"Credit Insurance: Expansion Ahead," *The Management Review* (March, 1953), p. 176.

"Credit Insurance Rules and Regulations Adopted by Insurance Commissioners," *Personal Finance Law Quarterly Report,* Vol. 8, No. 4 (Fall, 1954), p. 109.

"Credit: Less Stimulus for '56," *Business Week* (January 28, 1956), p. 48.

"Credit Life, A.&H. Practices, Theories Sharply Challenged," *The National Underwriter* (December 11, 1952), p. 19.

"Credit Life and Disability Insurance—Should It Be Sold in Connection with Small Loans?", *Conference of Personal Finance Law,* 1952–53.

"Credit Life Has 40-Fold Gain in Ten-Year Period," *The American Banker* (December 22, 1955).

"Credit Life Insurance Aids Time Purchases," *Woman's Wear Daily* (June 7, 1955).

"Cuna Mutual Insurance Society Annual Reports," Madison, Wis., 1954, 1955, and 1956.

DARR, J. REUBEN. "Refund Installment Loan Charges and Consumer Credit Insurance Premiums." New York: Bankers Security Life Insurance Society, 1956.

"Definite Rules on Credit Life and A&H Urged by NAIC Subcommittee," *National Underwriter* (December 12, 1952), p. 19.

DUNBAR, EDWARD A. "Group Life Insurance Approved in Vermont," *Personal Finance Law Quarterly Report,* Vol. 9, No. 3 (Summer, 1955), p. 82.

————. "Langer Committee Reports on Credit Insurance," *Personal Finance Law Quarterly Report,* Vol. 9, No. 2 (Spring, 1955), p. 58.

DUNKMAN, WILLIAM E. "Second Annual New York State Consumer Credit Conference," *Personal Finance Law Quarterly Report,* Vol. 9, No. 3 (Summer, 1955), p. 74.

EVANS, TOM. "Insurance Scheme Held Usurious in Kansas," *Personal Finance Quarterly Report,* Vol. 9, No. 2 (Spring, 1955), p. 39.

FAULKNER, E. J. "An Underwriter Looks at Insurance in Connection with Lending," *Quarterly Report* (Winter, 1951).

FEDERAL RESERVE BANK OF CHICAGO. "Changing Fashions in Department Store Credit," *Business Conditions* (December, 1955).

FRENCH, WALTER B. "Small Loans, An Investment for Banks." Cambridge: Bankers Publishing Co., 1937.

FRITZ, EDWARD C. "Damages Assessed Against Three Texas Lenders for Usury and Abusive Collection Efforts," *Personal Finance Law Quarterly Report,* Vol. 9, No. 3 (Summer, 1955), p. 99.

GANE, F. H. "A New Appraisal of the Small Loan Business," *Business Education World* (May, 1954), p. 9.

GOEBEL, SYL H. "Kentucky Insurance Commissioner Praises Credit Insurance," *Personal Finance Quarterly Report,* Vol. 8, No. 4 (Fall, 1954), p. 111.

GREENE, J. THOMAS. "Utah Amends Loan Laws," *Personal Finance Law Quarterly Report,* Vol. 9, No. 3 (Summer, 1955), p. 90.

GREGG, D. N. "An Analysis of Group Life Insurance." Philadelphia: University of Pennsylvania Press, 1950.

GROBBEN, M. M. *The Cooperative Loan Agency.* New York: Consumer Credit Institute of America, 1937.

HOUSEHOLD FINANCE CORPORATION. "Cost of Administering HFC Insurance Program," the results of a survey made, 1956.

"Household Finance Introduces Group Life: Again Scores Extra Insurance Charge," *National Underwriter* (March 20, 1953), p. 8.

HUBACHEK, F. B. "Annotations on Small Loan Laws." New York: Russel Sage Foundation, 1938.

————. "Progress and Problems in Regulation of Consumer Credit," *Law and Contemporary Problems,* Vol. 19, No. 1 (Winter, 1954).

————. "The Drift Toward a Consumer Credit Code," *The University of Chicago Law Review,* Vol. 16, No. 4 (Summer, 1949).

HUEBNER, S. S. "Life Insurance." New York: Appleton-Century-Crofts, Inc., 1950.

"Illinois Credit Insurance Regulations Invalid in Part," *Personal Finance Law Quarterly Review,* Vol. 9, No. 4 (Fall, 1955), p. 116.

ILSE, L. W. "Group Insurance and Employee Retirement Plans," New York: Prentice-Hall, Inc., 1953.

"In a Boom Built on Credit," *Business Week* (March 10, 1956).

"In the Best American Tradition," a brochure published by The Prudential Insurance Company of America, 4 pages.

"Injunction Sought Against South Carolina Lender," *Personal Finance Law Quarterly Report,* Vol. 8, No. 4 (Fall, 1954), p. 112.

"Installment Credit Outstanding," *Business Week* (October 15, 1955), p. 92.

INSTITUTE OF LIFE INSURANCE. "Credit Life Insurance in the United States" (June, 1954, and April, 1955).

"Insurance—Billion Dollar Baby," *Time* (July 21, 1952).

IRELAND, GAIL L. "Colorado Forges Ahead in Credit Insurance Recognition," *Personal Finance Law Quarterly Report,* Vol. 9, No. 3 (Summer, 1955), p. 80.

————. "Life Insurance Fact Book," New York, 1955, 1956.

JOHNSON, HAROLD. "Nebraska Has No Loan Shark Problem," *Law and Contemporary Problems,* Vol. 19, No. 1 (Winter, 1954).

"Justice Department Obtains Judgment Against Tie-In Insurance Practice," *Personal Finance Law Quarterly Report,* Vol. 8, No. 4 (Fall, 1954), p. 108.

KAVANAUGH, LUKE J. "Federal Report on Consumer Credit Insurance and Small Loans Analyzed," *The Industrial Banker* (April, 1955).

KEDZIE, DANIEL P. "Present Status, Characteristics and Trends," *Insurance Law Journal* (June, 1957), p. 334.

KENNEY, ROGER. "The Dangers in This Credit Life Insurance Squabble," *United States Investor* (December 22, 1956), p. 1.

KRAMER, ROBERT. *Law and Contemporary Problems,* Vol. 19, No. 1 (Winter, 1954), preface.

KRUEGER, HARRY, and WAGGONER, LELAND T. "The Life Insurance Policy Contract." Boston: Little, Brown and Co., 1953.

KULP, C. A. "Casualty Insurance." New York: The Ronald Press Co., 1956.

"Langer Committee Hearing on Credit Insurance Open in Kansas," *Personal Finance Law Quarterly Report,* Vol. 8, No. 4 (Fall, 1954), p. 99.

LATCHAW, J. R. "Worry-Proofing Your Borrowers," *Time Sales Financing,* Vol. 16, Nos. 3 and 4.

Law and Contemporary Problems, School of Law, Duke University, Vol. VII, No. 1 (Winter, 1941), Vol. 19, No. 1 (Winter, 1954).

"Legislative Probe of Credit Insurance Sought in Indiana," *National Underwriter* (November 18, 1955), p. 3.

"Life Insurance Ownership Among American Families 1951." Ann Arbor, Mich.: Survey Research Center, Institute for Social Research, University of Michigan, 1951.

LIND, STANLEY L. "Kansas Adopts Consumer Loan Act," *Personal Finance Law Quarterly Report,* Vol. 9, No. 3 (Summer, 1955), p. 69.

LONGGOOD, WILLIAM. "Watch Out for Those Gyp Car Deals," *The Saturday Evening Post* (October 29, 1955), p. 27.

MACLEAN, JOSEPH B. "Life Insurance," New York: McGraw-Hill Book Co., Inc., 1945.

MAGEE, JOHN H. *General Insurance.* Homewood, Ill.: Richard D. Irwin, Inc., 1953.

MCATEE, W. PETER. "New Mexico Revises Small Loan Law," *Personal Finance Law Quarterly Report,* Vol. 9, No. 3 (Summer, 1955), p. 85.

MCCAHAN, DAVID. *Accident and Sickness Insurance.* Philadelphia: University of Pennsylvania Press, 1954.

MCCAULEY, J. L. "Don't Be Confused About Credit Insurance," *The American Agency Bulletin* (April, 1955), p. 25.

MEHR, ROBERT I., and CAMMACK, EMERSON. "Principles of Insurance." Homewood, Ill.: Richard D. Irwin, Inc., 1953.

———, and OSLER, ROBERT W. *Modern Life Insurance.* New York: The Macmillan Co., 1956.

MICHELBACHER, G. F. *Casualty Insurance Principles.* 2nd ed.; New York: McGraw-Hill Book Co., Inc., 1942.

MORS, WALLACE P. "A&H As Credit Insurance—How Is Its Reputation?", *The A & H Underwriter* (May, 1955), p. 17.

———. "Consumer Instalment Credit Insurance," *The Insurance Law Journal* (May, 1956), p. 299.

———. "Small Loans and Credit Insurance," *Insurance Law Journal* (December, 1954), p. 778.

MOWBRAY, ALBERT H., and BLANCHARD, RALPH H. *Insurance, Its Theory and Practice in the United States.* New York: McGraw-Hill Book Co., Inc., 1955.

"NAIC Unit Studying Credit Cover Rules Advocates Uniformity," *National Underwriter* (September 4, 1953), p. 6.

NEIFEILD, M. R. "Institutional Organization of Consumer Credit," *Law and Contemporary Problems,* Vol. VIII, No. 1, (Winter, 1941).

"New Rules in Texas on Credit Insurance," *National Underwriter,* (December 12, 1952), p. 26.

"1955 Survey of Consumer Finances—Housing Arrangements of Consumers," *Federal Reserve Bulletin* (August, 1955).

"1955 Survey of Consumer Finances—Purchases of Durable Goods in 1954," *Federal Reserve Bulletin* (May, 1955).

"1955 Survey of Consumer Finances—the Financial Position of Consumers," *Federal Reserve Bulletin* (June, 1955).

PARISH, WILLIAM J. "Credit Insurance and the Small Loan Industry," *New Mexico Business,* Vol. 6, No. 6 (June, 1953), p. 3.

PEARSON, KARL G. "The Small Loan Business—Saint or Sinner," *Business Education World* (November and December, 1953), p. 10.

"Preliminary Findings of the 1955 Survey of Consumer Finances," *Federal Reserve Bulletin* (March, 1955).

Proceedings of the National Consumer Credit Conference for 1954. Los Angeles: University of Southern California Press, 1954.

"Prosperity on the Installment Plan," *National City Bank Letter* (July, 1955), pp. 80–83.

"Prudential Group-Creditor Coverage Takes $2 Billion in Less Than 25 Years," *National Underwriter* (November 28, 1952), p. 4.

"Prudential Group Creditors Life Insurance," a brochure by the Prudential Press, March, 1953.

PUBLIC AFFAIRS COMMITTEE. "Credit for Consumers," *Public Affairs Pamphlets,* No. 5. Washington, D.C., 1936.

RHODUS, H. LEE. "Consumer Credit Insurance—Cushion of Security," *The Insurance Educator* (November 11, 1952), p. 1265.

RIEGEL, ROBERT, and MILLER, JEROME S. *Insurance Principles and Practices.* 3rd ed.; New York: Prentice-Hall, Inc., 1947.

ROSENQUIST, ROY. "Creditor Life Insurance: Handful of Cos. Write Vast Volume on Borrowers, Installment-Plan Buyers," *National Underwriter* (October 23, 1953), p. 5.

SANBORN, THEODORE S. "Credit Insurance," *Northwest Insurance News* (August, 1955), p. 12.

————. "Credit Insurance Adds New Income for the Local Agent," *Northwest Insurance News* (September, 1955).

SCHWARTZ, MAX J. "Accident and Health Insurance Rates, Rating Plans, and Commissions," *Examination of Insurance Companies.* Albany, New York: New York State Insurance Department, 1955.

SHENKMAN, ELIA M. "Insurance Against Credit Risks," Westminster, England: P. S. King & Son, Ltd., 1935.

SHEPARD, R. D. "Thirty Six Year Story—Insuring Credit," *The Spectator,* Vol. 161 (July, 1953), p. 18.

"Six Points on Credit," *Insurance Index* (June, 1954), p. 27.

TAFT, FORD S. "Credit Insurance in Wyoming," *Personal Finance Law Quarterly Report,* Vol. 9, No. 3 (Summer, 1955), p. 83.

THROWER, RANDOLPH W. "Georgia Enacts Small Loan Law," *Personal Finance Law Quarterly Report,* Vol. 9, No. 2 (Spring, 1955), p. 33.

U.S. DEPARTMENT OF COMMERCE. *Survey of Current Business.* Vol. 35, No. 8, "Recent Trends in Consumer Credit" (August, 1955), p. 7.

UPGREN, ARTHUR R. *Why Things Look So Good.* Hanover, New Hampshire: Dartmouth College, 1956.

"Urge Early NAIC Action on Guides for Credit Covers," *National Underwriter* (April 30, 1954), p. 1.

VAN SLYCK, WILLARD N. "Insurance Security for Loans—Historical Development of Court-Made Law," *The Journal of the Bar Association of the State of Kansas,* Vol. XXIII, No. 3 (February, 1955), p. 239.

VERNON, DAVID H. "Regulated Credit Life and Disability Insurance and the Small Loan," *New York University Law Review,* Vol. 29, No. 5 (May, 1954), p. 1098.

VICKER, RAY. "How to Worry Proof Your Debts," *Better Homes and Gardens* (March, 1953).

"Warns Credit Insurers of Threatened Dual Regulation by States," *National Underwriter* (June 12, 1953), p. 8.

"Wisconsin Attorney General Rules Banks May Make Credit Insurance Available to Borrowers," *Personal Finance Law Quarterly Report,* Vol. 8, No. 4 (Fall, 1954), p. 113.

PROFESSIONAL JOURNALS

CENTER, CHARLES C. "An Experiment in State Insurance—The Wisconsin State Life Fund," *The Journal of the American Society of Chartered Life Underwriters,* Vol. 5, No. 3 (June, 1951).

GREGORY, JOHN E. "Credit Insurance," *The Casualty Actuarial Society,* Vol. VIII, p. 266–72.

KEDZIE, DANIEL P. "Marketing Consumer Credit Insurance," *Journal of Insurance* (July, 1957).

SOCIETY OF ACTUARIES. "Transactions," 1952 Reports, No. 2, pp. 70–182.

WHITTAKER, E. B. "Creditor Insurance Under Group & Allied Plans," *Record of the American Institute of Actuaries,* XXVI (1937), pp. 193–202.

WHITTAKER, EDMUND D. "Group Creditors Life Insurance," *Journal of the American Society of Chartered Life Underwriters* (June, 1953), pp. 219–24.

THESES, PAPERS, AND STUDIES

"Analysis of the Cost of Handling Credit Life Insurance," a cost study made by Driscoll, Millet & Co. of Philadelphia, sponsored by the Beneficial Management Corporation, Morristown, N.J., February 6, 1956.

"Creditors Group Life Insurance," results of a study by the State Farm Life Insurance Company, Bloomington, Ill., from 1950 to 1955.

DAUER, ERNST A. "Comparative Operating Experience of Consumer Installment Financing Agencies and Commercial Banks," 1929–41 Studies in Consumer Instalment Financing No. 10, National Bureau of Economic Research, 1944, pp. 109–114.

DICKERSON, O. D. "Long Term Guaranteed Renewable Disability Insurance," Harold R. Gordon Memorial Paper (June, 1955).

DUNBAR, EDWARD. "Consumer Instalment Credit Insurance," a paper given before the American Finance Association, New York (December 30, 1955).

DURAND, DAVID. *Risk Elements in Consumer Instalment Financing.* Studies in Instalment Financing, No. 8. New York: National Bureau of Economic Research, 1941.

JACOBSON, JAMES B. *An Analysis of Group Creditors Insurance.* A thesis presented to the faculty of the Department of Finance, University of Southern California, 1955.

MINICK, JOHN B. "Study of Insured and Uninsured Consumer Debts of Deceased Borrowers in the Kansas City Area" Chicago; Consumer Credit Insurance Association (February, 1957).

O'CONNELL, DONALD W. "The Insurability of Credit Risks," a Ph.D. dissertation presented to the faculty of the University of Illinois, 1952.

YOUSRI, ABBAS SOLIMAN. "The Activities of the CUNA Mutual Insurance Society," unpublished Masters thesis, University of Wisconsin, 1951.

CASES AND BRIEFS

Brief of Kansas State Industrial Union Council, As Amicus Curiae in Opposition to Defendant's Demurrers, *State of Kansas* ex rel. *Harold R. Fatzer, Attorney General, Plaintiff,* v. *P. H. Molitor, et al., Def.*

Memorandum Brief Amici Curiae (Old Republic Credit Life Insurance Company of Chicago, Illinois, The Credit Life Insurance Company of Springfield, Ohio, and the Kansas Association of Finance companies), District Court of Wyandotte County, Kansas, *State of Kansas, Harold Fatzer* v. *P. H. Molitor et al.*

Public Law 15, c. 20 (79th Cong. 1st Sess.).

United States v. *South-Eastern Underwriters Association et al.,* 322 U.S. 533 (1944).

GOVERNMENT REPORTS, BILLS, LAWS, AND RULINGS

"Annual Report on the Operations of Small Loan Cos., Discount Loan Cos., Foreign Exchange Cos., Community Currency Exchanges and Collection Agencies for 1954 and 1955," State of Wisconsin Dept. of Banking.

"Credit Life and Accident and Health Exhibit," a supplement to the Annual Statement filed with State Insurance Departments.

"Credit Life and Credit Accident and Health Insurance Rules and Regulations," Bulletin No. 172, Tallahassee, Florida: Office of the State Insurance Commissioner (April 20, 1956).

"Credit Life and Credit Accident and Health Insurance Rules and Regulations," Bulletin No. 172–Supplement A, Tallahassee, Florida: Office of the State Insurance Commissioner, June 4, 1956.

"Creditor's and Debtor's Group Life Insurance," *State of New York Insurance Department,* Circular letter of September 20, 1929, October 14, 1929, August 22, 1940, State of New York Insurance Department.

"Digest of Opinions of the Office of the Comptroller of the Currency Relating to Operations and Powers of National Banks," Washington, D.C., September, 1950, Par. 9420A.

DOWNEY, F. ROGER, "Report on Insurance Charges in Consumer Credit Transactions," submitted to the Superintendent of Insurance, State of New York, January 24, 1957.

Federal Reserve Bulletin, Vol. 41, No. 6 (June, 1955).

HOMAN, LILBURN C. "Special Report to Governor Edwin L. Mechem re: Small Loan Industry in New Mexico," 35 pages.

"Minimum Premiums for Group Creditors Insurance," State of New York Insurance Department, April 29, 1955.

"Oregon Credit Accident and Health Insurance Act," Chap. 125, Oregon Laws of 1955.

"Report of Examination," The Central National Life Insurance Company of Omaha, Nebraska, December 31, 1955, by the Nebraska Insurance Department, Lincoln, Nebraska.

"Report of Examination," The Old Republic Credit Life Insurance Company, December 31, 1952, by the Department of Insurance, State of Illinois, Springfield, Illinois.

"Report of the Subcommittee on Credit Life and Credit Accident and Health Insurance, *Proceedings of the National Association of Insurance Commissioners,* Vol. II (June 7–11, 1954).

"Rules and Regulations on Credit Insurance," Iowa Insurance Department, Bulletin F-10 (February 24, 1954).

Senate Bill No. 318, "To Provide for the Writing of Life and Accident and Health Insurance in Connection with the Making of Loans Authorized and Legal Under Article 2 and Article 3," Chap. 73, Colorado Revised Statutes, 1953.

"The Tie-In Sale of Credit Insurance in Connection with Small Loans and Other Transactions," Report of the Subcommittee on Antitrust and Monopoly Legislation of the Committee on the Judiciary, U.S. Senate (83rd Cong., 2nd Sess.).

Transcript of the Public Hearings Before the Colorado Committee on Fair Loan Practices, Denver, Colorado, December 18, 19, and 20, 1952.

Transcript of the Public Hearings Before the State Board of Insurance Commissioners on Credit Insurance, Austin, Texas, September 24, 1952.

Wisconsin Attorney General's Opinion, to G. M. Matthews, Commissioner of Banking, on the Sale of Consumer Credit Life Insurance by State Banks, June 29, 1954.

Wisconsin State Insurance Department Filings, Madison, Wisconsin.

Wisconsin Statutes, Chap. 206, 1953.

Addresses, Statements, and Memoranda

ADAMS, CLARIS. "Life Insurance and the Washington Scene," an address at the meeting of General Agents and Managers Conference of the National Association of Life Underwriters, Columbus, Ohio, March 21, 1955.

BOYER, PAUL F. Statement before the Credit Life Insurance Subcommittee of the Life Insurance Committee of the National Association of Insurance Commissioners, November 28, 1955, New York.

————. Written Statement on Behalf of Household Finance Corporation in a Public Hearing Before the Texas Board of Insurance Commissioners, April 3, 1956, Austin, Texas.

DAUER, ERNST. "The Consumer Credit Situation," an Address to the Robert Morris Associates, Dallas, Texas, November 14, 1955.

DUNBAR, EDWARD. Statement before the NAIC, St. Louis, Missouri, May 15, 1956.

————. "The Regulation of the Sale of Credit Life, Health and Accident Insurance by Licensed Lenders," a statement given at Washington University, St. Louis, Missouri, April 27, 1956.

————. Letter to the Members of the Subcommittee on Credit Life and Credit Accident and Health Insurance of the Life Committee of the National Association of Insurance Commissioners, dated May 28, 1956.

"Exhibit 'A'," a statement on the subject of Credit Life and Accident and Health Insurance by the CCIA to the NAIC Subcommittee to Study Rules and Regulations Pertaining to Credit Life and Accident & Health Insurance, at a Public Hearing, April 27, 1954.

Joint Statement of the American Life Convention and the Life Insurance Association of America before the Credit Life Insurance Subcommittee of the National Association of Insurance Commissioners, New York, November 28, 1955.

LARSON, J. EDWARD. "Abuses Arising From the Sale of Credit Life and Credit Accident and Health Insurance in Connection with Small Loans–from the Viewpoint of a State Administrative Official," an address given at Washington, University, St. Louis, Missouri, April 27, 1956.

"Minimum Reserves," statement of the CCIA given the NAIC Subcommittee to Study Rules & Regulations Pertaining to Credit Life and Credit Accident & Health Insurance at a public hearing, Chicago, April 26, 1954.

NYBORG, VICTOR H. "Self Regulation," Address before Consumer Credit Insurance Association, June 5, 1953.

PETERSON, CECIL N. Statement before the Senate Judiciary Committee of the State of Kansas, Topeka, February 16, 1955.

PIKE, ALBERT J. "Memorandum on Credit Life Insurance," published by Life Insurance Association of America, undated.

PRITCHARD, OWEN D. Statement before the Subcommittee on Credit Life Insurance of the Life Insurance Committee of the National Association of Insurance Commissioners, New York, November 28, 1955.

"Regulation of Credit Life and Credit Accident & Health Insurance," Statement of the CCIA given the NAIC Subcommittee to Study Rules and Regulations Pertaining to Credit Life and Accident and Health Insurance, at a Public Hearing, April 27, 1954.

SANBORN, THEODORE. "What Credit Life and Disability Insurance Mean to Wisconsin Bankers," an address delivered at the annual meeting of the Wisconsin Bankers Association, Milwaukee, June 21, 1954.

SCOTT, FRANK J. "Memorandum on the Origins of Credit Life Insurance," New York, undated.

SINCLAIR, J. S. "Are We Mortgaging Our Future Too Much?" *Vital Speeches* (May, 1956), p. 431.

"Statement by the Consumer Credit Insurance Association," *Proceedings of the National Association of Insurance Commissioners,* Vol. II (June 7–11, 1954).

"Statement on Credit Insurance," Submitted by the Indiana Consumer Finance Association, Inc., to the Subcommittee of the Indiana Legislative Advisory Commission, Indianapolis, March 15, 1956,

WHITTAKER, E. B. Statement before the Senate Judiciary Committee of the State of Kansas, February 15, 1955.

————. Statement on proposed Colorado Small Loan Legislation, March 9, 1953.

NEWSPAPERS

DAVID, KEN. Articles in *Topeka Daily Capital,* December 19, 1954, February 6, 16, 1955.

HANNA, PHIL S., "Consumer Credit Insurance Booms," *Chicago Daily News,* September 21, 1951.

Indianapolis Star, Various articles, January 28, 1955; February 5, 1955; November 1–4, 10–12, 1955; December 6, 22, 1955; January 19, 21, 1956; March 16, 1956.

VICKERS, RAY. "Credit Insurance," *The Wall Street Journal* (March 13, 1952).

INDEX

This book has been set on the Linotype in 12 and 10 point Garamond No. 3, leaded 1 point. Chapter numbers are in 24 point Garamont italic caps and lower case. Chapter titles are in 18 point Garamont italic caps. The size of the type page is 24 by 42 picas.